CONTENTS

A NOTE FROM JEAN NIDETCH

Are you the type of shopper who casts a careful eye on labels?

There's a 'label' on this book that you can be assured stands for Grade-A quality. I refer to the two simple words: Weight and Watchers. Together they stand for the largest weight-control company in the world, and the most respected.

If I may take a nostalgic journey, come with me to the apartment house I lived in, in Little Neck, New York. That's where our first meetings were held, back in 1962. We began with just six women . . . I went to the New York City Board of Health Obesity Clinic for help. The diet they gave me, which was to become the basis of the original Weight Watchers Food Plan, was well balanced. However, I sensed that something more than calorie counting was needed: the missing ingredient was the 'I-know-just-what-you-mean' that only comes from fellow sufferers.

Our recipe for success was something called group support. It was to become the hallmark of the Weight Watchers Organisation, for the hands joined together now encircle the globe. The six have multiplied astoundingly into more than twelve million. So universal was and is the need that today the sun seldom sets on Weight Watchers classes. They can be found in nearly every corner of the world. Our members span the decades (from teens to nineties) and encompass all races, religions, careers and social levels, for overweight is no respecter of these boundaries.

The help we offer extends far beyond the classes. Our 'label' appears on best-selling cookbooks and magazines. And wherever the name 'Weight Watchers' is seen or heard, you have the satisfaction of knowing it is backed up by the expertise of highly skilled professionals. Many of them have lent their nutritional knowledge and culinary abilities to the making of this cookbook.

But you don't have to be on a diet to find this book an invaluable 'partner'. What it does is take the burden of meal-planning off your shoulders by supplying well-balanced, carefully thought out menu plans. For the first time, we have divided a cookbook into daily menus – appropriately so, since eating successfully is a day-to-day challenge!

Now you have a chance to sample our exciting world for yourself and discover that it is possible to eat healthfully and control your weight without starvation, without boredom, without even having to forfeit many favourites. In a word: enjoyably!

Isn't it delicious to know that with this book that 'choice' is yours?

Jean Nidetch

Jean Nidetch
Founder
Weight Watchers International

Weight Watchers
365-DAY MENU
COOKBOOK

NEW ENGLISH LIBRARY

For information about the Weight Watchers Classroom Programme, contact: Weight Watchers U.K. Limited, 11–12 Fairacres, Dedworth Road, Windsor, Berkshire SL4 4UY. Telephone: Windsor (95) 56751.

First published in the USA in 1981 by New American Library.

First published in Great Britain in 1983 by New English Library.

This revised paperback edition first published in Great Britain in 1985 by New English Library.

NEL Books are published by
New English Library,
Mill Road, Dunton Green,
Sevenoaks, Kent.
Editorial office: 47 Bedford Square, London WC1B 3DP.

Line drawings by Christine Beadle

Jacket photograph by Andrew Whittuck

Typeset by South Bucks Photosetters Limited

Printed and bound by Cox & Wyman Ltd, Reading

British Library C.I.P.

Weight Watchers 365-day menu cookbook.——(Rev.ed.)
   1. Reducing diets——Recipes
   I. Weight Watchers
   641.5′635   RM222.2

   ISBN 0–450–05860–3

INTRODUCTION

Weight Watchers' first – and only – paperback was published in 1975. Ten years later, we are delighted to introduce you to another, with fifty-two menu plans and a collection of recipes which will prove more tempting and practical than ever. We feel sure that this book will be in constant use in your kitchen, whether you're cooking for one or for the whole family.

Many of us find it hard enough to plan appetising, well-balanced meals day after day, week after week, without having to think about calorie content as well, so any help must be a boon, if not a real salvation, from this daily 'headache'. And please don't worry about calories: these have been worked out for you; all you have to do is follow the plans!

Since there are fifty-two weekly menus, we decided to assume that Week One starts on January 1st, and you'll find that the food choices throughout the year reflect the seasons. Whenever you buy this book, you can turn to the relevant part of the year and start wherever you want. The menus are balanced within each week and you may swap one day's menu for another within the same week, but please don't swap from one week's plan to another half-way through the week or you may not receive the proper balance of nutrients.

The Weight Watchers Food Plan is more a way of life than a diet. It ensures that you remain in good health while you are losing weight and, when your ideal weight has been reached, you can make a few additions and still retain your weight loss. Moreover, it is a result of many years' research and is approved by the medical profession.

We have created this book in an easy-to-use format and we feel that it shows a true reflection of the way Weight Watchers wants its members to lead a 'normal' life and not isolate themselves as 'slimmers'. We recommend variety in the choice of foods and try to show through the menu suggestions that the taste, texture and appearance of the food we eat is just as vital to the success of a diet as the control of portion size.

So, enjoy yourself trying out all the menus, keep this book handy, refer to it often and we can promise you a much more relaxed and enjoyable time than you'd expect while following a successful slimming regime!

INFORMATION TO HELP YOU MAKE THE MOST OF THIS BOOK

These Menu Plans have been developed to meet the nutritional requirements of a complete week in accordance with the Weight Watchers Full Exchange Plan for Women.

Men and Teenagers may also follow these Plans but must make the following additions:
> At least 2 extra pieces of fruit every day, with a maximum of 3 if desired. Please note that 1 banana = 2 pieces of fruit. At least 1 extra slice of bread every day, with a maximum of 2 if desired.
> Teenagers: Please have an extra ½ pint of skim milk daily.

We suggest you check the Menu Plan and make a weekly shopping list so that before preparing a recipe you have every item to hand.

You may include the items given under 'Snacks at Planned Times' with your day's meals rather than take them as snacks.

In our recipes we have given you the choice of artificial sweeteners or sugar to suit you own taste.

Water, soda water and mineral water, in reasonable amounts, may be used at any time. Black coffee and tea may be used and you may add to these skim milk from the 1 pint a day which we have built into the Menu Plans.

As a general guide for meat, poultry and fish, buy 6 oz including skin and bone to obtain 4 oz cooked weight. The skin, fat and bones should be discarded. Grill or roast meat on a rack, after trimming away the fat, and discard the fats and juices.

Fresh, frozen or canned vegetables and fruit may be used, but frozen or canned fruit should be free of sugar or syrup. Buy fruit canned in natural juice.

Vegetables are a valuable source of vitamins and are essential in any balanced diet. They can be steamed, baked, grilled, or boiled. When boiling, always use as small an amount of water as possible; under-cooking is better than over-cooking.

Any cereal, except the sugar-coated ones, may be included on your shopping list.

Be sure to use a margarine high in polyunsaturates.

Fish canned in oil, brine or tomato sauce should be well drained before weighing.

For best results, weigh and measure every ingredient. Please don't guess! Make full use of kitchen scales, measuring jugs and spoons. Teaspoons hold 5ml and tablespoons 15 ml and measurements should be level. In recipes serving more than one person, the ingredients should be well mixed and the finished dish divided into equal portions.

Non-stick cookware makes it possible to cook without fat.

WEEK 1

If your New Year Resolution is to lose weight, then you've made an excellent start. In this book you'll find a guide to good eating, good health and satisfactory weight loss.

DAY 1

MORNING MEAL
4 oz (120 g) fruit cocktail
¾ oz (20 g) cornflakes
5 fl oz (150 ml) skim milk

MIDDAY MEAL
4 oz (120 g) cooked chicken, sliced, served on 1 slice (1 oz/30 g) bread, with lettuce and radish salad, with **Vinaigrette Dressing** (page 293)
½ medium grapefruit

EVENING MEAL
Prawns with Crispy Topping (page 268)
3 oz (90 g) broccoli
green salad with 2 teaspoons low-calorie mayonnaise
1 medium apple

SNACKS OR DRINKS AT PLANNED TIMES
15 fl oz (450 ml) skim milk

DAY2

MORNING MEAL
4 fl oz (120 ml) orange juice
2½ oz (75 g) cottage cheese
1 slice (1 oz/30 g) currant bread

MIDDAY MEAL
4 oz (120 g) grilled lamb's liver
3 oz (90 g) sliced onion, sauteed in 1½
   teaspoons vegetable oil
3 oz (90 g) green beans with diced red pepper
sparkling mineral water

EVENING MEAL
3 oz (90 g) grilled chicken
Cucumber and Tomato Salad (page 289)
2 oz (60 g) cooked noodles
4 oz (120 g) stewed apples with 1 oz (30 g)
   raisins

SNACKS OR DRINKS AT PLANNED TIMES
5 fl oz (150 ml) low-fat natural yogurt with 1
   teaspoon honey, ½ pint (300 ml) skim milk

DAY3

MORNING MEAL
4 fl oz (120 ml) grapefruit juice
2 poached eggs
1 slice (1 oz/30 g) wholemeal bread

MIDDAY MEAL
5 oz (150 g) cottage cheese
melba toast, up to 80 calories
1½ teaspoons margarine
green salad with lemon juice
4 oz (120 g) peach

EVENING MEAL
Baked Fish Casserole (page 267)
1 medium tomato, sliced on lettuce with
   cider vinegar
1 medium pear

SNACKS OR DRINKS AT PLANNED TIMES
¾ oz (20 g) scone, 7½ fl oz (225 ml) skim
   milk, 5 fl oz (150 ml) low-fat natural yogurt

DAY4

MORNING MEAL
4 fl oz (120 ml) grapefruit juice
¾ oz (20 g) wheat flakes
5 fl oz (150 ml) skim milk
1 slice (1 oz/30 g) wholemeal bread, toasted
1 teaspoon margarine
1 tablespoon marmalade

MIDDAY MEAL
4 breadcrumbed fish fingers, grilled
3 oz (90 g) carrots
1 teaspoon margarine
iceberg lettuce with lemon juice
1 medium apple

EVENING MEAL
Beef and Corn Casserole (page 256)
green salad with **Vinaigrette Dressing** (page 293)
4 oz (120 g) peaches

SNACKS OR DRINKS AT PLANNED TIMES
15 fl oz (450 ml) skim milk

DAY5

MORNING MEAL
1 medium orange
3 oz (90 g) baked beans
1 slice (1 oz/30 g) bread, toasted

MIDDAY MEAL
Mushroom Omelette (page 230)
3 oz (90 g) peas
1 oz (30 g) wholemeal roll
2 teaspoons low-fat spread
4 oz (120 g) fruit salad

EVENING MEAL
5 oz (150 g) poached cod fillet
2 teaspoons tomato relish
3 oz (90 g) leeks
3 oz (90 g) swede
1 teaspoon margarine
1 medium apple

SNACKS OR DRINKS AT PLANNED TIMES
½ pint (300 ml) skim milk, 5 fl oz (150 ml) low-fat natural yogurt

DAY 6

MORNING MEAL
4 fl oz (120 ml) orange juice
2½ oz (75 g) cottage cheese
1 slice (1 oz/30 g) bread with 1 teaspoon
    low-fat spread

MIDDAY MEAL
2 oz (60 g) canned tuna
1 hard-boiled egg
sliced tomato and onion salad with wine
    vinegar and pinch oregano
1½ teaspoons mayonnaise
1 slice (1 oz/30 g) bread
mineral water with lemon slice

EVENING MEAL
Sesame Chicken with Green Beans (page
    239
2 oz (60 g) cooked brown rice
green salad with lemon juice
1 medium orange

**SNACKS OR DRINKS
AT PLANNED TIMES**
½ pint (300 ml) skim milk, 5 fl oz (150 ml)
    low-fat natural yogurt, ¼ small pineapple

DAY 7

MORNING MEAL
½ medium banana
¾ oz (20 g) muesli
5 fl oz (150 ml) skim milk

MIDDAY MEAL
8 fl oz (240 ml) tomato juice
4 oz (120 g) roast pork
3 oz (90 g) Brussels sprouts
3 oz (90 g) baked jacket potato
2 teaspoons low-fat spread
2 oz (60 g) stewed apple
3 oz (90 g) baked onion, sprinkled with sage
4 fl oz (120 ml) white wine

EVENING MEAL
4 oz (120 g) sardines
2 teaspoons mayonnaise
sliced tomato and onion on green salad
1 slice (1 oz/30 g) wholemeal bread
mineral water with lemon slice

**SNACKS OR DRINKS
AT PLANNED TIMES**
5 fl oz (150 ml) skim milk, 5 fl oz (150 ml)
    low-fat natural yogurt, ½ oz (15 g) raisins

WEEK 2

Food is more than nourishment. It's relaxation, hospitality, pleasure. The wide variety of foods in these menu plans ensure that dull monotony is kept at bay.

DAY 1

MORNING MEAL
½ medium grapefruit
¾ oz (20 g) porridge oats cooked with water
5 fl oz (150 ml) skim milk

MIDDAY MEAL
4 oz (120 g) canned tuna served on lettuce leaves
2 teaspoons mayonnaise
3 oz (90 g) canned asparagus tips
1 oz (30 g) pitta bread
1 teaspoon margarine

EVENING MEAL
Lamb's Liver Creole (page 254)
2 oz (60 g) cooked rice
4 oz (120 g) fruit salad

SNACKS OR DRINKS AT PLANNED TIMES
1 medium orange, 5 fl oz (150 ml) skim milk, 5 fl oz (150 ml) low-fat natural yogurt

DAY 2

MORNING MEAL
4 fl oz (120 ml) orange juice
2½ oz (75 g) cottage cheese
1 slice (1 oz/30 g) brown bread

MIDDAY MEAL
Mushroom Omelette (page 230)
1 slice (1 oz/30 g) brown bread
1 teaspoon margarine
3 oz (90 g) broccoli

EVENING MEAL
5 oz (150 g) grilled chicken
3 oz (90 g) courgettes with oregano
3 oz (90 g) carrots
green salad with **Thousand Island Dressing**
(page 291)
½ medium banana

SNACKS OR DRINKS AT PLANNED TIMES
1 medium apple, ½ pint (300 ml) skim milk,
Coconut-Coffee Mounds (page 300)

DAY 3

MORNING MEAL
4 oz (120 g) grapefruit sections
¾ oz (20 g) cereal
5 fl oz (150 ml) skim milk

MIDDAY MEAL
Tomato Stuffed with Herb Cheese (page 226)
green salad with 1 teaspoon mayonnaise
1 (1 oz/30 g) bread roll
2 teaspoons low-fat spread
3 oz (90 g) grapes

EVENING MEAL
6 oz (180 g) grilled plaice
3 oz (90 g) baked jacket potato with 2½ fl oz
(75 ml) low-fat natural yogurt with chives
3 oz (90 g) spinach
chicory salad with **Vinaigrette Dressing**
(page 293)
1 medium pear

SNACKS OR DRINKS AT PLANNED TIMES
½ pint (300 ml) skim milk

DAY4

MORNING MEAL
4 fl oz (120 ml) orange juice
1 scrambled egg
2 teaspoons tomato ketchup
1 slice (1 oz/30 g) wholemeal bread

MIDDAY MEAL
3 oz (90 g) cold roast chicken
mixed green salad with sliced tomato
3 teaspoons salad dressing
1 slice (1 oz/30 g) wholemeal bread
2 inch (5 cm) wedge honeydew melon

EVENING MEAL
4 oz (120 g) grilled ham steak
3 oz (90 g) peas
3 oz (90 g) cauliflower
green salad with **Herb Dressing** (page 293)
3 oz (90 g) grapes

SNACKS OR DRINKS AT PLANNED TIMES
2½ fl oz (75 ml) low-fat natural yogurt with 1 digestive biscuit, 15 fl oz (450 ml) skim milk

DAY5

MORNING MEAL
1 medium orange
1 oz (30 g) Cheddar cheese
1 slice (1 oz/30 g) wholemeal bread

MIDDAY MEAL
3 tablespoons peanut butter
2 slices (1 oz/30 g each) white bread
3 oz (90 g) grapes

EVENING MEAL
4 oz (120 g) grilled veal chop
3 oz (90 g) Brussels sprouts
3 oz (90 g) carrots
1 medium pear

SNACKS OR DRINKS AT PLANNED TIMES
1 pint (600 ml) skim milk

DAY6

MORNING MEAL
Honey Stewed Prunes (page 298)
¾ oz (20 g) porridge oats cooked with water
5 fl oz (150 ml) skim milk

MIDDAY MEAL
4 oz (120 g) canned sardines served on
    lettuce
3 oz (90 g) tomato, sliced
1 oz (30 g) onion, sliced
3 teaspoons mayonnaise
5 fl oz (150 ml) low-fat natural yogurt

EVENING MEAL
4 oz (120 g) grilled beefburger
1 x 2 oz (60 g) bap
2 teaspoons tomato ketchup
1 pickled cucumber
Curried Cole Slaw (page 288)
1 medium orange

SNACKS OR DRINKS AT PLANNED TIMES
1 medium pear, 5 fl oz (150 ml) skim milk

DAY7

MORNING MEAL
½ medium grapefruit
1 poached egg
1 slice (1 oz/30 g) bread, toasted
2 teaspoons low-fat spread

MIDDAY MEAL
4 oz (120 g) grilled lemon sole with lemon
    juice
2 oz (60 g) cooked noodles
2 teaspoons low-fat spread
6 oz (180 g) broccoli
green salad
4 fl oz (120 ml) white wine
4 oz (120 g) peaches

EVENING MEAL
9 oz (270 g) baked beans
1 slice (1 oz/30 g) bread, toasted
1 teaspoon margarine
4 oz (120 g) fruit salad

SNACKS OR DRINKS AT PLANNED TIMES
½ pint (300 ml) skim milk and 5 fl oz (150 ml)
    low-fat natural yogurt

WEEK 3

Our ancestors used garlic (worn round the neck) to ward off evil spirits. Today we prefer to use it to enhance the flavour of savoury dishes. A little goes a long way – so use with caution.

DAY 1

MORNING MEAL
4 fl oz (120 ml) orange juice
¾ oz (20 g) wheat flakes served with 5 fl oz (150 ml) skim milk

MIDDAY MEAL
2 oz (60 g) Cheddar cheese
green salad with **Vinaigrette Dressing** (page 293)
3 oz (90 g) sweet corn
4 oz (120 g) mandarin orange sections sprinkled with 1 teaspoon shredded coconut

EVENING MEAL
6 oz (180 g) grilled veal chop
3 oz (90 g) Brussels sprouts
3 oz (90 g) grilled tomato
sliced chicory on lettuce with 1 teaspoon mayonnaise
Baked Apple (page 295)

SNACKS OR DRINKS AT PLANNED TIMES
5 fl oz (150 ml) skim milk, 2 cream crackers with 1 teaspoon margarine and 2 teaspoons grated Cheddar cheese, 5 fl oz (150 ml) low-fat natural yogurt

DAY2

MORNING MEAL
1 medium orange
2½ oz (75 g) curd cheese with 1 tablespoon
    jam
1 slice (1 oz/30 g) bread, toasted

MIDDAY MEAL
5 oz (150 g) corned beef
1 slice (1 oz/30 g) bread
tomato and cucumber salad with 2
    teaspoons vegetable oil
1 medium apple

EVENING MEAL
Mushroom Omelette (page 230)
3 oz (90 g) peas
3 oz (90 g) carrots
4 oz (120 g) pear

**SNACKS OR DRINKS
AT PLANNED TIMES**
2 oz (60 g) vanilla ice cream, 2 cream
    crackers, 1 pint (600 ml) skim milk

DAY3

MORNING MEAL
1 large tangerine
¾ oz (20 g) cereal with 5 fl oz (150 ml) skim
    milk

MIDDAY MEAL
1 hard-boiled egg
1 oz (30 g) Cheddar cheese
green salad with **Russian Dressing** (page
    292)
1 slice (1 oz/30 g) wholemeal bread
1 teaspoon margarine
1 medium orange

EVENING MEAL
6 oz (180 g) grilled cod
3 oz (90 g) broccoli
3 oz (90 g) carrots
3 oz (90 g) baked jacket potato
1 teaspoon margarine

**SNACKS OR DRINKS
AT PLANNED TIMES**
5 fl oz (150 ml) skim milk, 5 fl oz (150 ml)
    low-fat natural yogurt with ½ medium
    banana, sliced

DAY4

MORNING MEAL
4 fl oz (120 ml) orange juice
2½ oz (75 g) cottage cheese
crispbread, up to 80 calories

MIDDAY MEAL
Salmon Mousse (page 268)
chicory and watercress salad with lemon
　　juice
2 cream crackers
2 teaspoons low-fat spread
1 medium apple

EVENING MEAL
3 oz (90 g) grilled rump steak
3 oz (90 g) broccoli
3 oz (90 g) French beans
1 teaspoon low-fat spread
2 oz (60 g) cooked pasta shells
4 fl oz (120 ml) orange juice

**SNACKS OR DRINKS
AT PLANNED TIMES**
15 fl oz (450 ml) skim milk

DAY5

MORNING MEAL
4 oz (120 g) grapefruit sections
¾ oz (20 g) porridge oats cooked with water
5 fl oz (150 ml) skim milk

MIDDAY MEAL
5 oz (150 g) cottage cheese
sliced tomatoes on bed of lettuce
1 teaspoon vegetable oil
Garlic Bread (page 286)
Pear Frozen Yogurt (page 301)

EVENING MEAL
6 oz (180 g) grilled chicken livers sprinkled
　　with lemon juice
3 oz (90 g) peas with 1 teaspoon margarine
3 oz (90 g) cauliflower
2 oz (60 g) cooked rice
4 fl oz (120 ml) red or white wine

**SNACKS OR DRINKS
AT PLANNED TIMES**
1 medium orange, 5 fl oz (150 ml) skim milk

DAY6

MORNING MEAL
4 fl oz (120 ml) orange juice
1 poached egg on 1 slice (1 oz/30 g)
    wholemeal bread, toasted
1½ teaspoons margarine

MIDDAY MEAL
Curried Chicken Salad (page 243)
chicory and sliced red pepper salad with 1
    teaspoon low-calorie mayonnaise
1 oz (30 g) wholemeal roll

EVENING MEAL
3 oz (90 g) grilled plaice
3 oz (90 g) peas
3 oz (90 g) boiled potato, mashed
1 medium pear

SNACKS OR DRINKS AT PLANNED TIMES
½ pint (300 ml) skim milk, 5 fl oz (150 ml)
    low-fat natural yogurt, ½ oz (15 g) raisins

DAY7

MORNING MEAL
4 oz (120 g) grapefruit sections
2½ oz (75 g) curd cheese with chopped
    chives
1 slice (1 oz/30 g) wholemeal bread

MIDDAY MEAL
3 oz (90 g) roast chicken
3 oz (90 g) broccoli
tomato salad with lettuce, with 2 teaspoons
    mayonnaise

EVENING MEAL
4 oz (120 g) cooked tongue
3 oz (90 g) sliced beetroot and watercress
cucumber salad with 1 teaspoon mayonnaise
1 oz (30 g) wholemeal roll
2 canned pineapple slices

SNACKS OR DRINKS AT PLANNED TIMES
1 pint (600 ml) skim milk, 1 large mandarin
    orange, 1 digestive biscuit

WEEK 4

January 25th is Burns Night and in Scotland they celebrate it with haggis, neeps and tatties. If these aren't to your taste, then you're sure to find something else to please you in this week's selections.

DAY 1

MORNING MEAL
4 oz (120 g) orange sections
1 scrambled egg
1 slice (1 oz/30 g) wholemeal bread

MIDDAY MEAL
2 oz (60 g) Cheshire cheese
melba toast, up to 80 calories
1 medium tomato, sliced on shredded lettuce
   with **Cole Slaw Vinaigrette** (page 288)
5 oz (150 g) melon balls

EVENING MEAL
5 oz (150 g) grilled salmon steak
Courgettes Italian Style (page 279)
chicory salad with **Vinaigrette Dressing**
   (page 293)
4 oz (120 g) pear

SNACKS OR DRINKS AT PLANNED TIMES
½ pint (300 ml) skim milk, 1 digestive biscuit,
   5 fl oz (150 ml) low-fat natural yogurt

DAY 2

MORNING MEAL
½ medium grapefruit
¾ oz (20 g) muesli
5 fl oz (150 ml) skim milk

MIDDAY MEAL
4 oz (120 g) crab meat
green salad with sliced tomato
2 teaspoons mayonnaise
2 cream crackers
¼ small pineapple

EVENING MEAL
4 oz (120 g) grilled chicken with herbs and
lemon juice
3 oz (90 g) cauliflower
3 oz (90 g) carrots
1 teaspoon low-fat spread
½ medium banana with 2½ fl oz (75 ml) low-
fat natural yogurt

SNACKS OR DRINKS AT PLANNED TIMES
1 slice (1 oz/30 g) currant bread, toasted, with
1 teaspoon low-fat spread, ½ pint (300 ml)
skim milk

DAY 3

MORNING MEAL
4 fl oz (120 ml) orange juice
1 oz (30 g) Cheddar cheese
1 slice (1 oz/30 g) wholemeal bread

MIDDAY MEAL
Tuna Boats (page 263)
Bean Salad (page 289)
1 slice (1 oz/30 g) white bread
1 medium orange
5 fl oz (150 ml) low-fat natural yogurt

EVENING MEAL
3 oz (90 g) grilled beef sausages
4 oz (120 g) mushrooms
3 oz (90 g) grated beetroot on lettuce with
cider vinegar
½ pint (300 ml) beer

SNACKS OR DRINKS AT PLANNED TIMES
4 oz (120 g) fruit cocktail, ½ pint (300 ml) skim
milk

DAY 4

MORNING MEAL
4 oz (120 g) fruit salad
1 poached egg
1 slice (1 oz/30 g) brown bread, toasted
2 teaspoons low-fat spread

MIDDAY MEAL
4 oz (120 g) grilled liver
3 oz (90 g) cauliflower florets
green salad with **Vinaigrette Dressing** (page 293)
4 oz (120 g) apricots

EVENING MEAL
3 oz (90 g) sliced roast chicken, on 1 slice (1 oz/30 g) wholemeal bread with lettuce, tomato slices and 2 teaspoons salad dressing
3 oz (90 g) canned cream-style corn
3 oz (90 g) carrots
1 medium orange

SNACKS OR DRINKS AT PLANNED TIMES
½ pint (300 ml) skim milk, 5 fl oz (150 ml) low-fat natural yogurt

---

DAY 5

MORNING MEAL
½ medium grapefruit
¾ oz (20 g) porridge oats cooked with water
5 fl oz (150 ml) skim milk

MIDDAY MEAL
4 oz (120 g) grilled beefburger
3 oz (90 g) spinach
3 oz (90 g) carrots
green salad with **Russian Dressing** (page 292)

EVENING MEAL
Burns Supper
Cook-A-Leekie (page 219)
4 oz (120 g) cooked haggis
3 oz (90 g) swede mashed with 1 teaspoon low-fat spread and pinch nutmeg, salt and pepper
3 oz (90 g) cooked potatoes, mashed with 3 teaspoons low-fat spread and pinch each salt and pepper
5 oz (150 g) raspberries
1½ fl oz (45 ml) whisky

SNACKS OR DRINKS AT PLANNED TIMES
1 medium orange, 5 fl oz (150 ml) skim milk, 5 fl oz (150 ml) low-fat natural yogurt

DAY 6

MORNING MEAL
4 oz (120 g) grapefruit sections
¾ oz (20 g) cornflakes
5 fl oz (150 ml) skim milk

MIDDAY MEAL
Chicken Greek Style (page 241)
green salad with sliced red onion and
    Vinaigrette Dressing (page 293)
1 oz (30 g) bread roll
5 oz (150 g) stewed blackcurrants

EVENING MEAL
5 oz (150 g) curd cheese mixed with 2 oz (60
    g) cooked chopped chicken
1 slice (1 oz/30 g) brown bread, toasted
1 medium tomato
hearts of lettuce with **Russian Dressing**
    (page 292)
Baked Apple (page 295)

SNACKS OR DRINKS
AT PLANNED TIMES
5 fl oz (150 ml) skim milk, 5 fl oz (150 ml)
    low-fat natural yogurt

DAY 7

MORNING MEAL
1 medium orange, cut into wedges
2 oz (60 g) ham
1 slice (1 oz/30 g) rye bread

MIDDAY MEAL
Mushroom Omelette (page 230)
mixed salad with lemon juice
crispbread, up to 80 calories
4 oz (120 g) peaches with 5 fl oz (150 ml)
    low-fat natural yogurt

EVENING MEAL
Fillet of Sole Florentine (page 270)
3 oz (90 g) mashed swede
3 oz (90 g) carrot slices
sliced radishes and celery on shredded
    lettuce with 1 teaspoon mayonnaise,
    sprinkled with chopped chives

SNACKS OR DRINKS
AT PLANNED TIMES
½ pint (300 ml) skim milk, 1 medium apple

WEEK 5

Cinnamon gives a pungent flavour to dishes, both sweet and savoury. It's a simple, inexpensive way to 'lift' the taste of everyday foods. Try Cinnamon-Cheese Toast this week.

DAY1

MORNING MEAL
4 oz (120 g) canned crushed pineapple
¾ oz (20 g) cereal
5 fl oz (150 ml) skim milk

MIDDAY MEAL
Salmon Salad (page 265)
celery sticks, cucumber sticks, and 2 green olives
1 slice (1 oz/30 g) rye bread
2 teaspoons margarine

EVENING MEAL
4 oz (120 g) grilled calf liver
3 oz (90 g) courgettes
3 oz (90 g) green beans
4 oz (120 g) orange and grapefruit sections

SNACKS OR DRINKS AT PLANNED TIMES
15 fl oz (450 ml) skim milk, 1 digestive biscuit, 4 oz (120 g) pear

DAY 2

MORNING MEAL
2½ fl oz (75 ml) apple juice
¾ oz (20 g) cereal
5 fl oz (150 ml) skim milk

MIDDAY MEAL
Chilli-Cheese Rarebit (page 231)
green salad with **Vinaigrette Dressing** (page 293)

EVENING MEAL
6 oz (180 g) grilled haddock with lemon wedge
3 oz (90 g) sweet corn with 1 teaspoon margarine
3 oz (90 g) chopped spinach
1 medium orange

SNACKS OR DRINKS AT PLANNED TIMES
2 chopped dried dates with 5 fl oz (150 ml) low-fat natural yogurt, 5 fl oz (150 ml) skim milk

---

DAY 3

MORNING MEAL
4 oz (120 g) orange sections
Cinnamon-Cheese Toast (page 234)

MIDDAY MEAL
2 hard-boiled eggs
sliced red and green pepper rings on lettuce
2 teaspoons salad dressing
1 slice (1 oz/30 g) rye bread
1 teaspoon margarine

EVENING MEAL
5 oz (150 g) grilled chicken
3 oz (90 g) carrot slices with 3 oz (90 g) peas
green salad with 1 teaspoon mayonnaise
4 oz (120 g) fruit salad

SNACKS OR DRINKS AT PLANNED TIMES
4 oz (120 g) peaches, ½ pint (300 ml) skim milk, 5 fl oz (150 ml) low-fat natural yogurt

DAY4

MORNING MEAL
4 oz (120 g) grapefruit sections
¾ oz (20 g) cereal
5 fl oz (150 ml) skim milk

MIDDAY MEAL
4 oz (120 g) canned drained tuna
mixed salad with pepper rings
1 teaspoon margarine
1 slice (1 oz/30 g) rye bread
2 medium plums

EVENING MEAL
4 oz (120 g) grilled rump steak
3 oz (90 g) baked jacket potato
3 oz (90 g) broccoli spears
iceberg lettuce with **Russian Dressing** (page 292)
1 large mandarin orange

SNACKS OR DRINKS AT PLANNED TIMES
watercress and mushroom salad with **Vinaigrette Dressing** (page 293), 15 fl oz (450 ml) skim milk

---

DAY5

MORNING MEAL
4 oz (120 g) grapefruit sections
1 poached egg
1 slice (1 oz/30 g) wholemeal bread
1 teaspoon margarine

MIDDAY MEAL
Cream of Cauliflower Soup (page 216)
3 oz (90 g) sliced roast turkey
chicory salad with **Vinaigrette Dressing** (page 293)
1 medium pickled cucumber
1 oz (30 g) bread roll

EVENING MEAL
4 oz (120 g) grilled halibut
Green Beans and Tomatoes Hungarian Style (page 282)
crisp lettuce with cucumber slices and 2½ fl oz (75 ml) low-fat natural yogurt
4 oz (120 g) mandarin sections

SNACKS OR DRINKS AT PLANNED TIMES
12½ fl oz (375 ml) skim milk, 1 medium kiwi fruit

DAY6

MORNING MEAL
½ medium grapefruit
2 oz (60 g) smoked salmon with lemon
    wedge
1 slice (1 oz/30 g) brown bread
1 teaspoon low-fat spread

MIDDAY MEAL
2 oz (60 g) Edam cheese, sliced
melba toast, up to 80 calories
green salad with 2 teaspoons salad dressing
4 fl oz (120 ml) white wine

EVENING MEAL
4 oz (120 g) roast veal
3 oz (90 g) braised celery
3 oz (90 g) braised onion
3 teaspoons low-fat spread
2 oz (60 g) cooked rice

**SNACKS OR DRINKS
AT PLANNED TIMES**
1 medium banana with 5 fl oz (150 ml) low-fat
    natural yogurt, ½ pint (300 ml) skim milk

DAY7

MORNING MEAL
1 medium banana
2½ oz (75 g) curd cheese
1 slice (1 oz/30 g) wholemeal bread

MIDDAY MEAL
1 scrambled egg
3 oz (90 g) mushrooms, cooked in 1 teaspoon
    margarine
2 tablespoons peanut butter on 1 slice (1 oz/
    30 g) wholemeal bread

EVENING MEAL
Pork Goulash (page 247)
3 oz (90 g) leeks
½ medium grapefruit
½ pint (300 ml) cider or beer

**SNACKS OR DRINKS
AT PLANNED TIMES**
1 digestive biscuit, 5 fl oz (150 ml) low-fat
    natural yogurt with ½ teaspoon honey,
    7½ fl oz (225 ml) skim milk

WEEK 6

Mushrooms are a versatile vegetable and are available all the year round. Served in salads, pureed, or poached they add flavour and interest to meals.

DAY 1

MORNING MEAL
2½ fl oz (75 ml) pineapple juice
1 poached egg
1 slice (1 oz/30 g) white bread, toasted
1 teaspoon margarine

MIDDAY MEAL
2 oz (60 g) grated Cheddar cheese
3 oz (90 g) sliced beetroot
crisp lettuce with **Thousand Island Dressing** (page 291)
1 oz (30 g) wholemeal roll
1 teaspoon margarine
1 medium apple

EVENING MEAL
5 oz (150 g) steamed plaice
3 oz (90 g) carrots
3 oz (90 g) cabbage

SNACKS OR DRINKS AT PLANNED TIMES
4 oz (120 g) grapefruit sections, 15 fl oz (450 ml) skim milk, crispbread, up to 80 calories

DAY 2

MORNING MEAL
1 oz (30 g) dried apricots
¾ oz (20 g) porridge oats cooked with water
5 fl oz (150 ml) skim milk

MIDDAY MEAL
4 oz (120 g) sliced roast turkey with **Russian Dressing** (page 292)
4 oz (120 g) chilled cooked artichoke hearts
mixed salad with lemon juice
1 slice (1 oz/30 g) rye bread
1 teaspoon margarine
1 medium orange

EVENING MEAL
4 oz (120 g) grilled lamb's liver
3 oz (90 g) cauliflower
3 oz (90 g) spinach
1 medium apple

SNACKS OR DRINKS AT PLANNED TIMES
melba toast, up to 80 calories and 1 teaspoon margarine, 15 fl oz (450 ml) skim milk

---

DAY 3

MORNING MEAL
4 fl oz (120 ml) orange juice
1 boiled egg
1 slice (1 oz/30 g) bread
1 teaspoon margarine

MIDDAY MEAL
Cod-Vegetable Bake (page 260)
chicory and lettuce salad with 2 green olives, capers, and **Vinaigrette Dressing** (page 293)

EVENING MEAL
3 oz (90 g) grilled beefburger with 2 teaspoons ketchup mixed with 1 teaspoon mayonnaise
2 oz (60 g) bap
½ medium pickled cucumber, sliced
1 medium tomato, sliced
4 oz (120 g) fruit cocktail

SNACKS OR DRINKS AT PLANNED TIMES
5 fl oz (150 ml) low-fat natural yogurt, ½ medium banana, ½ pint (300 ml) skim milk

DAY4

MORNING MEAL
½ medium banana
¾ oz (20 g) bran flakes
5 fl oz (150 ml) skim milk

MIDDAY MEAL
2 oz (60 g) sliced Cheshire cheese, grilled on
1 slice (1 oz/30 g) wholemeal bread,
toasted
1 medium tomato, grilled

EVENING MEAL
6 oz (180 g) grilled trout
3 oz (90 g) peas
3 oz (90 g) poached mushrooms
3 oz (90 g) boiled potato
3 teaspoons margarine
4 oz (120 g) pear

SNACKS OR DRINKS AT PLANNED TIMES
1 medium orange, 15 fl oz (450 ml) skim milk

DAY5

MORNING MEAL
Honey-Stewed Prunes (page 298)
1 scrambled egg
1 slice (1 oz/30 g) wholemeal bread
1 teaspoon margarine

MIDDAY MEAL
2½ fl oz (75 ml) apple juice
3 oz (90 g) canned tuna
green pepper and cucumber slices with 1
teaspoon mayonnaise
melba toast, up to 80 calories

EVENING MEAL
4 oz (120 g) corned beef
3 oz (90 g) diced carrot
spinach and mushroom salad with
Vinaigrette Dressing (page 293)
½ medium grapefruit

SNACKS OR DRINKS AT PLANNED TIMES
5 fl oz (150 ml) low-fat natural yogurt, ½ pint
(300 ml) skim milk

DAY 6

MORNING MEAL
2½ fl oz (75 ml) pineapple juice
¾ oz (20 g) cereal
5 fl oz (150 ml) skim milk

MIDDAY MEAL
5 oz (150 g) cottage cheese mixed with 4 oz (120 g) canned crushed pineapple arranged on lettuce
1 medium tomato, sliced
crispbread, up to 80 calories
2 teaspoons low-fat spread

EVENING MEAL
2 hard-boiled eggs
4 oz (120 g) cooked roast chicken
green salad with 1 teaspoon mayonnaise
1 medium tomato, sliced

SNACKS OR DRINKS AT PLANNED TIMES
melba toast, up to 80 calories, **Mushroom Dip** (page 300), ½ pint (300 ml) beer or cider, 1 medium orange, 5 fl oz (150 ml) skim milk

DAY 7

MORNING MEAL
½ medium grapefruit
1 poached egg
1 slice (1 oz/30 g) bread, toasted
1 teaspoon margarine

MIDDAY MEAL
Chicken Kebabs (page 237)
celery and beansprout salad with 2 teaspoons salad dressing
1 large mandarin orange
4 fl oz (120 ml) white wine

EVENING MEAL
9 oz (270 g) baked beans
1 slice (1 oz/30 g) bread, toasted
1 medium tomato, sliced on a green salad with 1 teaspoon vegetable oil with wine vinegar

SNACKS OR DRINKS AT PLANNED TIMES
1 medium apple, 1 digestive biscuit, 1 pint (600 ml) skim milk

WEEK 7

Perhaps you don't associate pancakes with a slimming regime, but if they're taken as part of your whole week's plan – as on Day 2 here – you can happily indulge yourself on Shrove Tuesday.

DAY 1

MORNING MEAL
4 oz (120 g) canned fruit cocktail
¾ oz (20 g) puffed wheat
5 fl oz (150 ml) skim milk

MIDDAY MEAL
5 oz (150 g) cottage cheese
3 oz (90 g) beetroot
green salad with 2 teaspoons low-calorie mayonnaise
1 slice (1 oz/30 g) wholemeal bread
1 medium orange

EVENING MEAL
6 oz (180 g) grilled beefburger
3 oz (90 g) green beans
sliced tomato, cucumber and mushrooms on lettuce with 2 teaspoons mayonnaise

SNACKS OR DRINKS AT PLANNED TIMES
5 fl oz (150 ml) skim milk, 5 fl oz (150 ml) low-fat natural yogurt with 1 portion of stewed rhubarb

DAY 2

MORNING MEAL
¾ oz (20 g) muesli
½ medium banana
5 fl oz (150 ml) skim milk

MIDDAY MEAL
3 oz (90 g) baked beans
1 poached egg
1 slice (1 oz/30 g) wholemeal bread, toasted
1 teaspoon margarine
3 oz (90 g) poached mushrooms
1 medium grilled tomato
1 medium orange

EVENING MEAL
5 oz (150 g) melon balls
5 oz (150 g) sliced roast turkey
3 oz (90 g) sliced beetroot
tomato and onion salad with 1 teaspoon
    vegetable oil, wine vinegar and oregano
Pancakes with Lemon Juice (page 231)

**SNACKS OR DRINKS
AT PLANNED TIMES**
12½ fl oz (375 ml) skim milk

DAY 3

MORNING MEAL
4 fl oz (120 ml) orange juice
1 egg cooked in 1 teaspoon low-fat spread
1 slice (1 oz/30 g) wholemeal bread

MIDDAY MEAL
2 oz (60 g) Cheddar cheese toasted on 1 slice
    (1 oz/30 g) wholemeal bread
iceberg lettuce with 1 teaspoon imitation
    bacon bits and 2 teaspoons low-calorie
    mayonnaise
1 medium apple

EVENING MEAL
5 oz (150 g) grilled plaice
3 oz (90 g) artichoke hearts with 1 teaspoon
    low-fat spread
green salad with 1 teaspoon olive oil and 1
    tablespoon wine vinegar
4 oz (120 g) peaches
5 fl oz (150 ml) low-fat natural yogurt

**SNACKS OR DRINKS
AT PLANNED TIMES**
½ pint (300 ml) skim milk

DAY4

MORNING MEAL
4 fl oz (120 ml) orange juice
2½ oz (75 g) quark cheese with ½ oz (15 g) raisins
crispbread, up to 80 calories

MIDDAY MEAL
3 oz (90 g) sliced liver sausage
1 oz (30 g) sliced onion
lettuce and tomato salad with 1 teaspoon olive oil and 1 tablespoon vinegar
1 slice (1 oz/30 g) rye bread
1 teaspoon margarine
½ oz (15 g) dried apricots chopped and added to 5 fl oz (150 ml) low-fat natural yogurt

EVENING MEAL
4 oz (120 g) roast chicken
6 oz (180 g) courgettes
1 teaspoon margarine
5 oz (150 g) stewed blackcurrants
2 oz (60 g) vanilla ice cream

SNACKS OR DRINKS AT PLANNED TIMES
½ pint (300 ml) skim milk

DAY5

MORNING MEAL
½ medium grapefruit
¾ oz (20 g) bran flakes
5 fl oz (150 ml) skim milk

MIDDAY MEAL
Sweet and Sour Liver (page 246)
3 oz (90 g) cauliflower
3 oz (90 g) courgettes
1 teaspoon low-fat spread
5 fl oz (150 ml) low-fat natural yogurt

EVENING MEAL
4 oz (120 g) grilled cod with lemon wedge
3 oz (90 g) carrots
1 teaspoon low-fat spread
green salad with chopped onion
2 teaspoons salad cream
4 oz (120 g) stewed apples with ½ oz (15 g) raisins

SNACKS OR DRINKS AT PLANNED TIMES
2 oz (60 g) muffin, split and toasted with 1 teaspoon low-fat spread and 1 teaspoon honey, 5 fl oz (150 ml) skim milk

DAY 6

MORNING MEAL
1 medium orange
2½ oz (75 g) cottage cheese
1 slice (1 oz/30 g) currant bread

MIDDAY MEAL
4 oz (120 g) grilled chicken with lemon juice
    and mixed herbs
green salad with 1 teaspoon vegetable oil and
    wine vinegar
3 oz (90 g) green beans
3 oz (90 g) baked jacket potato
2 teaspoons low-fat spread
1 medium pear

EVENING MEAL
2 hard-boiled eggs
1 oz (30 g) Cheddar cheese
2 sticks celery
1 medium tomato
crispbread, up to 80 calories
2 teaspoons low-fat spread
4 oz (120 g) fruit salad

SNACKS OR DRINKS AT PLANNED TIMES
½ pint (300 ml) skim milk, 5 fl oz (150 ml)
    low-fat natural yogurt

DAY 7

MORNING MEAL
½ medium banana
¾ oz (20 g) porridge oats cooked with water
5 fl oz (150 ml) skim milk

MIDDAY MEAL
3 oz (90 g) roast pork
3 oz (90 g) carrots
3 oz (90 g) potatoes
2 teaspoons low-fat spread
1 medium baked apple
4 fl oz (120 ml) white wine

EVENING MEAL
5 oz (150 g) peeled prawns with 2 teaspoons
    low-calorie mayonnaise
3 oz (90 g) canned asparagus spears
tomato, cucumber and lettuce salad with
    lemon juice
crispbread, up to 80 calories
2 teaspoons low-fat spread
4 oz (120 g) orange sections

SNACKS OR DRINKS AT PLANNED TIMES
5 fl oz (150 ml) skim milk, 5 fl oz (150 ml)
    low-fat natural yogurt

WEEK 8

Fennel has a delicious, mild aniseed taste. Use it raw in salads or cooked with cheese and garlic. It goes very well with fish and chicken, too.

DAY 1

MORNING MEAL
4 oz (120 g) grapefruit sections
2½ oz (75 g) cottage cheese
1 medium tomato, sliced
melba toast, up to 80 calories

MIDDAY MEAL
3 oz (90 g) sliced cooked chicken
Fennel with Parmesan Cheese (page 278)
green salad with 1½ teaspoons vegetable oil
     with wine vinegar
1 oz (30 g) bread roll

EVENING MEAL
5 oz (150 g) uncooked liver sauteed with 3 oz
     (90 g) sliced onion in 1½ teaspoons
     vegetable oil
3 oz (90 g) green beans
1 medium pear

SNACKS OR DRINKS AT PLANNED TIMES
½ pint (300 ml) skim milk, 5 fl oz (150 ml)
     low-fat natural yogurt, 4 oz (120 g) fruit
     salad, 1 digestive biscuit

DAY 2

MORNING MEAL
4 fl oz (120 ml) orange juice
1 egg, scrambled with 1 teaspoon margarine
on 1 slice (1 oz/30 g) bread, toasted

MIDDAY MEAL
4 breadcrumbed fish fingers, grilled
3 oz (90 g) peas
3 oz (90 g) cauliflower
1 medium apple

EVENING MEAL
3 oz (90 g) roast chicken
3 oz (90 g) canned sweet corn
green salad with 2 teaspoons low-calorie
mayonnaise
½ medium banana, sliced into 5 fl oz (150 ml)
low-fat natural yogurt, sprinkled with
pinch of cinnamon

**SNACKS OR DRINKS
AT PLANNED TIMES**
½ pint (300 ml) skim milk, ¾ oz (20 g) plain
scone with 1 teaspoon margarine, 1
tablespoon jam

DAY 3

MORNING MEAL
½ medium banana
¾ oz (20 g) cereal with 1 oz (30 g) sultanas
5 fl oz (150 ml) skim milk

MIDDAY MEAL
5 oz (150 g) curd cheese on green salad
1 medium tomato, sliced with 2 teaspoons
vegetable oil, mixed with cider vinegar
1 oz (30 g) bread roll

EVENING MEAL
6 oz (180 g) grilled veal chop
3 oz (90 g) spinach with lemon juice
3 oz (90 g) courgettes
8 fl oz (240 ml) tomato juice

**SNACKS OR DRINKS
AT PLANNED TIMES**
15 fl oz (450 ml) skim milk, 1 oz (30 g) bread
roll with 1 teaspoon margarine and 1
teaspoon honey

DAY4

MORNING MEAL

1 medium orange
1 poached egg
1 slice (1 oz/30 g) bread, toasted
1 teaspoon low-fat spread

MIDDAY MEAL

3 oz (90 g) canned salmon with green salad,
    sliced tomato and cucumber
2 small satsumas

EVENING MEAL

Chicken Provencale (page 236)
3 oz (90 g) baked jacket potato
lettuce and grated carrot salad with 1
    teaspoon salad cream
4 fl oz (120 ml) white wine
Cherry Tarts (page 294)

**SNACKS OR DRINKS
AT PLANNED TIMES**

½ pint (300 ml) skim milk, 5 fl oz (150 ml)
    low-fat natural yogurt

DAY5

MORNING MEAL

4 oz (120 g) canned grapefruit sections
¾ oz (20 g) cereal with 5 fl oz (150 ml) skim
    milk

MIDDAY MEAL

5 oz (150 g) cottage cheese
mixed salad with low-calorie salad dressing,
    up to 50 calories
1 (1 oz/30 g) wholemeal roll
2 teaspoons low-fat spread
1 medium apple

EVENING MEAL

6 oz (180 g) grilled veal
3 oz (90 g) peas
3 oz (90 g) carrots
2 teaspoons low-fat spread
4 oz (120 g) peaches

**SNACKS OR DRINKS
AT PLANNED TIMES**

crispbread, up to 80 calories, with 2
    teaspoons low-fat spread, 5 fl oz (150 ml)
    skim milk, 5 fl oz (150 ml) low-fat natural
    yogurt

DAY6

MORNING MEAL
4 fl oz (120 ml) orange juice
2½ oz (75 g) cottage cheese lightly grilled on
    1 slice (1 oz/30 g) wholemeal bread,
    toasted

MIDDAY MEAL
2-egg omelette, cooked with 1 teaspoon
    vegetable oil, filled with 3 oz (90 g)
    poached mushrooms
3 oz (90 g) courgettes
2 cream crackers
2 teaspoons low-fat spread

EVENING MEAL
5 oz (150 g) baked trout with lemon wedges
3 oz (90 g) peas
3 oz (90 g) sweet corn
sliced chicory with **Vinaigrette Dressing**
    (page 293)
4 fl oz (120 ml) white wine
Coconut-Coffee Mounds (page 300)

SNACKS OR DRINKS AT PLANNED TIMES
Baked Apple (page 295), 5 fl oz (150 ml)
    low-fat natural yogurt with 1 oz (30 g)
    raisins, 5 fl oz (150 ml) skim milk

DAY7

MORNING MEAL
4 oz (120 g) grapefruit sections
¾ oz (20 g) porridge oats cooked with water
5 fl oz (150 ml) skim milk

MIDDAY MEAL
4 oz (120 g) grilled beef steak
3 oz (90 g) boiled and mashed potatoes with 2
    teaspoons margarine
3 oz (90 g) peas
1 grilled tomato
1 medium orange

EVENING MEAL
4 oz (120 g) grilled lemon sole
3 oz (90 g) green beans
3 oz (90 g) carrot slices

SNACKS OR DRINKS AT PLANNED TIMES
½ medium banana, 5 fl oz (150 ml) low-fat
    natural yogurt, 1 slice (1 oz/30 g) bread, 2
    teaspoons low-fat spread, 5 fl oz (150 ml)
    skim milk

WEEK 9

The leek is a versatile vegetable. Its subtle taste of onion gives a marvellous flavour to casseroles or it goes well as the vegetable served with your main course.

DAY 1

MORNING MEAL

Honey-Stewed Prunes (page 298)
1 boiled egg
1 slice (1 oz/30 g) wholemeal bread, toasted
1 teaspoon margarine

MIDDAY MEAL

Chick Pea Croquettes (page 273)
salad of sliced tomato on shredded lettuce
    with 2 teaspoons low-calorie mayonnaise
2 water biscuits
4 oz (120 g) pear

EVENING MEAL

5 oz (150 g) grilled cod steak
3 oz (90 g) broccoli spears with lemon wedge
mixed salad with 2 teaspoons low-calorie
    mayonnaise
4 fl oz (120 ml) white wine

SNACKS OR DRINKS AT PLANNED TIMES

½ medium grapefruit, ½ pint (300 ml) skim
    milk

DAY 2

MORNING MEAL 1 oz (30 g) dried apricots, chopped, with ¾ oz (20 g) muesli
5 fl oz (150 ml) low-fat natural yogurt

MIDDAY MEAL 4 oz (120 g) canned tuna
mixed green salad with 1 teaspoon mayonnaise
1 medium tomato
1 slice (1 oz/30 g) bread
1 teaspoon margarine
1 medium apple

EVENING MEAL 4 oz (120 g) roast beef
2 oz (60 g) cooked brown rice
3 oz (90 g) green beans
lettuce and cucumber salad with **Vinaigrette Dressing** (page 293)
4 oz (120 g) orange sections

SNACKS OR DRINKS AT PLANNED TIMES ½ pint (300 ml) skim milk

DAY 3

MORNING MEAL **Oatmeal with Spiced Fruit Ambrosia** (page 285)

MIDDAY MEAL 4 oz (120 g) grilled, thinly-sliced liver
1 medium onion, sauteed for 2-3 minutes in 1 teaspoon vegetable oil
3 oz (90 g) cauliflower
3 oz (90 g) grilled tomatoes
1 slice (1 oz/30 g) bread with 1 teaspoon margarine

EVENING MEAL 4 oz (120 g) grilled veal steak
3 oz (90 g) boiled potato
3 oz (90 g) green beans
1 teaspoon margarine
4 oz (120 g) orange sections

SNACKS OR DRINKS AT PLANNED TIMES 5 fl oz (150 ml) skim milk, 5 fl oz (150 ml) low-fat natural yogurt, 4 oz (120 g) canned pineapple

DAY4

MORNING MEAL	½ medium grapefruit **Welsh Rarebit** (page 227)

MIDDAY MEAL	5 oz (150 g) cottage cheese on lettuce leaves
	    with 1 medium tomato, sliced
	1 slice (1 oz/30 g) bread
	1 medium orange, sliced with 5 fl oz (150 ml)
	    low-fat natural yogurt

EVENING MEAL	**Cream of Asparagus and Leek Soup** (page 220) 5 oz (150 g) grilled plaice 3 oz (90 g) carrot slices 3 oz (90 g) broccoli 1 teaspoon margarine 4 oz (120 g) apple
SNACKS OR DRINKS AT PLANNED TIMES	9 fl oz (270 ml) skim milk, 1 digestive biscuit

---

DAY5

MORNING MEAL	2 inch (5 cm) wedge honeydew melon 1 egg, scrambled with 1 teaspoon margarine 1 slice (1 oz/30 g) bread, toasted

MIDDAY MEAL	3 oz (90 g) canned sardines
	3-4 green pepper and onion rings on lettuce
	    with 1 teaspoon mayonnaise
	crispbread, up to 80 calories
	5 fl oz (150 ml) low-fat natural yogurt with
	    coffee flavouring and sweetener to taste

EVENING MEAL	4 oz (120 g) grilled beef steak 3 oz (90 g) baked beans 3 oz (90 g) Brussels sprouts 1 teaspoon margarine 1 medium orange
SNACKS OR DRINKS AT PLANNED TIMES	2 medium plums, ½ pint (300 ml) skim milk

DAY6

MORNING MEAL
4 fl oz (120 ml) grapefruit juice
¾ oz (20 g) cornflakes
5 fl oz (150 ml) skim milk

MIDDAY MEAL
5 oz (150 g) cooked chicken
Chinese Cabbage and Tomato Medley
(page 280)
melba toast, up to 80 calories
1 medium pear

EVENING MEAL
2-egg omelette cooked in 2 teaspoons
vegetable oil, filled with 1 oz (30 g)
Cheddar cheese, grated
3 oz (90 g) peas
1 slice (1 oz/30 g) wholemeal bread
1 medium apple

SNACKS OR DRINKS AT PLANNED TIMES
15 fl oz (450 ml) skim milk, 4 fl oz (120 ml) red
wine

DAY7

MORNING MEAL
4 oz (120 g) orange and grapefruit sections
1 poached egg
1 slice (1 oz/30 g) bread
1 teaspoon margarine

MIDDAY MEAL
4 oz (120 g) grilled haddock
3 oz (90 g) steamed mushrooms
watercress and sliced cucumber
Pineapple-Orange 'Cream' (page 299)

EVENING MEAL
Beef Pie (page 258)
3 oz (90 g) cauliflower dotted with 1 teaspoon
margarine

SNACKS OR DRINKS AT PLANNED TIMES
5 oz (150 g) strawberries with 5 fl oz (150 ml)
low-fat natural yogurt, 1 digestive biscuit,
5 fl oz (150 ml) skim milk

WEEK 10

Always keep vegetables in the kitchen –
fresh or frozen -- ready to use in prepared
dishes or in our Vegetable Medley Soup
on Day 7.

DAY 1

MORNING MEAL	½ medium grapefruit 1 poached egg 1 slice (1 oz/30 g) bread, toasted 2 teaspoons low-fat spread
MIDDAY MEAL	3 oz (90 g) grilled lemon sole 3 oz (90 g) peas green salad with **Vinaigrette Dressing** (page 293) 1 large mandarin orange
EVENING MEAL	4 oz (120 g) grilled pork fillet 3 oz (90 g) boiled potatoes 3 oz (90 g) green beans 1 teaspoon margarine
SNACKS OR DRINKS AT PLANNED TIMES	5 fl oz (150 ml) low-fat natural yogurt with 1 tablespoon jam, ½ pint (300 ml) skim milk, 4 oz (120 g) pineapple

DAY 2

MORNING MEAL
4 oz (120 g) stewed apple with 1 teaspoon honey
1 tablespoon peanut butter spread on crispbread, up to 80 calories

MIDDAY MEAL
3 oz (90 g) grilled halibut
3 oz (90 g) peas
1 slice (1 oz/30 g) white bread
1 teaspoon margarine
shredded lettuce with 2 sliced tomatoes

EVENING MEAL
4 oz (120 g) sliced roast chicken
3 oz (90 g) green beans
beansprouts and carrot salad with
  Vinaigrette Dressing (page 293)
4 fl oz (120 ml) white wine
Pineapple Sorbet (page 301)

SNACKS OR DRINKS AT PLANNED TIMES
½ pint (300 ml) skim milk, 1 medium orange and 2 cream crackers

DAY 3

MORNING MEAL
¾ oz (20 g) bran flakes with ½ medium banana, sliced
5 fl oz (150 ml) skim milk

MIDDAY MEAL
Pitta Bread Sandwich (page 228)
carrot and celery sticks
1 medium orange

EVENING MEAL
6 oz (180 g) grilled fillet of lemon sole
6 oz (180 g) carrots and courgettes
1 oz (30 g) bread roll
3 teaspoons low-fat spread
2 oz (60 g) vanilla ice cream

SNACKS OR DRINKS AT PLANNED TIMES
15 fl oz (450 ml) skim milk

DAY4

MORNING MEAL
4 oz (120 g) apple
¾ oz (20 g) porridge oats cooked with water
5 fl oz (150 ml) skim milk

MIDDAY MEAL
4 oz (120 g) canned tuna
sliced tomatoes on lettuce with 1 teaspoon
  mayonnaise
melba toast, up to 80 calories
4 oz (120 g) fruit cocktail with 5 fl oz (150 ml)
  low-fat natural yogurt

EVENING MEAL
4 oz (120 g) roast chicken
3 oz (90 g) spinach
3 oz (90 g) carrots
2 teaspoons margarine

SNACKS OR DRINKS AT PLANNED TIMES
4 oz (120 g) grapefruit sections, 5 fl oz (150
  ml) skim milk

DAY5

MORNING MEAL
4 fl oz (120 ml) orange juice
¾ oz (20 g) cornflakes
5 fl oz (150 ml) skim milk

MIDDAY MEAL
1 oz (30 g) Cheddar cheese, grilled on 1 slice
  (1 oz/30 g) bread, toasted and topped with
  1 poached egg
green salad with **Vinaigrette Dressing** (page
  293)

EVENING MEAL
6 oz (180 g) steamed plaice
3 oz (90 g) peas
green pepper rings on lettuce with 2
  teaspoons mayonnaise
4 oz (120 g) mandarin orange sections with
  5 fl oz (150 ml) low-fat natural yogurt

SNACKS OR DRINKS AT PLANNED TIMES
5 fl oz (150 ml) skim milk, 8 fl oz (240 ml)
  tomato juice with 2 water biscuits

DAY6

MORNING MEAL
Honey-Stewed Prunes (page 298)
2½ oz (75 g) cottage cheese
1 slice (1 oz/30 g) bread
2 teaspoons low-fat spread

MIDDAY MEAL
3 oz (90 g) grilled beefburger
1 tablespoon relish, any type
1 slice (1 oz/30 g) rye bread
2 teaspoons low-fat spread
Curried Cole Slaw (page 288)
1 medium orange

EVENING MEAL
Liver Pate (page 254)
2 grilled tomatoes
green salad with **Vinaigrette Dressing** (page 293)
5 fl oz (150 ml) low-fat natural yogurt

SNACKS OR DRINKS AT PLANNED TIMES
½ pint (300 ml) skim milk

DAY7

MORNING MEAL
2½ fl oz (75 ml) pineapple juice
1 scrambled egg cooked with 1 teaspoon margarine
1 slice (1 oz/30 g) brown bread, toasted

MIDDAY MEAL
Vegetable Medley Soup (page 222)
5 oz (150 g) grilled lamb chop
3 oz (90 g) broccoli

EVENING MEAL
Baked Cheese Souffle (page 226)
mixed salad with **Vinaigrette Dressing** (page 293)
1 medium orange

SNACKS OR DRINKS AT PLANNED TIMES
1 medium apple with 5 fl oz (150 ml) low-fat natural yogurt, 7½ fl oz (225 ml) skim milk

WEEK 11

Potatoes were once regarded as an exotic delicacy, grown only (in the 1500s) in the gardens of the Royal household and the nobility. For us they're a nourishing and inexpensive staple food.

DAY 1

MORNING MEAL
4 fl oz (120 ml) orange juice
2½ oz (75 g) cottage cheese
1 slice (1 oz/30 g) raisin bread
1 teaspoon low-fat spread

MIDDAY MEAL
3 oz (90 g) crab meat
green salad
1 medium tomato
2 teaspoons low-calorie mayonnaise
1 oz (30 g) pitta bread
1 medium pear

EVENING MEAL
4 oz (120 g) grilled lamb's liver
3 oz (90 g) cauliflower
3 oz (90 g) courgettes
2 teaspoons low-fat spread
¼ small pineapple

SNACKS OR DRINKS AT PLANNED TIMES
1 slice (1 oz/30 g) wholemeal bread with 1 teaspoon low-fat spread and 1 teaspoon honey, 5 fl oz (150 ml) low-fat natural yogurt, ½ pint (300 ml) skim milk

DAY 2

MORNING MEAL
½ medium banana
¾ oz (20 g) muesli
5 fl oz (150 ml) skim milk

MIDDAY MEAL
4 oz (120 g) sliced roast chicken
3 oz (90 g) sliced cucumber and green pepper
1 slice (1 oz/30 g) rye bread
2 teaspoons mayonnaise
5 fl oz (150 ml) low-fat natural yogurt with 1
    teaspoon honey and 1 oz (30 g) sultanas

EVENING MEAL
Cod with Lemon (page 260)
2 oz (60 g) cooked rice
3 oz (90 g) green beans
4 oz (120 g) orange sections

**SNACKS OR DRINKS
AT PLANNED TIMES**
5 fl oz (150 ml) skim milk

DAY 3

MORNING MEAL
4 oz (120 g) orange sections
1 oz (30 g) Cheddar cheese
1 slice (1 oz/30 g) bread

MIDDAY MEAL
3 oz (90 g) grilled beefburger
tomato and onion salad with 1 teaspoon olive
    oil and wine vinegar
1 oz (30 g) bread roll
4 oz (120 g) peaches

EVENING MEAL
4 oz (120 g) cooked chicken
3 oz (90 g) peas with 1 teaspoon margarine
green salad with 1 teaspoon mayonnaise
¼ pint (150 ml) raspberry jelly and 5 oz
    (150 g) raspberries

**SNACKS OR DRINKS
AT PLANNED TIMES**
½ pint (300 ml) skim milk, 5 fl oz (150 ml)
    low-fat natural yogurt

DAY4

MORNING MEAL
2½ fl oz (75 ml) apple juice
¾ oz (20 g) porridge oats cooked in water
with 5 fl oz (150 ml) skim milk and 1
teaspoon golden syrup

MIDDAY MEAL
3 eggs, scrambled in 1 teaspoon margarine
3 oz (90 g) poached mushrooms
1 slice (1 oz/30 g) wholemeal bread, toasted
1 teaspoon margarine
1 medium orange

EVENING MEAL
5 oz (150 g) roast beef
3 oz (90 g) baked jacket potato with 1
teaspoon margarine
3 oz (90 g) green beans
¼ small pineapple

SNACKS OR DRINKS AT PLANNED TIMES
5 fl oz (150 ml) skim milk, 5 fl oz (150 ml)
low-fat natural yogurt

DAY5

MORNING MEAL
½ medium grapefruit
1 oz (30 g) Cheddar cheese on 1 slice (1 oz/
30 g) bread, toasted

MIDDAY MEAL
3 oz (90 g) tuna mixed with 2 teaspoons
mayonnaise
green pepper, tomato and onion salad with
iceberg lettuce and lemon juice
1 slice (1 oz/30 g) wholemeal bread
1 teaspoon low-fat spread

EVENING MEAL
4 oz (120 g) sliced roast chicken
3 oz (90 g) spinach
3 oz (90 g) carrots
1 oz (30 g) French bread
1 teaspoon low-fat spread
4 oz (120 g) pineapple

SNACKS OR DRINKS AT PLANNED TIMES
½ pint (300 ml) skim milk, 5 fl oz (150 ml)
low-fat natural yogurt, 1 oz (30 g) sultanas,
1 portion stewed rhubarb

DAY6

MORNING MEAL
½ medium grapefruit
¾ oz (20 g) cornflakes
5 fl oz (150 ml) skim milk

MIDDAY MEAL
2 hardboiled eggs
1 oz (30 g) Cheddar cheese
mixed salad with 1 tablespoon mayonnaise
4 oz (120 g) fruit salad

EVENING MEAL
Irish Stew (page 255)
4 oz (120 g) peaches
2 oz (60 g) vanilla ice cream

SNACKS OR DRINKS AT PLANNED TIMES
5 fl oz (150 ml) skim milk, 5 fl oz (150 ml) low-fat natural yogurt, 2½ oz (75 g) cottage cheese with 2 cream crackers

DAY7

MORNING MEAL
½ medium grapefruit
1 poached egg
1 oz (30 g) muffin, toasted
1 teaspoon margarine

MIDDAY MEAL
Ginger-Grilled Chicken (page 238)
3 oz (90 g) mange tout peas, sliced celery, cucumber and mushroom salad with **Vinaigrette Dressing** (page 293)
3 oz (90 g) sweet corn
1 medium apple

EVENING MEAL
3 oz (90 g) peeled prawns
2 oz (60 g) cooked pasta shells mixed with 1 tablespoon chopped red pepper and 2 teaspoons low-calorie mayonnaise
tomato and lettuce salad
5 fl oz (150 ml) low-fat natural yogurt with 1 oz (30 g) chopped dried apricots

SNACKS OR DRINKS AT PLANNED TIMES
½ pint (300 ml) skim milk

WEEK 12

Sauteed vegetables must be cooked over a good heat and kept in constant motion in the cooking pan. They're delicious. We've borrowed the method from the Chinese.

DAY 1

MORNING MEAL
½ medium grapefruit
¾ oz (20 g) cornflakes
5 fl oz (150 ml) skim milk

MIDDAY MEAL
5 oz (150 g) cottage cheese
2 oz (60 g) ham
mixed salad with 2 teaspoons mayonnaise
2 oz (60 g) bread roll

EVENING MEAL
4 oz (120 g) roast chicken
3 oz (90 g) peas
3 oz (90 g) cabbage
1 teaspoon margarine
Baked Apple (page 295)

SNACKS OR DRINKS AT PLANNED TIMES
5 fl oz (150 ml) skim milk, 5 fl oz (150 ml) low-fat natural yogurt, 1 medium orange

DAY 2

MORNING MEAL
4 fl oz (120 ml) orange juice
1 poached egg
1 slice (1 oz/30 g) wholemeal bread

MIDDAY MEAL
4 oz (120 g) tuna
2 teaspoons mayonnaise
iceberg lettuce with sliced tomatoes
3 oz (90 g) beetroot
crispbread, up to 80 calories, with 2 teaspoons low-fat spread

EVENING MEAL
3 oz (90 g) grilled veal
3 oz (90 g) baked jacket potato
4 fl oz (120 ml) red wine
4 oz (120 g) fruit salad

SNACKS OR DRINKS AT PLANNED TIMES
4 oz (120 g) pear, ½ pint (300 ml) skim milk, 5 fl oz (150 ml) low-fat natural yogurt

DAY 3

MORNING MEAL
2 inch (5 cm) wedge honeydew melon
1 oz (30 g) Cheddar cheese, grilled on 1 slice (1 oz/30 g) wholemeal bread, toasted

MIDDAY MEAL
2 oz (60 g) sliced cooked chicken and 1 sliced hard-boiled egg
mixed salad with 2 teaspoons salad dressing

EVENING MEAL
4 oz (120 g) grilled haddock with lemon wedges
3 oz (90 g) sliced beetroot
3 oz (90 g) spinach
green salad with 2 teaspoons salad dressing
1 slice (1 oz/30 g) wholemeal bread
2 teaspoons low-fat spread
1 medium orange

SNACKS OR DRINKS AT PLANNED TIMES
½ pint (300 ml) skim milk, 5 fl oz (150 ml) low-fat natural yogurt, 1 oz (30 g) raisins

DAY4

MORNING MEAL
½ medium banana
¾ oz (20 g) muesli
5 fl oz (150 ml) skim milk

MIDDAY MEAL
Chicken Livers Sauteed in Wine (page 257)
sliced cucumber and tomato salad
1 oz (30 g) wholemeal roll
1 teaspoon margarine
4 oz (120 g) pear

EVENING MEAL
4 oz (120 g) veal escalope
1 teaspoon vegetable oil
3 oz (90 g) broccoli
3 oz (90 g) potatoes
4 oz (120 g) grapefruit and orange sections

SNACKS OR DRINKS AT PLANNED TIMES
5 fl oz (150 ml) skim milk, 5 fl oz (150 ml) low-fat natural yogurt, 1 portion stewed rhubarb

DAY5

MORNING MEAL
4 fl oz (120 ml) orange juice
1 boiled egg
1 slice (1 oz/30 g) bread, toasted
1 teaspoon margarine

MIDDAY MEAL
4 oz (120 g) grilled cod
3 oz (90 g) green beans
3 oz (90 g) carrots
1 teaspoon margarine
1 slice (1 oz/30 g) wholemeal bread
1 teaspoon margarine
5 oz (150 g) blackcurrants with **Custard** (page 297)

EVENING MEAL
3 oz (90 g) cooked ham
3 oz (90 g) poached mushrooms
1 medium grilled tomato
1 medium apple

SNACKS OR DRINKS AT PLANNED TIMES
5 fl oz (150 ml) skim milk, 5 fl oz (150 ml) low-fat natural yogurt

DAY 6

MORNING MEAL
1 medium orange
2½ oz (75 g) cottage cheese
1 slice (1 oz/30 g) raisin bread, toasted
1 teaspoon low-fat spread

MIDDAY MEAL
Chicken Teriyaki (page 240)
2 oz (60 g) cooked rice
beansprouts, sliced onions and green
    peppers, sauteed in 1 teaspoon vegetable
    oil
2 inch (5 cm) wedge honeydew melon

EVENING MEAL
3 oz (90 g) grilled plaice
1 medium grilled tomato
3 oz (90 g) broccoli
cucumber, radish and green pepper slices on
    lettuce with 2 teaspoons salad dressing

SNACKS OR DRINKS AT PLANNED TIMES
½ pint (300 ml) skim milk, 5 fl oz (150 ml)
    low-fat natural yogurt with ½ oz (15 g)
    raisins

DAY 7

MORNING MEAL
½ medium grapefruit
¾ oz (20 g) porridge oats cooked with water,
    served with 5 fl oz (150 ml) skim milk

MIDDAY MEAL
6 oz (180 g) grilled rump steak
3 oz (90 g) kale
3 oz (90 g) baked jacket potato
2 teaspoons low-fat spread
green salad with 1 teaspoon mayonnaise
4 fl oz (120 ml) red wine
4 oz (120 g) pear

EVENING MEAL
2 oz (60 g) Cheddar cheese toasted on 1 slice
    (1 oz/30 g) bread
green pepper, tomato and onion slices with 1
    teaspoon olive oil, wine vinegar and pinch
    oregano
5 fl oz (150 ml) low-fat natural yogurt with 1
    teaspoon honey and 2 dried dates,
    chopped

SNACKS OR DRINKS AT PLANNED TIMES
5 fl oz (150 ml) skim milk

WEEK 13

'Boil-in-the-bag' fish meals such as on Day 2 this week should only be used once a week. Plan them for a busy day.

DAY 1

MORNING MEAL
4 oz (120 g) apricots
2½ oz (75 g) cottage cheese
1 slice (1 oz/30 g) wholemeal bread

MIDDAY MEAL
2-egg omelette with pinch mixed herbs cooked in 1 teaspoon vegetable oil
3 oz (90 g) grilled mushrooms
2 medium grilled tomatoes
crispbread, up to 80 calories
1 teaspoon low-fat spread
1 medium orange

EVENING MEAL
5 oz (150 g) grilled halibut
3 oz (90 g) carrots
iceberg lettuce with 1 teaspoon mayonnaise
1 oz (30 g) bread roll
1 teaspoon low-fat spread
4 oz (120 g) stewed apple with **Custard** (page 297)

SNACKS OR DRINKS AT PLANNED TIMES
5 fl oz (150 ml) skim milk, 5 fl oz (150 ml) low-fat natural yogurt

DAY2

MORNING MEAL
4 fl oz (120 ml) orange juice
¾ oz (20 g) cornflakes
5 fl oz (150 ml) skim milk

MIDDAY MEAL
2 oz (60 g) Cheddar cheese
1 boiled egg
green salad with sliced tomatoes and onions
    with 2 teaspoons salad dressing and 1
    tablespoon wine vinegar
1 slice (1 oz/30 g) bread
1 teaspoon margarine
4 oz (120 g) fruit cocktail

EVENING MEAL
1 portion boil-in-the-bag fish in sauce (any
    type)
3 oz (90 g) carrots
3 oz (90 g) green beans
2 teaspoons low-fat spread

**SNACKS OR DRINKS
AT PLANNED TIMES**
5 fl oz (150 ml) skim milk, 5 fl oz (150 ml)
    low-fat natural yogurt, 5 oz (150 g)
    blackcurrants, 1 digestive biscuit, 2½ oz
    (75 g) curd cheese

DAY3

MORNING MEAL
½ medium grapefruit
1 egg, scrambled in 1 teaspoon margarine
1 slice (1 oz/30 g) wholemeal bread, toasted
1 teaspoon margarine

MIDDAY MEAL
3 oz (90 g) grilled chicken
2 grilled tomatoes
3 oz (90 g) peas
2 oz (60 g) cooked noodles

EVENING MEAL
4 oz (120 g) roast beef
3 oz (90 g) baked jacket potato with 2½ fl oz
    (75 ml) low-fat natural yogurt and chopped
    chives
tomato, lettuce and onion salad with 1
    teaspoon vegetable oil and 1 tablespoon
    wine vinegar
4 oz (120 g) pineapple with 2½ fl oz (75 ml)
    low-fat natural yogurt

**SNACKS OR DRINKS
AT PLANNED TIMES**
½ pint (300 ml) skim milk, 1 medium apple

DAY4

MORNING MEAL
1 medium orange
¾ oz (20 g) bran flakes
5 fl oz (150 ml) skim milk

MIDDAY MEAL
shredded iceberg lettuce
1 hard-boiled egg, sliced
1 oz (30 g) grated Cheddar cheese and
    tomato wedges with **Vinaigrette
    Dressing** (page 293)
crispbread, up to 80 calories
1 teaspoon margarine
¼ pint (150 ml) orange jelly with 4 oz (120 g)
    orange slices

EVENING MEAL
6 oz (180 g) grilled haddock with lemon
    wedges
3 oz (90 g) broad beans
3 oz (90 g) potatoes
2 teaspoons low-fat spread
5 oz (150 g) raspberries

**SNACKS OR DRINKS
AT PLANNED TIMES**
5 fl oz (150 ml) skim milk, 5 fl oz (150 ml)
    low-fat yogurt

DAY5

MORNING MEAL
½ medium grapefruit
2½ oz (75 g) cottage cheese
1 oz (30 g) French bread

MIDDAY MEAL
3 oz (90 g) cold roast chicken
tomato and watercress salad with 1
    teaspoon vegetable oil and wine vinegar
1 slice (1 oz/30 g) wholemeal bread
1 teaspoon low-fat spread
4 oz (120 g) fresh fruit salad

EVENING MEAL
4 oz (120 g) grilled lamb's liver
3 oz (90 g) sliced onion, sauteed in 1 teaspoon
    margarine
3 oz (90 g) carrots
1 teaspoon low-fat spread
5 fl oz (150 ml) low-fat natural yogurt with ½
    medium banana

**SNACKS OR DRINKS
AT PLANNED TIMES**
½ pint (300 ml) skim milk, 1 digestive biscuit

DAY6

MORNING MEAL
1 medium orange
¾ oz (20 g) muesli
5 fl oz (150 ml) skim milk

MIDDAY MEAL
Curried Kidney Beans (page 276)
lettuce and onion salad with **Vinaigrette Dressing** (page 293)
1 oz (30 g) pitta bread
5 fl oz (150 ml) low-fat natural yogurt with ½ oz (15 g) raisins

EVENING MEAL
6 oz (180 g) grilled veal
3 oz (90 g) celery hearts
1 oz (30 g) French bread
1 teaspoon low-fat spread
½ medium cantaloupe melon

SNACKS OR DRINKS AT PLANNED TIMES
5 fl oz (150 ml) skim milk

DAY7

MORNING MEAL
4 fl oz (120 ml) orange juice
1 oz (30 g) Cheddar cheese grilled on 1 slice (1 oz/30 g) wholemeal bread, toasted

MIDDAY MEAL
3 oz (90 g) sardines
green salad with sliced tomatoes and sliced onions
2 teaspoons low-calorie mayonnaise
4 oz (120 g) pineapple

EVENING MEAL
4 oz (120 g) grilled rump steak
4 oz (120 g) cooked rice
3 oz (90 g) courgettes
iceberg lettuce with 2 teaspoons olive oil and wine vinegar
4 oz (120 g) peaches
4 fl oz (120 ml) red wine

SNACKS OR DRINKS AT PLANNED TIMES
5 fl oz (150 ml) low-fat natural yogurt, ½ pint (300 ml) skim milk

WEEK 14

The lettuce family includes many interesting relatives – round, cos, iceberg, endive, cress, escarole etc. Try them in your salads this week.

DAY 1

MORNING MEAL
4 fl oz (120 ml) orange juice
1 poached egg
1 slice (1 oz/30 g) wholemeal bread
1 teaspoon margarine

MIDDAY MEAL
3 oz (90 g) grilled haddock
3 oz (90 g) carrots
3 oz (90 g) potatoes
1 teaspoon margarine
½ medium cantaloupe melon

EVENING MEAL
4 oz (120 g) roast chicken
3 oz (90 g) cauliflower
3 oz (90 g) Brussels sprouts
1 teaspoon margarine
1 medium apple

SNACKS OR DRINKS AT PLANNED TIMES
5 fl oz (150 ml) low-fat natural yogurt, ½ pint (300 ml) skim milk

DAY 2

MORNING MEAL
8 fl oz (240 ml) tomato juice
1 oz (30 g) Cheddar cheese
1 slice (1 oz/30 g) bread
1 teaspoon margarine

MIDDAY MEAL
3 oz (90 g) cold chicken
tomato and cucumber slices on lettuce with
    1 teaspoon low-calorie mayonnaise
1 slice (1 oz/30 g) wholemeal bread
4 oz (120 g) peaches

EVENING MEAL
4 oz (120 g) roast lamb
3 oz (90 g) broccoli
3 oz (90 g) celery
1½ teaspoons margarine
½ medium grapefruit

SNACKS OR DRINKS
AT PLANNED TIMES
½ pint (300 ml) skim milk, 5 fl oz (150 ml)
    low-fat natural yogurt

DAY 3

MORNING MEAL
½ medium banana
¾ oz (20 g) bran flakes
5 fl oz (150 ml) skim milk

MIDDAY MEAL
5 oz (150 g) uncooked chicken livers, sauteed
    in 1 teaspoon vegetable oil
Bacon-Flavoured Potato Salad (page 284)
1 slice (1 oz/30 g) wholemeal bread
1 teaspoon margarine
4 oz (120 g) fruit cocktail

EVENING MEAL
4 oz (120 g) grilled haddock
3 oz (90 g) peas
2 oz (60 g) cooked sliced mushrooms

SNACKS OR DRINKS
AT PLANNED TIMES
5 fl oz (150 ml) low-fat natural yogurt, 1
    medium orange, 5 fl oz (150 ml) skim milk

DAY4

MORNING MEAL
2½ fl oz (75 ml) apple juice
2½ oz (75 g) cottage cheese
1 oz (30 g) bread roll

MIDDAY MEAL
3-egg omelette cooked in 1 teaspoon
  vegetable oil, filled with 1 oz (30 g)
  Cheddar cheese
1 slice (1 oz/30 g) wholemeal bread
2 teaspoons low-fat spread

EVENING MEAL
9 oz (270 g) baked beans
1 slice (1 oz/30 g) bread
3 oz (90 g) courgettes
1 teaspoon margarine
green salad with wine vinegar
1 medium orange

**SNACKS OR DRINKS
AT PLANNED TIMES**
5 oz (150 g) strawberries, 5 fl oz (150 ml)
  low-fat natural yogurt, ½ pint (300 ml)
  skim milk

DAY5

MORNING MEAL
4 oz (120 g) grapefruit
¾ oz (20 g) cornflakes
5 fl oz (150 ml) skim milk

MIDDAY MEAL
4 oz (120 g) peeled prawns
1 tablespoon low-calorie seafood sauce
3 oz (90 g) green beans
1 slice (1 oz/30 g) wholemeal bread
2 teaspoons margarine
2 oz (60 g) stewed apple

EVENING MEAL
4 oz (120 g) grilled pork chop
2 oz (60 g) cooked apple, pureed
3 oz (90 g) cauliflower
2 teaspoons low-fat spread
4 fl oz (120 ml) red wine

**SNACKS OR DRINKS
AT PLANNED TIMES**
1 medium pear, 1 digestive biscuit, 15 fl oz
  (450 ml) skim milk

DAY 6

MORNING MEAL
1 medium orange
1 boiled egg
crispbread, up to 80 calories

MIDDAY MEAL
3 tablespoons peanut butter
1 slice (1 oz/30 g) wholemeal bread
tomato, lettuce and cucumber salad with
  lemon juice
1 medium pear

EVENING MEAL
4 oz (120 g) sliced roast chicken
3 oz (90 g) spinach
3 oz (90 g) carrots
4 oz (120 g) pineapple

SNACKS OR DRINKS AT PLANNED TIMES
5 fl oz (150 ml) low-fat natural yogurt, ½ pint
  (300 ml) skim milk

DAY 7

MORNING MEAL
½ medium banana
¾ oz (20 g) muesli
5 fl oz (150 ml) skim milk

MIDDAY MEAL
4 oz (120 g) grilled rump steak
3 oz (90 g) courgettes
3 oz (90 g) broccoli
2 teaspoons low-fat spread
4 oz (120 g) fruit salad
2 oz (60 g) vanilla ice cream

EVENING MEAL
2 breadcrumbed fish cakes, grilled
3 oz (90 g) baked beans
green salad with 2 teaspoons low-calorie
  mayonnaise
1 oz (30 g) bread roll
2 teaspoons low-fat spread
8 fl oz (240 ml) tomato juice

SNACKS OR DRINKS AT PLANNED TIMES
5 fl oz (150 ml) low-fat natural yogurt, 5 fl oz
  (150 ml) skim milk

WEEK 15

Easter and the Jewish Passover share one symbol – the egg. New birth, new life and the new season are all reflected in this festival week.

DAY 1

MORNING MEAL	4 fl oz (120 ml) orange juice **Matzo Brei** (page 224)
MIDDAY MEAL	5 oz (150 g) quark cheese green salad with sliced tomato and cucumber 1 teaspoon mayonnaise 1 slice (1 oz/30 g) wholemeal bread 1 medium orange mineral water with twist of lemon
EVENING MEAL	5 oz (150 g) grilled herring 3 oz (90 g) mushrooms sauteed in 1 teaspoon oil 3 oz (90 g) carrots 5 fl oz (150 ml) low-fat natural yogurt
SNACKS OR DRINKS AT PLANNED TIMES	½ pint (300 ml) skim milk, 2 oz (60 g) vanilla ice cream with 4 oz (120 g) mandarin oranges

DAY 2

MORNING MEAL
4 fl oz (120 ml) orange juice
¾ oz (20 g) cereal with 5 fl oz (150 ml) skim milk

MIDDAY MEAL
4 oz (120 g) grilled chicken
3 oz (90 g) green beans
green salad with sliced tomato
2 teaspoons mayonnaise
1 medium apple

EVENING MEAL
4 oz (120 g) grilled ham
3 oz (90 g) cooked potatoes
3 oz (90 g) carrots
1 teaspoon margarine

SNACKS OR DRINKS AT PLANNED TIMES
½ pint (300 ml) skim milk, 4 oz (120 g) apricots, 1 digestive biscuit, 2½ fl oz (75 ml) low-fat natural yogurt

DAY 3

MORNING MEAL
4 fl oz (120 ml) orange juice
1 boiled egg
1 slice (1 oz/30 g) bread
1 teaspoon margarine

MIDDAY MEAL
3 oz (90 g) canned tuna
Curried Cole Slaw (page 288)
3 oz (90 g) sweet corn
1 medium orange

EVENING MEAL
4 oz (120 g) grilled veal
3 oz (90 g) mange tout peas
1 medium tomato, sliced
green salad with 2 teaspoons vegetable oil, plus wine vinegar

SNACKS OR DRINKS AT PLANNED TIMES
Pear Frozen Yogurt (page 301), ½ pint (300 ml) skim milk

DAY4

MORNING MEAL
4 oz (120 g) grapefruit sections
2½ oz (75 g) soft cheese
1 slice (1 oz/30 g) currant bread
1 teaspoon margarine

MIDDAY MEAL
3 oz (90 g) sliced roast turkey or chicken
1 medium tomato, sliced
shredded lettuce
1 slice (1 oz/30 g) wholemeal bread
1 teaspoon margarine
4 oz (120 g) fruit salad

EVENING MEAL
4 oz (120 g) grilled rump steak
3 oz (90 g) baked jacket potato with 1
   teaspoon margarine
3 oz (90 g) onion
3 oz (90 g) spinach

SNACKS OR DRINKS AT PLANNED TIMES
5 oz (150 g) raspberries, 5 fl oz (150 ml) low-
   fat natural yogurt, ½ pint (300 ml) skim
   milk

DAY5

MORNING MEAL
2½ fl oz (75 ml) apple juice
1 oz (30 g) Cheddar cheese
1 slice (1 oz/30 g) wholemeal bread

MIDDAY MEAL
5 oz (150 g) grilled cod steak
3 oz (90 g) courgettes
1 slice (1 oz/30 g) wholemeal bread
1 teaspoon margarine
1 medium orange

EVENING MEAL
Vegetable-Cheese Platter (page 233)
sliced cucumber
2 teaspoons mayonnaise
½ pint (300 ml) lager or cider

SNACKS OR DRINKS AT PLANNED TIMES
5 fl oz (150 ml) low-fat natural yogurt, 7½ fl oz
   (225 ml) skim milk, 1 medium apple

DAY6

MORNING MEAL
½ medium banana, sliced
¾ oz (20 g) cereal
5 fl oz (150 ml) skim milk

MIDDAY MEAL
4 oz (120 g) grilled chicken livers
2 medium tomatoes, grilled
1 oz (30 g) wholemeal roll
2 teaspoons low-fat spread
4 oz (120 g) fruit salad

EVENING MEAL
Chicken Capri with Potatoes (page 235)
3 oz (90 g) courgettes
green salad with 2 teaspoons low-calorie
   mayonnaise

SNACKS OR DRINKS AT PLANNED TIMES
1 medium orange, 5 fl oz (150 ml) low-fat
   natural yogurt, 5 fl oz (150 ml) skim milk

DAY7

MORNING MEAL
Swedish Apple Bake (page 295)

MIDDAY MEAL
3 oz (90 g) sliced roast beef
1 medium tomato, sliced green pepper rings
   on lettuce with 1 teaspoon mayonnaise
1 slice (1 oz/30 g) wholemeal bread
4 oz (120 g) orange sections

EVENING MEAL
4 oz (120 g) grilled lemon sole
3 oz (90 g) carrots dotted with 1 teaspoon
   margarine
green salad with **Vinaigrette Dressing** (page
   293)
2 inch (5 cm) wedge honeydew melon

SNACKS OR DRINKS AT PLANNED TIMES
5 fl oz (150 ml) low-fat natural yogurt, ½ pint
   (300 ml) skim milk, 1 digestive biscuit

WEEK 16

Spring lamb is one of the meat dishes of this season and it deserves special attention in cooking. We suggest orange and rosemary to enhance its flavour.

DAY 1

MORNING MEAL	4 fl oz (120 ml) grapefruit juice 1 boiled egg 1 slice (1 oz/30 g) bread 2 teaspoons margarine
MIDDAY MEAL	3 oz (90 g) canned tuna with lettuce, tomato and cucumber 1 slice (1 oz/30 g) bread 1 teaspoon margarine 1 medium apple
EVENING MEAL	4 oz (120 g) cooked chicken breast 3 oz (90 g) cauliflower 3 oz (90 g) peas 2 oz (60 g) boiled rice 1 medium orange
SNACKS OR DRINKS AT PLANNED TIMES	½ pint (300 ml) skim milk, 5 fl oz (150 ml) low-fat natural yogurt

DAY2

MORNING MEAL
4 fl oz (120 ml) grapefruit juice
¾ oz (20 g) cornflakes served with 5 fl oz (150 ml) skim milk

MIDDAY MEAL
5 oz (150 g) cottage cheese with spring onions, celery, lettuce and tomato with 2 teaspoons salad dressing
1 slice (1 oz/30 g) bread
1 teaspoon margarine
1 medium apple

EVENING MEAL
6 oz (180 g) poached haddock
3 oz (90 g) poached mushrooms
1 (1 oz/30 g) granary roll
1 teaspoon margarine
1 medium pear

SNACKS OR DRINKS AT PLANNED TIMES
15 fl oz (450 ml) skim milk

DAY3

MORNING MEAL
1 medium orange
1 oz (30 g) Cheddar cheese grilled on 1 slice (1 oz/30 g) wholemeal bread, toasted

MIDDAY MEAL
2 hard-boiled eggs, sliced lettuce, tomato and cucumber, chopped, with 2 teaspoons salad dressing
crispbread, up to 80 calories
1 teaspoon margarine
1 medium apple

EVENING MEAL
5 oz (150 g) grilled lamb's liver
3 oz (90 g) onion, cut in rings and sauteed in 1 teaspoon vegetable oil
3 oz (90 g) carrots
2 oz (60 g) cooked rice
4 fl oz (120 ml) grapefruit juice

SNACKS OR DRINKS AT PLANNED TIMES
½ pint (300 ml) skim milk, 5 fl oz (150 ml) low-fat natural yogurt

DAY4

MORNING MEAL
½ medium grapefruit
1 scrambled egg with 1 medium tomato
1 slice (1 oz/30 g) bread, toasted
1 teaspoon margarine

MIDDAY MEAL
3 oz (90 g) canned sardines, with lettuce, tomato and cucumber, with 1 teaspoon vegetable oil
2 water biscuits
2 teaspoons low-fat spread
3 oz (90 g) grapes

EVENING MEAL
4 oz (120 g) thick slice ham, grilled with 4 oz (120 g) pineapple slices
3 oz (90 g) peas
3 oz (90 g) broccoli

SNACKS OR DRINKS AT PLANNED TIMES
½ pint (300 ml) skim milk, 5 fl oz (150 ml) low-fat natural yogurt

---

DAY5

MORNING MEAL
½ medium grapefruit
¾ oz (20 g) muesli with 5 fl oz (150 ml) skim milk

MIDDAY MEAL
1 (2 oz/60 g) bap spread with 2 teaspoons margarine and filled with 2 oz (60 g) grated Cheddar cheese, lettuce and tomato slices
1 medium banana

EVENING MEAL
Piquant Lemon Sole (page 264)
3 oz (90 g) courgettes
3 oz (90 g) spring greens
2 oz (60 g) vanilla ice cream

SNACKS OR DRINKS AT PLANNED TIMES
15 fl oz (450 ml) skim milk

DAY 6

MORNING MEAL
4 fl oz (120 ml) orange juice
2½ oz (75 g) curd cheese mixed with 1
    teaspoon chopped chives and spread on 1
    slice (1 oz/30 g) brown bread, toasted

MIDDAY MEAL
4 fish fingers, breadcrumbed, spread with 1
    teaspoon margarine, and grilled
3 oz (90 g) peas
3 oz (90 g) baked beans
4 oz (120 g) fruit cocktail

EVENING MEAL
3 oz (90 g) grilled rump steak
3 oz (90 g) broccoli
3 oz (90 g) carrots dotted with 2 teaspoons
    margarine
1 medium apple

**SNACKS OR DRINKS
AT PLANNED TIMES**
½ pint (300 ml) skim milk, 5 fl oz (150 ml)
    low-fat natural yogurt

DAY 7

MORNING MEAL
4 fl oz (120 ml) orange juice
¾ oz (20 g) wheat flakes served with 5 fl oz
    (150 ml) skim milk

MIDDAY MEAL
Orange Lamb with Rosemary (page 246)
3 oz (90 g) spring greens
2 oz (60 g) boiled rice

EVENING MEAL
4 oz (120 g) canned salmon with mixed salad
    and 3 oz (90 g) diced beetroot with 2
    teaspoons mayonnaise
1 digestive biscuit crumbled into 5 fl oz (150
    ml) low-fat natural yogurt with 1 oz (30 g)
    sultanas

**SNACKS OR DRINKS
AT PLANNED TIMES**
5 fl oz (150 ml) skim milk

WEEK 17

Courgettes feature on Day 5. They're really just miniature marrows and need short cooking. They absorb well the flavour of tomato, garlic and basil in **Courgettes Italian Style**

DAY 1

MORNING MEAL	½ medium grapefruit 1 egg, scrambled in 1 teaspoon low-fat spread 1 medium grilled tomato 1 slice (1 oz/30 g) bread 2 teaspoons low-fat spread
MIDDAY MEAL	5 oz (150 g) sliced roast chicken 3 oz (90 g) carrots 3 oz (90 g) courgettes 1 teaspoon low-fat spread **Baked Apple** (page 295)
EVENING MEAL	5 oz (150 g) cottage cheese mixed salad 4 oz (120 g) mandarin oranges with 5 fl oz (150 ml) low-fat natural yogurt
SNACKS OR DRINKS AT PLANNED TIMES	½ pint (300 ml) skim milk, 2 oz (60 g) hot cross bun, 2 teaspoons low-fat spread

DAY 2

MORNING MEAL

4 fl oz (120 ml) orange juice
¾ oz (20 g) porridge oats cooked with water
and ½ oz (15 g) raisins
5 fl oz (150 ml) skim milk

MIDDAY MEAL

4 oz (120 g) grilled plaice with 1 teaspoon
margarine
3 oz (90 g) green beans
1 medium grilled tomato
1 slice (1 oz/30 g) wholemeal bread

EVENING MEAL

4 oz (120 g) grilled ham steak
3 oz (90 g) swede
3 oz (90 g) boiled potato, mashed together
with 2 teaspoons margarine
3 oz (90 g) carrots
6 oz (180 g) peaches

**SNACKS OR DRINKS
AT PLANNED TIMES**

5 fl oz (150 ml) low-fat natural yogurt, 5 fl oz
(150 ml) skim milk

DAY 3

MORNING MEAL

½ medium grapefruit
2½ oz (75 g) cottage cheese
1 slice (1 oz/30 g) wholemeal bread
2 teaspoons low-fat spread

MIDDAY MEAL

4 oz (120 g) tuna fish
Curried Cole Slaw (page 288)
1 oz (30 g) bread roll
3 oz (90 g) white grapes

EVENING MEAL

3 oz (90 g) grilled veal
3 oz (90 g) broccoli with 1 teaspoon
margarine
mixed green salad with 1 teaspoon vegetable
oil

**SNACKS OR DRINKS
AT PLANNED TIMES**

½ medium banana sliced into 5 fl oz (150 ml)
low-fat natural yogurt, ½ pint (300 ml)
skim milk

DAY4

MORNING MEAL

½ medium banana, sliced
¾ oz (20 g) cereal
5 fl oz (150 ml) skim milk
1 slice (1 oz/30 g) wholemeal bread
2 teaspoons low-fat spread
½ teaspoon honey

MIDDAY MEAL

8 fl oz (240 ml) tomato juice
4 oz (120 g) liver sausage
mixed salad with 3 oz (90 g) diced beetroot
2 teaspoons low-calorie mayonnaise

EVENING MEAL

4 oz (120 g) roast turkey
3 oz (90 g) white cabbage
3 oz (90 g) carrots
1 medium baked onion
4 oz (120 g) orange sections

SNACKS OR DRINKS AT PLANNED TIMES

1 slice (1 oz/30 g) currant bread, 1 teaspoon margarine, 5 fl oz (150 ml) low-fat natural yogurt, 5 fl oz (150 ml) skim milk

---

DAY5

MORNING MEAL

4 oz (120 g) peaches, chopped and combined with 2½ oz (75 g) cottage cheese
1 slice (1 oz/30 g) currant bread

MIDDAY MEAL

3 tablespoons peanut butter
crispbread, up to 80 calories
1 medium tomato, sliced with onion rings
1 medium apple

EVENING MEAL

4 oz (120 g) poached cod
3 oz (90 g) spinach
Courgettes Italian Style (page 279)
2 oz (60 g) cooked pasta shells
1 medium orange

SNACKS OR DRINKS AT PLANNED TIMES

5 fl oz (150 ml) low-fat natural yogurt, ½ pint (300 ml) skim milk

DAY 6

MORNING MEAL
1 medium apple
1 oz (30 g) Edam cheese
1 slice (1 oz/30 g) wholemeal bread
2 teaspoons low-fat spread

MIDDAY MEAL
Cream of Cauliflower Soup (page 216)
3 oz (90 g) tuna fish
mixed green salad with **Vinaigrette
    Dressing** (page 293)
1 medium orange, diced
5 fl oz (150 ml) low-fat natural yogurt

EVENING MEAL
Lamb's Liver Creole (page 254)
3 oz (90 g) peas
2 oz (60 g) cooked rice
4 oz (120 g) apricots
2 oz (60 g) vanilla ice cream

**SNACKS OR DRINKS
AT PLANNED TIMES**
7½ fl oz (225 ml) skim milk, 2 cream crackers,
    2 teaspoons low-fat spread, 1 teaspoon
    grated Parmesan cheese

DAY 7

MORNING MEAL
Swedish Apple Bake (page 295)
5 fl oz (150 ml) low-fat natural yogurt

MIDDAY MEAL
4 oz (120 g) roast beef
3 oz (90 g) parsnips
3 oz (90 g) savoy cabbage
3 oz (90 g) carrots
2 teaspoons low-fat spread
2 medium plums

EVENING MEAL
1 oz (30 g) Cheddar cheese
2 hard-boiled eggs
1 medium tomato
mixed green salad
2 teaspoons mayonnaise

**SNACKS OR DRINKS
AT PLANNED TIMES**
1 digestive biscuit, ½ pint (300 ml) skim milk,
    1 medium orange

WEEK 18

After the holiday period you will probably want to relax, so this week the meals are quick and easy to prepare.

DAY 1

MORNING MEAL
4 fl oz (120 ml) orange juice
¾ oz (20 g) cornflakes
5 fl oz (150 ml) skim milk

MIDDAY MEAL
4 oz (120 g) grilled cod
3 oz (90 g) broccoli
1 slice (1 oz/30 g) wholemeal bread
1 teaspoon margarine
1 medium apple

EVENING MEAL
4 oz (120 g) roast chicken
3 oz (90 g) spinach
3 oz (90 g) cooked potatoes
2 teaspoons margarine

SNACKS OR DRINKS AT PLANNED TIMES
1 medium orange, 5 fl oz (150 ml) low-fat
natural yogurt, 5 fl oz (150 ml) skim milk

DAY 2

MORNING MEAL
½ medium grapefruit
1 oz (30 g) Cheddar cheese
1 slice (1 oz/30 g) bread

MIDDAY MEAL
3 oz (90 g) cold roast chicken
mixed salad
1 teaspoon mayonnaise
1 oz (30 g) French bread

EVENING MEAL
4 oz (120 g) grilled lamb's liver
3 oz (90 g) broccoli
2 teaspoons low-fat spread
green salad
2 teaspoons salad dressing
1 medium orange

SNACKS OR DRINKS AT PLANNED TIMES
½ medium banana, ½ pint (300 ml) skim milk, 5 fl oz (150 ml) low-fat natural yogurt

---

DAY 3

MORNING MEAL
4 fl oz (120 ml) orange juice
1 boiled egg
1 slice (1 oz/30 g) wholemeal bread
1 teaspoon margarine

MIDDAY MEAL
5 oz (150 g) cottage cheese
lettuce with sliced tomato
2 cream crackers
4 oz (120 g) fruit cocktail

EVENING MEAL
5 oz (150 g) steamed plaice
3 oz (90 g) green beans
2 teaspoons low-fat spread
green salad with 1 teaspoon vegetable oil and wine vinegar

SNACKS OR DRINKS AT PLANNED TIMES
½ pint (300 ml) skim milk, 5 fl oz (150 ml) low-fat natural yogurt, 1 medium apple

DAY4

MORNING MEAL
1 medium orange
¾ oz (20 g) muesli
5 fl oz (150 ml) skim milk

MIDDAY MEAL
4 oz (120 g) mussels
lettuce with celery and cucumber
3 teaspoons salad cream
1 oz (30 g) French bread
1 portion stewed rhubarb

EVENING MEAL
4 oz (120 g) roast chicken
3 oz (90 g) cooked potatoes
3 oz (90 g) broccoli
3 teaspoons low-fat spread
green salad
4 oz (120 g) fruit cocktail

SNACKS OR DRINKS AT PLANNED TIMES
½ medium banana, 5 fl oz (150 ml) low-fat natural yogurt, 5 fl oz (150 ml) skim milk

---

DAY5

MORNING MEAL
8 fl oz (240 ml) tomato juice
1 oz (30 g) Edam cheese
1 slice (1 oz/30 g) wholemeal bread

MIDDAY MEAL
4 oz (120 g) cold roast chicken
lettuce
1 medium tomato
2 teaspoons mayonnaise
2 cream crackers
1 medium apple

EVENING MEAL
3 oz (90 g) roast lamb
3 oz (90 g) carrots
3 oz (90 g) cauliflower
1 teaspoon margarine

SNACKS OR DRINKS AT PLANNED TIMES
5 fl oz (150 ml) low-fat natural yogurt, ½ pint (300 ml) skim milk, 4 oz (120 g) peaches

DAY6

MORNING MEAL
½ medium grapefruit
1 poached egg
1 slice (1 oz/30 g) wholemeal bread
1 teaspoon margarine

MIDDAY MEAL
9 oz (270 g) baked beans
3 oz (90 g) poached mushrooms
1 slice (1 oz/30 g) wholemeal bread
1 teaspoon margarine

EVENING MEAL
4 oz (120 g) peeled prawns
lettuce with tomato, onion and cucumber
2 teaspoons salad dressing
3 oz (90 g) grapes

SNACKS OR DRINKS AT PLANNED TIMES
4 oz (120 g) fruit cocktail, 5 fl oz (150 ml)
   low-fat natural yogurt, ½ pint (300 ml)
   skim milk

DAY7

MORNING MEAL
3 oz (90 g) grapes
¾ oz (20 g) porridge oats cooked with water
5 fl oz (150 ml) skim milk

MIDDAY MEAL
5 oz (150 g) roast chicken
3 oz (90 g) green beans
3 oz (90 g) carrots
2 teaspoons low-fat spread

EVENING MEAL
3-egg omelette filled with 3 oz (90 g)
   poached, chopped mushrooms
2 teaspoons margarine
2 oz (60 g) bread roll
4 oz (120 g) peaches

SNACKS OR DRINKS AT PLANNED TIMES
1 medium orange, 5 fl oz (150 ml) skim milk,
   5 fl oz (150 ml) low-fat natural yogurt

WEEK 19

The merry month of May brings the May Bank Holiday and the historic echoes of May Queens. Young girls believed that if they washed their faces in the morning dew it would improve their complexions – perhaps it's safer to rely on a healthy diet!

DAY 1

MORNING MEAL
4 oz (120 g) sliced peaches
2½ oz (75 g) curd cheese
crispbread, up to 80 calories
1 teaspoon margarine

MIDDAY MEAL
4 oz (120 g) canned salmon
sliced tomato and onion rings on lettuce with
    2 teaspoons mayonnaise
1 slice (1 oz/30 g) rye bread, toasted
5 fl oz (150 ml) low-fat natural yogurt with 1
    tablespoon jam

EVENING MEAL
6 oz (180 g) butter beans
1 oz (30 g) grated Cheddar cheese
3 oz (90 g) green beans
1 slice (1 oz/30 g) brown bread
4 fl oz (120 ml) orange juice

SNACKS OR DRINKS AT PLANNED TIMES
1 medium apple, ½ pint (300 ml) skim milk

DAY 2

MORNING MEAL
4 oz (120 g) grapefruit sections
¾ oz (20 g) cornflakes
5 fl oz (150 ml) skim milk

MIDDAY MEAL
4 oz (120 g) grilled lamb's liver
1 teaspoon vegetable oil
3 oz (90 g) sliced courgettes
green salad with **Vinaigrette Dressing** (page 293)
1 medium pear

EVENING MEAL
4 oz (120 g) grilled mackerel
3 oz (90 g) peas
1 medium tomato, halved and grilled
1 slice (1 oz/30 g) wholemeal bread
1 teaspoon margarine
4 fl oz (120 ml) white wine

SNACKS OR DRINKS AT PLANNED TIMES
15 fl oz (450 ml) skim milk, 1 medium apple

DAY 3

MORNING MEAL
2½ fl oz (75 ml) apple juice
1 scrambled egg
1 slice (1 oz/30 g) bread, toasted
1 teaspoon margarine

MIDDAY MEAL
3 oz (90 g) roast chicken
3 oz (90 g) peas
2 oz (60 g) cooked rice, with 2 teaspoons margarine
1 medium orange

EVENING MEAL
4 oz (120 g) grilled plaice
3 oz (90 g) spinach
3 oz (90 g) sliced carrots
5 oz (150 g) gooseberries

SNACKS OR DRINKS AT PLANNED TIMES
crispbread, up to 80 calories, with 1 tablespoon jam, 5 fl oz (150 ml) low-fat natural yogurt, ½ pint (300 ml) skim milk

DAY4

MORNING MEAL
4 fl oz (120 ml) grapefruit juice
1 oz (30 g) Cheddar cheese, grilled on 1 slice (1 oz/30 g) wholemeal bread

MIDDAY MEAL
4 oz (120 g) boiled frankfurters with 1 teaspoon French mustard
3 oz (90 g) sauerkraut
3 oz (90 g) peas dotted with 2 teaspoons margarine
4 oz (120 g) mandarin oranges
½ pint (300 ml) lager or cider

EVENING MEAL
3 oz (90 g) grilled veal
3 oz (90 g) sliced courgettes, dotted with 1 teaspoon margarine
2 oz (60 g) cooked noodles
1 medium peach

SNACKS OR DRINKS AT PLANNED TIMES
5 fl oz (150 ml) low-fat natural yogurt, ½ pint (300 ml) skim milk

---

DAY5

MORNING MEAL
½ medium banana, sliced
¾ oz (20 g) cornflakes
5 fl oz (150 ml) skim milk

MIDDAY MEAL
5 oz (150 g) poached halibut
3 oz (90 g) green beans
3 oz (90 g) cauliflower
3 oz (90 g) boiled potatoes
3 teaspoons low-fat spread
5 oz (150 g) strawberries

EVENING MEAL
3-egg omelette with mixed fresh herbs cooked in 1½ teaspoons vegetable oil with 3 oz (90 g) baked beans
1 medium apple

SNACKS OR DRINKS AT PLANNED TIMES
15 fl oz (450 ml) skim milk

DAY6

MORNING MEAL
1 medium pear
1 oz (30 g) Edam cheese
crispbread, up to 80 calories

MIDDAY MEAL
5 oz (150 g) cottage cheese with mixed salad
　　of lettuce, watercress, sliced tomatoes
　　and cucumber
1 tablespoon mayonnaise
2 medium plums

EVENING MEAL
5 oz (150 g) grilled haddock
3 oz (90 g) green beans
1 medium tomato, halved and grilled
3 oz (90 g) boiled potatoes
1 medium orange

SNACKS OR DRINKS AT PLANNED TIMES
5 fl oz (150 ml) low-fat natural yogurt, ½ pint
　　(300 ml) skim milk

DAY7

MORNING MEAL
½ medium grapefruit
¾ oz (20 g) puffed rice
5 fl oz (150 ml) skim milk

MIDDAY MEAL
5 oz (150 g) roast leg of lamb
3 oz (90 g) baked jacket potato
3 oz (90 g) green beans
3 oz (90 g) cauliflower
2 teaspoons margarine
4 oz (120 g) peaches and 2½ fl oz (75 ml)
　　low-fat natural yogurt

EVENING MEAL
1 hard-boiled egg with 2 oz (60 g) sardines
3 oz (90 g) beetroot
tomato, cucumber and grated carrot on
　　lettuce with 1 teaspoon low-calorie
　　mayonnaise
1 oz (30 g) French bread with 1 teaspoon
　　low-fat spread
4 oz (120 g) stewed apple

SNACKS OR DRINKS AT PLANNED TIMES
5 fl oz (150 ml) skim milk, 2½ fl oz (75 ml)
　　low-fat natural yogurt

WEEK 20

Nutmeg is usually associated with sweet dishes, but it's delicious too in vegetable dishes and with egg. Try it in Spinach Frittata – an Italian omelette – on Day 4.

DAY 1

MORNING MEAL
½ medium cantaloupe melon
¾ oz (20 g) cornflakes
5 fl oz (150 ml) skim milk

MIDDAY MEAL
Macaroni-Cheese Salad (page 223)
green salad with 2 teaspoons salad dressing
1 medium peach

EVENING MEAL
6 oz (180 g) grilled chicken
3 oz (90 g) onion rings, grilled
3 oz (90 g) broccoli
1 tablespoon tomato relish
3 oz (90 g) boiled potatoes dotted with 1
    teaspoon margarine
5 oz (150 g) strawberries

**SNACKS OR DRINKS
AT PLANNED TIMES**
12½ fl oz (375 ml) skim milk

DAY 2

MORNING MEAL
4 fl oz (120 ml) orange juice
1 poached egg
1 slice (1 oz/30 g) wholemeal bread, toasted
1 teaspoon margarine

MIDDAY MEAL
3 oz (90 g) sliced cooked chicken with lettuce, tomatoes and spring onions
2 teaspoons low-calorie mayonnaise
½ medium banana, sliced into 1 serving **Custard** (page 297)

EVENING MEAL
4 oz (120 g) grilled haddock, dotted with 1 teaspoon margarine
3 oz (90 g) carrots
3 oz (90 g) boiled potatoes
4 oz (120 g) fruit salad

SNACKS OR DRINKS AT PLANNED TIMES
5 fl oz (150 ml) low-fat natural yogurt, 5 fl oz (150 ml) skim milk

DAY 3

MORNING MEAL
½ medium grapefruit
Cinnamon-Cheese Toast (page 234)

MIDDAY MEAL
3 oz (90 g) peeled prawns with lettuce, cucumber, tomatoes and 4 teaspoons low-calorie mayonnaise
3 oz (90 g) sweet corn
3 oz (90 g) grapes

EVENING MEAL
4 oz (120 g) grilled liver
3 oz (90 g) onion
3 oz (90 g) poached mushrooms
1 medium tomato
1 teaspoon margarine
1 medium apple

SNACKS OR DRINKS AT PLANNED TIMES
5 fl oz (150 ml) low-fat natural yogurt, ½ pint (300 ml) skim milk

DAY4

MORNING MEAL

1 medium orange
¾ oz (20 g) porridge oats, cooked with water
5 fl oz (150 ml) skim milk

MIDDAY MEAL

Spinach Frittata (page 232)
green salad with 1 teaspoon vegetable oil,
    mixed with vinegar
1 slice (1 oz/30 g) wholemeal bread
1 teaspoon low-fat spread
1 portion stewed rhubarb
2 oz (60 g) vanilla ice cream

EVENING MEAL

8 fl oz (240 ml) tomato juice
6 oz (180 g) grilled mackerel
3 oz (90 g) courgettes
3 oz (90 g) boiled potatoes
4 oz (120 g) peaches

SNACKS OR DRINKS AT PLANNED TIMES

15 fl oz (450 ml) skim milk

DAY5

MORNING MEAL

4 fl oz (120 ml) orange juice
1 oz (30 g) Cheddar cheese grilled on 1 slice
    (1 oz/30 g) bread, toasted

MIDDAY MEAL

3 oz (90 g) cold cooked chicken
mixed salad with 2 teaspoons salad cream
5 fl oz (150 ml) low-fat natural yogurt with 5 oz
    (150 g) strawberries and 1 digestive
    biscuit

EVENING MEAL

4 oz (120 g) grilled trout
3 oz (90 g) spinach dotted with 2 teaspoons
    margarine
3 oz (90 g) carrots
1 medium orange

SNACKS OR DRINKS AT PLANNED TIMES

½ pint (300 ml) skim milk

DAY 6

MORNING MEAL	½ medium grapefruit ¾ oz (20 g) wheat flakes 5 fl oz (150 ml) skim milk
MIDDAY MEAL	3 tablespoons peanut butter 2 oz (60 g) wholemeal bread roll celery and cucumber sticks 1 medium apple
EVENING MEAL	5 oz (150 g) grilled rump steak 3 oz (90 g) poached mushrooms 3 oz (90 g) peas 1 medium tomato, halved and grilled 4 oz (120 g) fruit salad
SNACKS OR DRINKS AT PLANNED TIMES	15 fl oz (450 ml) skim milk

DAY 7

MORNING MEAL	4 fl oz (120 ml) orange juice 1 boiled egg 1 slice (1 oz/30 g) wholemeal bread, toasted 1 teaspoon margarine
MIDDAY MEAL	3 oz (90 g) roast beef 1 tablespoon horseradish relish 3 oz (90 g) baked onion 3 oz (90 g) broccoli 3 oz (90 g) baked jacket potato 1 teaspoon margarine 4 oz (120 g) pineapple 4 fl oz (120 ml) red wine
EVENING MEAL	4 oz (120 g) tuna with lettuce, tomato, cucumber, spring onions, and watercress 2 teaspoons salad dressing 1 medium apple
SNACKS OR DRINKS AT PLANNED TIMES	5 fl oz (150 ml) low-fat natural yogurt, ½ pint (300 ml) skim milk

WEEK 21

Chinese-style pancakes contain no flour but consist of a mouth-watering mixture of rice and vegetables stirred into beaten eggs. Soy sauce adds something special.

DAY 1

MORNING MEAL
4 oz (120 g) grapefruit sections
¾ oz (20 g) cereal
5 fl oz (150 ml) skim milk

MIDDAY MEAL
Chinese-Style Pancakes (page 225)
3 oz (90 g) green beans
1 slice (1 oz/30 g) wholemeal bread
1 teaspoon margarine
4 oz (120 g) cherries

EVENING MEAL
6 oz (180 g) grilled veal
3 oz (90 g) peas
1 teaspoon margarine
1 portion stewed rhubarb with 2 oz (60 g)
   vanilla ice cream

SNACKS OR DRINKS AT PLANNED TIMES
2½ fl oz (75 ml) low-fat natural yogurt with 5
   oz (150 g) strawberries, ½ pint (300 ml)
   skim milk

DAY 2

MORNING MEAL
2 medium apricots, stewed with 1 teaspoon honey
2½ oz (75 g) curd cheese
1 slice (1 oz/30 g) wholemeal bread, toasted

MIDDAY MEAL
4 oz (120 g) grilled chicken livers
Bean Salad (page 289)
1 slice (1 oz/30 g) wholemeal bread
1 teaspoon margarine
1 medium peach

EVENING MEAL
3 oz (90 g) smoked mackerel
sliced tomato and onion rings with 1 teaspoon oil mixed with lemon juice
Curried Cole Slaw (page 288)
5 oz (150 g) strawberries

SNACKS OR DRINKS AT PLANNED TIMES
5 fl oz (150 ml) low-fat natural yogurt, ½ pint (300 ml) skim milk

---

DAY 3

MORNING MEAL
4 fl oz (120 ml) grapefruit juice
¾ oz (20 g) porridge oats cooked with water
5 fl oz (150 ml) skim milk

MIDDAY MEAL
Broccoli Quiche (page 229)
mixed salad with ½ oz (15 g) grated Cheddar cheese, 2 teaspoons low-calorie mayonnaise
5 oz (150 g) strawberries with 2½ fl oz (75 ml) low-fat natural yogurt

EVENING MEAL
½ medium cantaloupe melon
6 oz (180 g) grilled cod
3 oz (90 g) boiled potatoes
3 oz (90 g) poached mushrooms
3 oz (90 g) peas
2 teaspoons low-fat spread

SNACKS OR DRINKS AT PLANNED TIMES
7 fl oz (210 ml) skim milk

DAY4

MORNING MEAL
8 fl oz (240 ml) tomato juice
2½ oz (75 g) cottage cheese
crispbread, up to 80 calories

MIDDAY MEAL
4 oz (120 g) canned sardines
mixed salad with 3 teaspoons salad dressing
2 water biscuits
1 teaspoon low-fat spread
4 oz (120 g) cherries

EVENING MEAL
3 oz (90 g) grilled chicken breast
3 oz (90 g) butter beans
3 oz (90 g) carrots
1 medium tomato, halved and grilled
1 teaspoon margarine
½ medium banana
Custard (page 297)

SNACKS OR DRINKS AT PLANNED TIMES
15 fl oz (450 ml) skim milk

DAY5

MORNING MEAL
Oatmeal with Spiced Fruit Ambrosia (page 285)

MIDDAY MEAL
3 tablespoons crunchy peanut butter on 1 slice (2 oz/60 g) wholemeal bread, toasted
2-3 celery sticks
1 medium orange

EVENING MEAL
4 oz (120 g) grilled ham
3 oz (90 g) courgettes
3 oz (90 g) baked beans
5 oz (150 g) gooseberries

SNACKS OR DRINKS AT PLANNED TIMES
5 fl oz (150 ml) low-fat natural yogurt, 5 fl oz (150 ml) skim milk

DAY6

MORNING MEAL
4 oz (120 g) orange sections
1 egg scrambled in 1 teaspoon margarine, on
  1 slice (1 oz/30 g) bread, toasted

MIDDAY MEAL
3 oz (90 g) cold sliced chicken with lettuce,
  tomatoes and cucumber
3 oz (90 g) beetroot
2 teaspoons salad dressing
5 fl oz (150 ml) low-fat natural yogurt
1 medium peach
1 digestive biscuit

EVENING MEAL
4 oz (120 g) grilled haddock with 1 teaspoon
  margarine
3 oz (90 g) green beans
3 oz (90 g) poached mushrooms
5 oz (150 g) strawberries

**SNACKS OR DRINKS
AT PLANNED TIMES**
½ pint (300 ml) skim milk

DAY7

MORNING MEAL
4 fl oz (120 ml) orange juice
2½ oz (75 g) cottage cheese
1 slice (1 oz/30 g) wholemeal bread, toasted

MIDDAY MEAL
3 oz (90 g) roast veal
3 oz (90 g) peas
3 oz (90 g) turnips
3 oz (90 g) boiled potatoes dotted with 1
  teaspoon margarine
5 fl oz (150 ml) low-fat natural yogurt
5 oz (150 g) strawberries
4 fl oz (120 ml) white wine

EVENING MEAL
4 oz (120 g) liver sausage
mixed salad
4 teaspoons salad dressing
4 oz (120 g) fruit salad

**SNACKS OR DRINKS
AT PLANNED TIMES**
½ pint (300 ml) skim milk

WEEK 22

Kedgeree is a recipe from the days of the British Raj. We've created a milder version with smoked haddock, but it still makes a very satisfying breakfast.

DAY 1

MORNING MEAL	¾ oz (20 g) muesli and 1 medium apple, peeled, cored and diced, served with 5 fl oz (150 ml) skim milk
MIDDAY MEAL	4 oz (120 g) ham with cucumber, tomato and lettuce low-calorie salad dressing, up to 50 calories 3 oz (90 g) sweet corn 2 cream crackers 1 teaspoon margarine 1 medium peach
EVENING MEAL	5 oz (150 g) raw fillet plaice dipped in 1 tablespoon seasoned flour and sauteed in 2 teaspoons vegetable oil 3 oz (90 g) peas 3 oz (90 g) carrots 1 medium orange
SNACKS OR DRINKS AT PLANNED TIMES	15 fl oz (450 ml) skim milk

DAY 2

MORNING MEAL
2 inch (5 cm) wedge honeydew melon
1 boiled egg
1 slice (1 oz/30 g) bread, toasted and spread
  with 2 teaspoons low-fat spread

MIDDAY MEAL
3 oz (90 g) canned tuna with mixed green
  salad, with 2 teaspoons low-calorie
  mayonnaise
1 medium orange

EVENING MEAL
4 oz (120 g) sliced turkey breast
3 oz (90 g) baked jacket potato with 2
  teaspoons low-fat spread
3 oz (90 g) courgettes
1 tablespoon relish (any type)
3 oz (90 g) grapes

**SNACKS OR DRINKS
AT PLANNED TIMES**
5 fl oz (150 ml) low-fat natural yogurt, ½ pint
  (300 ml) skim milk

DAY 3

MORNING MEAL
¾ oz (20 g) cornflakes with ½ medium
  banana sliced and served with 5 fl oz (150
  ml) skim milk

MIDDAY MEAL
5 oz (150 g) cottage cheese mixed with 1
  medium orange, peeled and diced
mixed green salad with 2 teaspoons
  mayonnaise
crispbread, up to 80 calories
1 teaspoon margarine

EVENING MEAL
5 oz (150 g) grilled liver
3 oz (90 g) green beans
5 oz (150 g) strawberries

**SNACKS OR DRINKS
AT PLANNED TIMES**
15 fl oz (450 ml) skim milk, 2½ oz (75 g) curd
  cheese with 2 cream crackers

DAY4

MORNING MEAL
4 fl oz (120 ml) orange juice
1 oz (30 g) Cheddar cheese sliced and grilled on 1 slice (1 oz/30 g) bread, toasted

MIDDAY MEAL
3 oz (90 g) sliced liver sausage with tomatoes and cucumber with 2 teaspoons vegetable oil mixed with cider vinegar
½ medium banana

EVENING MEAL
4 breadcrumbed fish fingers sauteed in 1 teaspoon vegetable oil
3 oz (90 g) baked beans
1 medium tomato, halved and grilled
4 oz (120 g) mandarin oranges

SNACKS OR DRINKS AT PLANNED TIMES
5 fl oz (150 ml) low-fat natural yogurt, ½ pint (300 ml) skim milk

---

DAY5

MORNING MEAL
4 fl oz (120 ml) orange juice
¾ oz (20 g) wheat flakes served with 5 fl oz (150 ml) skim milk

MIDDAY MEAL
cheese and ham sandwich made with 2 slices (2 oz/60 g) bread with 2 teaspoons low-fat spread, 2 oz Cheddar cheese with 1 oz (30 g) sliced ham
1 medium apple

EVENING MEAL
7 oz (210 g) raw chicken breast cut into strips and sauteed in 2 teaspoons vegetable oil
3 oz (90 g) peas
3 oz (90 g) courgettes
1 medium orange

SNACKS OR DRINKS AT PLANNED TIMES
15 fl oz (450 ml) skim milk

DAY6

MORNING MEAL
2 inch (5 cm) wedge honeydew melon
2 oz (60 g) canned sardines mashed with 2
  teaspoons tomato ketchup on 1 slice
  (1 oz/30 g) bread, toasted

MIDDAY MEAL
Macaroni with Cheese and Peanut Sauce
(page 283)
mixed salad with low-calorie salad dressing,
  up to 50 calories
1 medium orange

EVENING MEAL
3-egg omelette cooked in 1 teaspoon
  vegetable oil, and filled with 3 oz (90 g)
  poached mushrooms
3 oz (90 g) peas
mixed green salad with lemon juice
4 oz (120 g) fruit cocktail

**SNACKS OR DRINKS
AT PLANNED TIMES**
5 fl oz (150 ml) low-fat natural yogurt, 8 fl oz
  (240 ml) skim milk

DAY7

MORNING MEAL
1 medium orange
Kedgeree and Mushroom Grill (page 284)

MIDDAY MEAL
4 oz (120 g) roast lamb
3 oz (90 g) baked jacket potato
2 teaspoons low-fat spread
3 oz (90 g) peas
3 oz (90 g) carrots
4 oz (120 g) peach

EVENING MEAL
3 oz (90 g) peeled prawns on mixed green
  salad with 3 teaspoons salad dressing
1 medium pear

**SNACKS OR DRINKS
AT PLANNED TIMES**
5 fl oz (150 ml) low-fat natural yogurt, ½ pint
  (300 ml) skim milk

WEEK 23

The description 'Florentine' applied to any dish means that it contains cooked spinach. We suggest Fillet of Sole Florentine for your midday meal on Day 2.

DAY 1

MORNING MEAL
½ medium grapefruit
¾ oz (20 g) cereal
5 fl oz (150 ml) skim milk

MIDDAY MEAL
Baked Cheese Souffle (page 226)
green salad with 2 teaspoons mayonnaise
2 inch (5 cm) wedge honeydew melon

EVENING MEAL
6 oz (180 g) cooked chicken breast
3 oz (90 g) mange tout peas
3 oz (90 g) carrots
1 oz (30 g) bread roll
2 teaspoons low-fat spread
4 fl oz (120 ml) white wine
1 medium apple

SNACKS OR DRINKS AT PLANNED TIMES
15 fl oz (450 ml) skim milk

DAY 2

MORNING MEAL
4 fl oz (120 ml) orange juice
2 slices (2 oz/60 g) wholemeal bread, toasted
2 teaspoons low-fat spread
1 tablespoon marmalade

MIDDAY MEAL
Fillet of Sole Florentine (page 270)
3 oz (90 g) green beans
4 oz (120 g) fruit cocktail

EVENING MEAL
4 oz (120 g) lean ham
mixed salad with 1 teaspoon vegetable oil
    and wine vinegar
2 cream crackers
1 medium apple

SNACKS OR DRINKS AT PLANNED TIMES
5 fl oz (150 ml) low-fat natural yogurt, ½ pint
    (300 ml) skim milk

DAY 3

MORNING MEAL
5 oz (150 g) strawberries
1 boiled egg
1 slice (1 oz/30 g) wholemeal bread, toasted
1 teaspoon margarine

MIDDAY MEAL
3 oz (90 g) sliced roast turkey breast
tomato slices and green pepper rings on
    lettuce
1 oz (30 g) pitta bread
1 teaspoon mayonnaise
½ medium banana

EVENING MEAL
4 oz (120 g) grilled veal
3 oz (90 g) baked jacket potato with 1
    teaspoon margarine
3 oz (90 g) broccoli
Curried Cole Slaw (page 288)

SNACKS OR DRINKS AT PLANNED TIMES
1 medium kiwi fruit, 1 pint (600 ml) skim milk

DAY4

MORNING MEAL
2 inch (5 cm) wedge honeydew melon
¾ oz (20 g) cornflakes
5 fl oz (150 ml) skim milk

MIDDAY MEAL
4 oz (120 g) grilled lamb's liver
3 oz (90 g) spinach
3 oz (90 g) mushrooms
1 oz (30 g) bread roll
2 teaspoons low-fat spread
5 oz (150 g) strawberries

EVENING MEAL
4 oz (120 g) roast lamb
3 oz (90 g) sliced carrots
3 oz (90 g) green beans
2 teaspoons margarine
5 oz (150 g) raspberries

SNACKS OR DRINKS AT PLANNED TIMES
5 fl oz (150 ml) low-fat natural yogurt, 5 fl oz (150 ml) skim milk

DAY5

MORNING MEAL
4 fl oz (120 ml) orange juice
1 scrambled egg
1 slice (1 oz/30 g) wholemeal bread, toasted
1 teaspoon margarine

MIDDAY MEAL
3 oz (90 g) tuna
mixed salad with 3 teaspoons low-calorie mayonnaise
1 medium peach

EVENING MEAL
4 oz (120 g) grilled chicken
3 oz (90 g) boiled new potatoes
3 oz (90 g) peas dotted with 1 teaspoon low-fat spread
4 oz (120 g) fruit cocktail

SNACKS OR DRINKS AT PLANNED TIMES
2 oz (60 g) vanilla ice cream, 5 fl oz (150 ml) low-fat natural yogurt, ½ pint (300 ml) skim milk

DAY6

MORNING MEAL
4 fl oz (120 ml) grapefruit juice
1 boiled egg
1 slice (1 oz/30 g) wholemeal bread, toasted
2 teaspoons low-fat spread

MIDDAY MEAL
2½ oz (75 g) cottage cheese
1 oz (30 g) Cheddar cheese, grated
2 cream crackers
mixed salad with 1 teaspoon vegetable oil
and cider vinegar
4 oz (120 g) peaches

EVENING MEAL
5 oz (150 g) grilled fillet of plaice
3 oz (90 g) carrots
3 oz (90 g) courgettes dotted with 1 teaspoon
margarine
Pear Frozen Yogurt (page 301)

**SNACKS OR DRINKS
AT PLANNED TIMES**
½ pint (300 ml) skim milk

DAY7

MORNING MEAL
2½ fl oz (75 ml) apple juice
¾ oz (20 g) wheat flakes
5 fl oz (150 ml) skim milk

MIDDAY MEAL
Sauteed Chick Peas Italian Style (page 274)
2 oz (60 g) cooked brown rice
3 oz (90 g) spinach
1 teaspoon margarine
4 oz (120 g) cherries

EVENING MEAL
4 oz (120 g) grilled beef steak
3 oz (90 g) boiled potatoes dotted with 1
teaspoon low-fat spread
3 oz (90 g) onion rings
3 oz (90 g) poached mushrooms
1 tomato, halved and grilled
5 oz (150 g) strawberries

**SNACKS OR DRINKS
AT PLANNED TIMES**
15 fl oz (450 ml) skim milk, 2 oz (60 g) Cheddar
cheese

WEEK 24

Risotto is an Italian rice speciality. In our version a variety of vegetables, cooked in stock, are poured over rice and cheese to make a complete meal.

DAY 1

MORNING MEAL	2½ oz (75 g) cottage cheese 4 oz (120 g) peaches 1 slice (1 oz/30 g) currant bread
MIDDAY MEAL	3 oz (90 g) cold roast lamb with **Mint Sauce** (page 291) 3 oz (90 g) sweet corn green salad with 1 teaspoon mayonnaise 1 medium orange, sliced into 5 fl oz (150 ml) low-fat natural yogurt
EVENING MEAL	4 oz (120 g) grilled lamb's liver 1 oz (30 g) lean grilled back bacon 3 oz (90 g) green beans 3 oz (90 g) carrots 2 teaspoons margarine 1 medium pear
SNACKS OR DRINKS AT PLANNED TIMES	½ pint (300 ml) skim milk

DAY2

MORNING MEAL
¾ oz (20 g) bran flakes
1 oz (30 g) raisins
5 fl oz (150 ml) skim milk
2 medium tomatoes, grilled on 1 slice (1 oz/
30 g) bread, toasted
1 teaspoon margarine

MIDDAY MEAL
5 oz (150 g) cottage cheese and 1 oz (30 g)
chopped ham, mixed, grilled on 1 slice
(1 oz/30 g) wholemeal bread
2 pickled onions
Worcestershire sauce
2 sticks celery
5 fl oz (150 ml) low-fat natural yogurt with 1
portion stewed rhubarb

EVENING MEAL
5 oz (150 g) cold roast chicken
mixed salad with 2 teaspoons mayonnaise
1 medium orange

**SNACKS OR DRINKS
AT PLANNED TIMES**
5 fl oz (150 ml) skim milk, 3 oz (90 g) grapes

DAY3

MORNING MEAL
½ medium grapefruit
1 poached egg on 1 oz (30 g) crumpet
2 teaspoons low-fat spread

MIDDAY MEAL
3 oz (90 g) cockles
green salad
1 tomato
1 teaspoon low-calorie mayonnaise
crispbread, up to 80 calories
4 oz (120 g) peaches

EVENING MEAL
4 oz (120 g) grilled frankfurters
Savoury Cabbage (page 279)
3 oz (90 g) boiled potatoes
½ pint (300 ml) lager
5 fl oz (150 ml) low-fat natural yogurt with rum
flavouring and 1 oz (30 g) raisins

**SNACKS OR DRINKS
AT PLANNED TIMES**
½ pint (300 ml) skim milk

DAY4

MORNING MEAL
4 fl oz (120 ml) orange juice
¾ oz (20 g) cornflakes
5 fl oz (150 ml) skim milk

MIDDAY MEAL
Curried Vegetables (page 281)
4 oz (120 g) chicken, grilled with lemon juice,
tandoori spice and 1 teaspoon margarine
4 oz (120 g) pineapple with 5 fl oz (150 ml)
low-fat natural yogurt

EVENING MEAL
4 oz (120 g) grilled kipper fillets
1 slice (1 oz/30 g) wholemeal bread
2 teaspoons margarine
3 oz (90 g) green beans
1 medium pear

**SNACKS OR DRINKS
AT PLANNED TIMES**
5 fl oz (150 ml) skim milk

DAY5

MORNING MEAL
2½ oz (75 g) cottage cheese
4 oz pineapple
crispbread, up to 80 calories

MIDDAY MEAL
2 oz (60 g) tuna fish
1 hard-boiled egg, green salad with 1
tablespoon mayonnaise
1 medium tomato, sliced
3 oz (90 g) beetroot
1 medium apple

EVENING MEAL
1 portion boil-in-the-bag fish in sauce (any
type)
4 oz (120 g) cooked rice
3 oz (90 g) broccoli
1 medium orange

**SNACKS OR DRINKS
AT PLANNED TIMES**
1 pint (600 ml) skim milk

DAY6

MORNING MEAL
2 scrambled eggs
1 teaspoon margarine
1 slice (1 oz/30 g) bread, toasted

MIDDAY MEAL
9 oz (270 g) baked beans, heated with 1 oz
(30 g) sultanas and curry powder to taste,
on 1 slice (1 oz/30 g) bread, toasted
green salad with 1 tomato, sliced
2 teaspoons mayonnaise

EVENING MEAL
Cheese and Vegetable Risotto (page 234)
5 fl oz (150 ml) low-fat natural yogurt with 2
teaspoons honey

SNACKS OR DRINKS AT PLANNED TIMES
½ pint (300 ml) skim milk, 1 medium orange

DAY7

MORNING MEAL
½ medium grapefruit
1 egg, scrambled with 2 teaspoons low-fat
spread
1 slice (1 oz/30 g) bread
2 medium grilled tomatoes

MIDDAY MEAL
2 inch (5 cm) wedge honeydew melon
4 oz (120 g) grilled salmon
3 oz (90 g) new potatoes
3 oz (90 g) peas
2 teaspoons low-fat spread
5 fl oz (150 ml) low-fat natural yogurt with 5 oz
(150 g) raspberries

EVENING MEAL
Swiss Cheese Bake (page 228)

SNACKS OR DRINKS AT PLANNED TIMES
½ pint (300 ml) skim milk

WEEK 25

If you're a 'plain cook' who wants to create a gourmet impression for some special occasion, try our Chicken Provencale on Day 2.

DAY 1

MORNING MEAL
½ medium grapefruit
1 boiled egg
1 slice (1 oz/30 g) wholemeal bread
2 teaspoons low-fat spread

MIDDAY MEAL
Liver Pate (page 254)
mixed green salad tossed with **Vinaigrette Dressing** (page 293)

EVENING MEAL
Beef Pie (page 258)
3 oz (90 g) carrots
1 medium pear

SNACKS OR DRINKS AT PLANNED TIMES
½ pint (300 ml) skim milk, 5 fl oz (150 ml) low-fat natural yogurt

DAY 2

MORNING MEAL
½ medium grapefruit
1 oz (30 g) grated Cheddar cheese, grilled on
    1 slice (1 oz/30 g) wholemeal bread,
    toasted

MIDDAY MEAL
2 poached eggs served on 6 oz (180 g)
    spinach dotted with 2 teaspoons low-fat
    spread
2½ oz (75 g) quark or cottage cheese mixed
    with 4 oz (120 g) apricots, diced
1 digestive biscuit

EVENING MEAL
Chicken Provencale (page 236)
2 oz (60 g) cooked pasta shells
3 oz (90 g) French beans
2 teaspoons low-fat spread
¼ small fresh pineapple

SNACKS OR DRINKS AT PLANNED TIMES
½ pint (300 ml) skim milk, 5 fl oz (150 ml)
    low-fat natural yogurt

DAY 3

MORNING MEAL
4 fl oz (120 ml) orange juice
¾ oz (20 g) muesli
5 fl oz (150 ml) skim milk

MIDDAY MEAL
4 oz (120 g) cooked, flaked cod, 1 diced celery
    stick, seeded and diced red pepper, 2 oz
    (60 g) cooked pasta shells, 2 teaspoons
    olive oil
3 oz (90 g) grapes

EVENING MEAL
4 oz (120 g) grilled lamb chop
3 oz (90 g) boiled potato mashed with 2
    teaspoons low-fat spread
3 oz (90 g) cauliflower
1 grilled tomato
½ medium banana

SNACKS OR DRINKS AT PLANNED TIMES
15 fl oz (450 ml) skim milk

DAY4

MORNING MEAL
½ medium banana, sliced with ¾ oz (20 g) cornflakes
5 fl oz (150 ml) skim milk

MIDDAY MEAL
2½ oz (75 g) cottage cheese sprinkled with chives
1 oz (30 g) grated Edam cheese served on shredded iceberg lettuce
2 cream crackers
4 teaspoons low-fat spread
1 medium apple

EVENING MEAL
½ medium grapefruit
6 oz (180 g) roast chicken
1 oz (30 g) grilled lean bacon
3 oz (90 g) courgettes
3 oz (90 g) baked jacket potato
2 teaspoons low-fat spread

SNACKS OR DRINKS AT PLANNED TIMES
15 fl oz (450 ml) skim milk

DAY5

MORNING MEAL
½ medium grapefruit
2½ oz (75 g) cottage cheese grilled on 1 slice (1 oz/30 g) wholemeal bread, toasted

MIDDAY MEAL
4 oz (120 g) canned mackerel
mixed salad with lemon juice
1 slice (1 oz/30 g) wholemeal bread

EVENING MEAL
2 inch (5 cm) wedge honeydew melon
Baked Prawns Thermidor (page 261)
3 oz (90 g) broccoli
3 oz (90 g) carrots
2 small satsumas

SNACKS OR DRINKS AT PLANNED TIMES
5 fl oz (150 ml) low-fat natural yogurt, 7½ fl oz (225 ml) skim milk

DAY6

MORNING MEAL   1 oz (30 g) raisins mixed with ¾ oz (20 g)
porridge oats cooked with water
5 fl oz (150 ml) skim milk

MIDDAY MEAL   2-egg omelette cooked in 1½ teaspoons
vegetable oil and filled with 3 oz (90 g)
skinned and diced tomatoes
3 oz (90 g) peas
1 slice (1 oz/30 g) wholemeal bread
1 medium orange

EVENING MEAL   **Italian Veal and Peppers** (page 242)
2 oz (60 g) cooked pasta shells
3 oz (90 g) broccoli
4 oz (120 g) peaches
2 oz (60 g) vanilla ice cream

SNACKS OR DRINKS   15 fl oz (450 ml) skim milk
AT PLANNED TIMES

DAY7

MORNING MEAL   1 medium orange sliced with ¾ oz (20 g)
muesli
5 fl oz (150 ml) skim milk

MIDDAY MEAL   4 oz (120 g) lean roast beef with **Spicy Plum
Sauce** (page 292)
3 oz (90 g) courgettes
3 oz (90 g) parsnips
3 oz (90 g) roast potato cooked with 2
teaspoons vegetable oil
Pear Frozen Yogurt (page 301)

EVENING MEAL   Danish sandwich
1 slice (1 oz/30 g) rye bread, spread with 2
teaspoons low-calorie mayonnaise,
topped with lettuce, tomato and
cucumber slices and 4 oz (120 g) canned
brislings

SNACKS OR DRINKS   5 fl oz (150 ml) skim milk
AT PLANNED TIMES

WEEK 26

Tomatoes are useful and so versatile. Canned tomatoes, used whole or pureed, are part of many good casseroles. Fresh tomatoes are much improved by the addition of a little basil.

DAY 1

MORNING MEAL
1 medium orange
¾ oz (20 g) cereal
5 fl oz (150 ml) skim milk

MIDDAY MEAL
Tomato Stuffed with Herb Cheese (page 226)
1 slice (1 oz/30 g) rye bread
1 teaspoon margarine
½ medium banana, sliced and set in ¼ pint (150 ml) lemon jelly

EVENING MEAL
6 oz (180 g) grilled chicken breast
3 oz (90 g) carrots
3 oz (90 g) broad beans
green salad with **Vinaigrette Dressing** (page 293)
1 oz (30 g) bread roll
1 teaspoon margarine
4 oz (120 g) cherries

SNACKS OR DRINKS AT PLANNED TIMES
15 fl oz (450 ml) skim milk

DAY 2

MORNING MEAL
2½ fl oz (75 ml) apple juice
1 egg, scrambled in 1 teaspoon margarine
1 slice (1 oz/30 g) wholemeal bread

MIDDAY MEAL
3 oz (90 g) cooked chicken
3 oz (90 g) marrow
3 oz (90 g) whole baby carrots dotted with 1
    teaspoon margarine
green salad with **Russian Dressing** (page
    292)
1 medium peach

EVENING MEAL
4 oz (120 g) grilled trout with 2 teaspoons
    horseradish relish
2 oz (60 g) cooked noodles
3 oz (90 g) courgettes
5 oz (150 g) strawberries with 2½ fl oz (75 ml)
    low-fat natural yogurt

**SNACKS OR DRINKS
AT PLANNED TIMES**
15 fl oz (450 ml) skim milk

DAY 3

MORNING MEAL
½ medium grapefruit
2½ oz (75 g) cottage cheese
1 slice (1 oz/30 g) wholemeal bread

MIDDAY MEAL
4 oz (120 g) poached salmon
Cucumber and Tomato Salad (page 289)
4 oz (120 g) apple, stewed
2 oz (60 g) vanilla ice cream

EVENING MEAL
Mexican Beef Patties (page 250)
3 oz (90 g) beetroot
3 oz (90 g) green beans
3 oz (90 g) boiled potatoes dotted with 1½
    teaspoons margarine
4 oz (120 g) mandarin oranges

**SNACKS OR DRINKS
AT PLANNED TIMES**
5 fl oz (150 ml) low-fat natural yogurt, ½ pint
    (300 ml) skim milk

DAY 4

MORNING MEAL ½ medium banana sliced on ¾ oz (20 g) muesli with 5 fl oz (150 ml) skim milk

MIDDAY MEAL 4 oz (120 g) grilled chicken livers
3 oz (90 g) onion rings
3 oz (90 g) broccoli dotted with 1 teaspoon margarine
3 oz (90 g) baked beans
5 oz (150 g) blackcurrants

EVENING MEAL 4 oz (120 g) grilled plaice with 1 tablespoon seafood dressing
3 oz (90 g) spinach
1 teaspoon margarine
5 oz (150 g) strawberries

SNACKS OR DRINKS AT PLANNED TIMES 2 water biscuits with 2 teaspoons low-fat spread, 15 fl oz (450 ml) skim milk

DAY 5

MORNING MEAL 4 fl oz (120 ml) orange juice
1 boiled egg
1 slice (1 oz/30 g) wholemeal bread, toasted
1 teaspoon margarine

MIDDAY MEAL 5 oz (150 g) cottage cheese with mixed salad
2 teaspoons salad cream
2 water biscuits
5 oz (150 g) strawberries
5 fl oz (150 ml) low-fat natural yogurt

EVENING MEAL 5 oz (150 g) grilled beef steak
1 tomato, halved and grilled
3 oz (90 g) broccoli dotted with 1 teaspoon margarine
5 oz (150 g) dessert gooseberries

SNACKS OR DRINKS AT PLANNED TIMES ½ pint (300 ml) skim milk

DAY6

MORNING MEAL
2 medium apricots, stoned and diced on ¾ oz
    (20 g) cereal
5 fl oz (150 ml) skim milk

MIDDAY MEAL
Mushroom Omelette (page 230)
green salad with green pepper rings and
    Vinaigrette Dressing (page 293)
1 slice (1 oz/30 g) wholemeal bread with 1
    teaspoon margarine
5 oz (150 g) strawberries

EVENING MEAL
6 oz (180 g) grilled veal chop
3 oz (90 g) broad beans
3 oz (90 g) carrots
3 oz (90 g) boiled potatoes
4 oz (120 g) black cherries

SNACKS OR DRINKS
AT PLANNED TIMES
15 fl oz (450 ml) skim milk

DAY7

MORNING MEAL
4 fl oz (120 ml) orange juice
1 oz (30 g) Cheddar cheese, sliced and grilled
    on 1 slice (1 oz/30 g) bread, toasted

MIDDAY MEAL
3 oz (90 g) grilled mackerel
3 oz (90 g) courgettes
3 oz (90 g) beetroot
green salad with 2 teaspoons oil with wine
    vinegar
1 medium peach

EVENING MEAL
Sesame Chicken with Green Beans (page
    239)
3 oz (90 g) sliced carrots
3 oz (90 g) boiled potatoes
5 oz (150 g) redcurrants

SNACKS OR DRINKS
AT PLANNED TIMES
5 fl oz (150 ml) low-fat natural yogurt, ½ pint
    (300 ml) skim milk

WEEK 27

Oregano is a native of Mediterranean regions, but we are now familiar with its slightly bitter taste in pizza and bolognaise sauce. Enjoy it in Chicken Greek Style on Day 6.

DAY 1

MORNING MEAL
4 fl oz (120 ml) grapefruit juice
¾ oz (20 g) cornflakes
5 fl oz (150 ml) skim milk

MIDDAY MEAL
5 oz (150 g) cottage cheese, 1 oz (30 g) raisins, tossed together and served on shredded lettuce
crispbread, up to 80 calories
2 teaspoons low-fat spread

EVENING MEAL
1 portion boil-in-the-bag fish in sauce (any type)
3 oz (90 g) baked beans
3 oz (90 g) carrots dotted with 4 teaspoons low-fat spread
Rice Pudding (page 302)

SNACKS OR DRINKS AT PLANNED TIMES
11 fl oz (330 ml) skim milk

DAY 2

MORNING MEAL
4 fl oz (120 ml) grapefruit juice
1 tablespoon peanut butter spread on 1 slice
(1 oz/30 g) wholemeal bread, toasted

MIDDAY MEAL
celery and bean soup made with 6 oz (180 g)
canned celery and 6 fl oz (180 ml) beef
stock made with ½ stock cube. Bring to
the boil and puree in blender. Reheat,
adding 6 oz (180 g) canned red kidney
beans
Pineapple Cheesecake (page 296)

EVENING MEAL
2 inch (5 cm) wedge honeydew melon
4 oz (120 g) grilled lamb's liver
1 oz (30 g) grilled lean bacon
3 oz (90 g) broccoli
1 small satsuma

**SNACKS OR DRINKS
AT PLANNED TIMES**
5 fl oz (150 ml) skim milk, 5 fl oz (150 ml)
low-fat natural yogurt

DAY 3

MORNING MEAL
2 inch (5 cm) wedge honeydew melon
¾ oz (20 g) cornflakes
5 fl oz (150 ml) skim milk

MIDDAY MEAL
mixed green salad with 2 hard-boiled eggs,
sliced, 1 tablespoon mayonnaise
1 medium orange
1 digestive biscuit

EVENING MEAL
6 oz (180 g) roast chicken
3 oz (90 g) peas
4 oz (120 g) apricots

**SNACKS OR DRINKS
AT PLANNED TIMES**
1 digestive biscuit, 5 fl oz (150 ml) skim milk,
5 fl oz (150 ml) low-fat natural yogurt

DAY4

MORNING MEAL
1 medium orange
2½ oz (75 g) cottage cheese lightly grilled on
1 slice (1 oz/30 g) wholemeal bread,
toasted

MIDDAY MEAL
Toss together, 3 oz (90 g) cold cooked
chicken, diced, 3 oz (90 g) canned, red
kidney beans, 1 diced celery stick, 1
grated carrot, 1 medium grated apple,
sprinkled with lemon juice, 4 teaspooons
salad cream

EVENING MEAL
Lamb Kebabs (page 248)
2 oz (60 g) hot cooked rice
1 tomato, sliced with onion rings and
Vinaigrette Dressing (page 293)
1 medium pear
2 oz (60 g) vanilla ice cream

SNACKS OR DRINKS AT PLANNED TIMES
15 fl oz (450 ml) skim milk

DAY5

MORNING MEAL
1 oz (30 g) raisins mixed with ¾ oz (20 g)
porridge oats cooked with water
5 fl oz (150 ml) skim milk

MIDDAY MEAL
toss together, 3 oz (90 g) drained sardines, 1
hard-boiled egg, sliced, 1 sliced tomato,
onion rings, with 2 teaspoons
mayonnaise, tucked into 1 x 2 oz (60 g)
pitta bread

EVENING MEAL
4 oz (120 g) grapefruit sections
4 oz (120 g) grilled trout
Chinese Cabbage and Tomato Medley
(page 280)

SNACKS OR DRINKS AT PLANNED TIMES
5 oz (150 g) blackberries, 5 fl oz (150 ml)
low-fat natural yogurt, 5 fl oz (150 ml) skim
milk

DAY6

MORNING MEAL
3 oz (90 g) grapes
¾ oz (20 g) muesli
5 fl oz (150 ml) skim milk

MIDDAY MEAL
4 oz (120 g) grilled beefburger
2 oz (60 g) bap
2 teaspoons low-fat spread
2 teaspoons tomato ketchup
1 medium apple

EVENING MEAL
Chicken Greek Style (page 241)
3 oz (90 g) green beans
3 oz (90 g) cauliflower
2 teaspoons low-fat spread
1 medium orange

SNACKS OR DRINKS AT PLANNED TIMES
15 fl oz (450 ml) skim milk

DAY7

MORNING MEAL
4 oz (120 g) peaches
2½ oz (75 g) cottage cheese
1 slice (1 oz/30 g) wholemeal bread, toasted

MIDDAY MEAL
3 oz (90 g) roast turkey breast
Fennel with Parmesan Cheese (page 278)
3 oz (90 g) carrots
3 oz (90 g) baked jacket potato
2 teaspoons low-fat spread
Cherry Tarts (page 294)

EVENING MEAL
Salmon Salad (page 265)
1 medium orange
5 fl oz (150 ml) low-fat natural yogurt

SNACKS OR DRINKS AT PLANNED TIMES
½ pint (300 ml) skim milk

WEEK 28

We've provided five cold midday meals this week, so you can picnic outside or take a packed lunch to work.

DAY 1

MORNING MEAL
4 fl oz (120 ml) orange juice
¾ oz (20 g) cornflakes with 5 fl oz (150 ml) skim milk

MIDDAY MEAL
Cheddar salad made with 2 oz (60 g) Cheddar cheese grated over green salad with 4 teaspoons salad cream
1 slice (1 oz/30 g) bread
2 teaspoons low-fat spread
1 medium orange

EVENING MEAL
4 oz (120 g) grilled beef sausages
6 oz (180 g) baked beans
1 tomato, halved and grilled
4 oz (120 g) pineapple

SNACKS OR DRINKS AT PLANNED TIMES
15 fl oz (450 ml) skim milk, 1 digestive biscuit

DAY 2

MORNING MEAL
4 fl oz (120 ml) orange juice
1 egg, scrambled in 1 teaspoon low-fat
   spread
1 slice (1 oz/30 g) bread, toasted
1 teaspoon low-fat spread

MIDDAY MEAL
salmon salad made with 3 oz (90 g) canned
   salmon on mixed salad with 2 teaspoons
   salad dressing
3 oz (90 g) beetroot
crispbread, up to 80 calories, spread with 2
   teaspoons low-fat spread
1 medium apple

EVENING MEAL
4 oz (120 g) roast chicken
3 oz (90 g) Brussels sprouts
3 oz (90 g) carrots
4 oz (120 g) apricots

SNACKS OR DRINKS AT PLANNED TIMES
½ pint (300 ml) skim milk, 5 fl oz (150 ml)
   low-fat natural yogurt

DAY 3

MORNING MEAL
½ medium banana sliced over ¾ oz (20 g)
   muesli with 5 fl oz (150 ml) skim milk

MIDDAY MEAL
4 oz (120 g) cooked chicken and green salad
   dressed with 2 teaspoons low-calorie
   mayonnaise
2 cream crackers with 2 teaspoons low-fat
   spread
1 medium orange

EVENING MEAL
1 portion boil-in-bag fish in sauce (any type)
3 oz (90 g) peas
3 oz (90 g) boiled potatoes dotted with 2
   teaspoons low-fat spread
4 oz (120 g) peaches

SNACKS OR DRINKS AT PLANNED TIMES
15 fl oz (450 ml) skim milk

DAY4

MORNING MEAL
1 medium orange
1 boiled egg
1 slice (1 oz/30 g) bread, toasted, spread with
   2 teaspoons low-fat spread

MIDDAY MEAL
3 oz (90 g) fresh crab
green salad with low-calorie salad dressing,
   up to 50 calories
crispbread, up to 80 calories
1 medium apple

EVENING MEAL
5 oz (150 g) uncooked liver, sliced, and 3 oz
   (90 g) onion, sliced, sauteed in
   2 teaspoons vegetable oil
1 oz (30 g) lean back bacon, grilled
3 oz (90 g) carrots
½ medium banana

SNACKS OR DRINKS AT PLANNED TIMES
½ pint (300 ml) skim milk, 5 fl oz (150 ml)
   low-fat natural yogurt

DAY5

MORNING MEAL
4 fl oz (120 ml) grapefruit juice
2 tablespoons crunchy peanut butter spread
   on crispbread, up to 80 calories

MIDDAY MEAL
cottage cheese salad made with 5 oz (150 g)
   cottage cheese mixed with diced
   cucumber, diced red pepper, celery and
   1 oz (30 g) raisins

EVENING MEAL
Savoury Mince with Noodles (page 257)
mixed green salad with lemon juice
3 oz (90 g) grapes

SNACKS OR DRINKS AT PLANNED TIMES
½ pint (300 ml) skim milk, 5 fl oz (150 ml)
   low-fat natural yogurt

DAY 6

MORNING MEAL
½ medium grapefruit
¾ oz (20 g) porridge oats cooked with water
and served with 5 fl oz (150 ml) skim milk

MIDDAY MEAL
8 fl oz (240 ml) tomato juice
9 oz (270 g) baked beans served on 1 slice
(1 oz/30 g) bread toasted and spread with
2 teaspoons low-fat spread
1 grilled tomato
2 oz (60 g) vanilla ice cream

EVENING MEAL
5 oz (150 g) grilled hake steak
3 oz (90 g) carrots
3 oz (90 g) peas
3 oz (90 g) boiled potatoes dotted with
4 teaspoons low-fat spread
½ medium banana

**SNACKS OR DRINKS
AT PLANNED TIMES**
15 fl oz (450 ml) skim milk

DAY 7

MORNING MEAL
½ medium grapefruit
1 oz (30 g) Cheddar cheese sliced and grilled
on 1 slice (1 oz/30 g) bread, toasted

MIDDAY MEAL
4 oz (120 g) lean roast pork
3 oz (90 g) braised leeks
3 oz (90 g) Brussels sprouts
3 oz (90 g) baked jacket potato with
2 teaspoons low-fat spread
Apple Meringue (page 297)

EVENING MEAL
3-egg omelette cooked in 2 teaspoons
vegetable oil and filled with 1 tomato,
chopped
3 oz (90 g) poached mushrooms
green salad with lemon juice
1 medium orange

**SNACKS OR DRINKS
AT PLANNED TIMES**
½ pint (300 ml) skim milk, 5 fl oz (150 ml)
low-fat natural yogurt

WEEK 29

Does a fruit sundae sound too good to be true? We've calculated the ingredients very carefully so that it keeps within your weekly intake. Go ahead – spoil yourself!

DAY 1

MORNING MEAL
½ medium grapefruit
1 oz (30 g) lean back bacon
3 oz (90 g) baked beans
1 slice (1 oz/30 g) bread, toasted
1 teaspoon low-fat spread

MIDDAY MEAL
2 oz (60 g) Cheddar cheese
2½ oz (75 g) cottage cheese
2 celery sticks
green salad with lemon juice
2 cream crackers
½ medium banana

EVENING MEAL
2 breadcrumbed fish cakes, grilled with 3 teaspoons low-fat spread
3 oz (90 g) carrots
3 oz (90 g) cauliflower dotted with 2 teaspoons low-fat spread
3 oz (90 g) grapes

SNACKS OR DRINKS AT PLANNED TIMES
½ pint (300 ml) skim milk, 5 fl oz (150 ml) low-fat natural yogurt

DAY 2

MORNING MEAL
4 fl oz (120 ml) orange juice
¾ oz (20 g) muesli with 5 fl oz (150 ml) skim milk

MIDDAY MEAL
2 slices (2 oz/60 g) wholemeal bread spread with 2 teaspoons low-fat spread, with 4 oz (120 g) sardines
3 oz (90 g) tomato, sliced
cucumber and onion rings
1 teaspoon low-calorie mayonnaise
1 medium pear

EVENING MEAL
Pork Chops with Orange Slices (page 252)
3 oz (90 g) finely shredded cabbage, sauteed in 3 teaspoons low-fat spread
3 oz (90 g) parsnips

SNACKS OR DRINKS AT PLANNED TIMES
5 fl oz (150 ml) skim milk and 5 fl oz (150 ml) low-fat natural yogurt

---

DAY 3

MORNING MEAL
½ medium grapefruit
1 boiled egg
1 slice (1 oz/30 g) wholemeal bread, toasted
1 teaspoon low-fat spread

MIDDAY MEAL
3 oz (90 g) cooked chicken
2 sticks celery, chopped, mixed with 1 medium red apple, cored and chopped and 4 teaspoons salad dressing
green salad
1 oz (30 g) bread roll

EVENING MEAL
4 oz (120 g) grilled beefburger
3 oz (90 g) grilled sliced onion
3 oz (90 g) peas
1 teaspoon low-fat spread
½ medium banana

SNACKS OR DRINKS AT PLANNED TIMES
5 fl oz (150 ml) low-fat natural yogurt, ½ pint (300 ml) skim milk

DAY4

MORNING MEAL
4 fl oz (120 ml) orange juice
¾ oz (20 g) cornflakes
5 fl oz (150 ml) skim milk

MIDDAY MEAL
4 oz (120 g) canned tuna
3 oz (90 g) sweet corn
sliced cucumber and onion rings with 4
    teaspoons low-calorie mayonnaise and 1
    tablespoon wine vinegar
4 oz (120 g) peaches

EVENING MEAL
Casseroled Liver (page 250)
3 oz (90 g) spring greens
1 medium apple

SNACKS OR DRINKS AT PLANNED TIMES
5 fl oz (150 ml) skim milk, 5 fl oz (150 ml)
    low-fat natural yogurt

DAY5

MORNING MEAL
¾ oz (20 g) bran flakes with 1 oz (30 g)
    sultanas
5 fl oz (150 ml) skim milk

MIDDAY MEAL
2-egg omelette cooked in 2 teaspoons
    vegetable oil
3 oz (90 g) poached mushrooms
1 oz (30 g) bread roll
2 teaspoons low-fat spread
1 medium orange

EVENING MEAL
4 oz (120 g) grilled beef sausages
6 oz (180 g) baked beans
1 tomato, halved and grilled
4 oz (120 g) fruit cocktail

SNACKS OR DRINKS AT PLANNED TIMES
5 fl oz (150 ml) skim milk, 5 fl oz (150 ml)
    low-fat natural yogurt

DAY6

MORNING MEAL
4 fl oz (120 ml) orange juice
1 oz (30 g) Cheddar cheese, grilled on 1 slice
   (1 oz/30 g) bread, toasted

MIDDAY MEAL
5 oz (150 g) cottage cheese
6 oz (180 g) finely shredded cabbage, grated
   carrot and thinly sliced onion, with 4
   teaspoons salad cream

EVENING MEAL
Baked Cod (page 262)
3 oz (90 g) green beans
2 oz (60 g) cooked rice
1 medium banana

SNACKS OR DRINKS AT PLANNED TIMES
½ pint (300 ml) skim milk, 5 fl oz (150 ml)
   low-fat natural yogurt

DAY7

MORNING MEAL
½ medium grapefruit
1 egg, scrambled in 1 teaspoon low-fat
   spread
1 small grilled tomato
1 slice (1 oz/30 g) bread, toasted
1 teaspoon low-fat spread
1 teaspoon honey

MIDDAY MEAL
3 oz (90 g) cooked chicken
3 oz (90 g) Brussels sprouts
3 oz (90 g) carrots
3 oz (90 g) baked jacket potato
2 teaspoons low-fat spread
Fruit Sundae (page 299)

EVENING MEAL
4 oz (120 g) canned salmon
2 sliced tomatoes
green salad
2 teaspoons salad cream

SNACKS OR DRINKS AT PLANNED TIMES
½ pint (300 ml) skim milk, 5 fl oz (150 ml)
   low-fat natural yogurt

Fish is an excellent source of protein, low in fat and calories. It can be cooked and flavoured in so many ways that you're sure to find a method to please you.

DAY 1

MORNING MEAL
1 medium apple, diced into ¾ oz (20 g) muesli
5 fl oz (150 ml) skim milk

MIDDAY MEAL
1 egg, scrambled in 1 teaspoon margarine, cooled and topped with 2 oz (60 g) peeled prawns, 1 teaspoon low-calorie mayonnaise and served on 1 slice (1 oz/ 30 g) wholemeal bread with 1 teaspoon low-fat spread
green salad
½ pint (300 ml) lager
2 medium plums

EVENING MEAL
4 oz (120 g) beef burger served on 6 oz (180 g) spinach and topped with 1 oz (30 g) melted Cheddar cheese
3 oz (90 g) cooked potatoes
1 teaspoon margarine
4 fl oz (120 ml) orange juice

SNACKS OR DRINKS AT PLANNED TIMES
5 fl oz (150 ml) skim milk, 5 fl oz (150 ml) low-fat natural yogurt

DAY 2

MORNING MEAL
5 oz (150 g) blackberries on 2½ oz (75 g) cottage cheese
1 slice (1 oz/30 g) wholemeal bread
1 teaspoon margarine

MIDDAY MEAL
9 oz (270 g) baked beans on 1 slice (1 oz/30 g) bread, toasted
2 teaspoons low-fat spread
3 oz (90 g) poached mushrooms
4 oz (120 g) orange sections
5 fl oz (150 ml) low-fat natural yogurt

EVENING MEAL
Skate with Lemon Sauce (page 269)
3 oz (90 g) boiled potatoes, mashed with 1 teaspoon low-fat spread
3 oz (90 g) green beans
3 oz (90 g) carrots
2 inch (5 cm) wedge honeydew melon

SNACKS OR DRINKS AT PLANNED TIMES
½ pint (300 ml) skim milk

DAY 3

MORNING MEAL
1 oz (30 g) raisins
¾ oz (20 g) porridge oats cooked with water and served with 5 fl oz (150 ml) skim milk

MIDDAY MEAL
Soused Herring (page 264)
6 oz (180 g) cooked potatoes, diced and mixed with 4 teaspoons low-calorie mayonnaise and chopped chives
3 oz (90 g) beetroot with onion rings
8 fl oz (240 ml) tomato juice

EVENING MEAL
4 oz (120 g) grilled lamb chop
3 oz (90 g) green beans
3 oz (90 g) courgettes
1 medium grilled tomato
1 teaspoon margarine
2 medium plums stewed with **Custard** (page 297)

SNACKS OR DRINKS AT PLANNED TIMES
½ pint (300 ml) skim milk

DAY4

MORNING MEAL
½ medium banana
¾ oz (20 g) bran flakes
5 fl oz (150 ml) skim milk

MIDDAY MEAL
2-egg omelette cooked in 1 teaspoon
    vegetable oil and filled with 3 oz (90 g)
    poached mushrooms
green salad
1 oz (30 g) French bread with 2 teaspoons
    low-fat spread
5 oz (150 g) strawberries with 5 fl oz (150 ml)
    low-fat natural yogurt

EVENING MEAL
6 oz (180 g) grilled chicken seasoned with
    barbecue spice and lemon juice
small tomatoes, onions, mushrooms, and
    cubes of green pepper skewered
    alternately and brushed with 1 teaspoon
    vegetable oil and garlic salt
2 oz (60 g) cooked rice
2 inch (5 cm) wedge honeydew melon

SNACKS OR DRINKS AT PLANNED TIMES
5 fl oz (150 ml) skim milk

DAY5

MORNING MEAL
1 tablespoon peanut butter
½ medium banana and 1 teaspoon honey on
    1 slice (1 oz/30 g) wholemeal bread

MIDDAY MEAL
2 oz (60 g) Cheddar cheese grated over green
    salad with 1 medium sliced tomato, 3 oz
    (90 g) beetroot
2 teaspoons low-calorie mayonnaise
4 oz (120 g) stewed apple with 2½ fl oz (75
    ml) low-fat natural yogurt

EVENING MEAL
5 oz (150 g) grilled plaice
6 oz (180 g) baked jacket potato with 2½ fl oz
    (75 ml) low-fat natural yogurt and chopped
    chives
3 oz (90 g) cauliflower
3 oz (90 g) courgettes
2 teaspoons low-fat spread
4 fl oz (120 ml) orange juice

SNACKS OR DRINKS AT PLANNED TIMES
½ pint (300 ml) skim milk

DAY6

MORNING MEAL
4 oz (120 g) apricots
¾ oz (20 g) wheat flakes with 5 fl oz (150 ml)
   skim milk

MIDDAY MEAL
8 fl oz (240 ml) tomato juice
4 breadcrumbed fish fingers, grilled
3 oz (90 g) sweet corn
3 oz (90 g) baked beans
2 medium tomatoes, grilled

EVENING MEAL
5 oz (150 g) uncooked lamb's liver, sauteed in
   1 teaspoon vegetable oil with 1 medium
   onion, sliced
3 oz (90 g) green beans
3 oz (90 g) marrow
2 teaspoons margarine
2½ oz (75 g) blackberries and 2 oz (60 g)
   apples, stewed, with 5 fl oz (150 ml) low-
   fat natural yogurt

**SNACKS OR DRINKS
AT PLANNED TIMES**
5 fl oz (150 ml) skim milk

DAY7

MORNING MEAL
4 fl oz (120 ml) orange juice
1 egg scrambled in 1 teaspoon low-fat spread
1 oz (30 g) lean back bacon, grilled
1 oz (30 g) granary roll

MIDDAY MEAL
2 inch (5 cm) wedge honeydew melon
3 oz (90 g) roast beef
3 oz (90 g) turnips
3 oz (90 g) carrots
3 oz (90 g) green beans
4 oz (120 g) fruit salad

EVENING MEAL
Kipper Pate (page 266) and green salad with
   lemon juice
2 oz (60 g) granary roll
1 teaspoon low-fat spread

**SNACKS OR DRINKS
AT PLANNED TIMES**
5 fl oz (150 ml) low-fat natural yogurt, with
   coffee flavouring, 7½ fl oz (225 ml) skim
   milk

Parsley soup is an interesting way of using a herb which many of us associate only with fish. Parsley grows well in a window-box set in shady, moist conditions.

DAY 1

MORNING MEAL
½ medium grapefruit
1 poached egg
1 slice (1 oz/30 g) bread, toasted
1 teaspoon margarine

MIDDAY MEAL
Chick Pea Croquettes (page 273)
1 tomato, halved and grilled
green salad with onion and pepper rings
1 teaspoon vegetable oil with wine vinegar
1 oz (30 g) pitta bread
4 oz (120 g) fruit salad

EVENING MEAL
5 oz (150 g) baked hake
3 oz (90 g) carrots
3 oz (90 g) courgettes
green salad with **Vinaigrette Dressing** (page 293)
1 medium peach

SNACKS OR DRINKS AT PLANNED TIMES
½ pint (300 ml) skim milk

DAY2

MORNING MEAL ½ medium banana, sliced on ¾ oz (20 g)
cornflakes with 5 fl oz (150 ml) skim milk

MIDDAY MEAL 5 oz (150 g) cottage cheese
1 tomato sliced with onion rings
Vinaigrette Dressing (page 293)
2 cream crackers
1 teaspoon margarine
1 medium apple

EVENING MEAL 6 oz (180 g) grilled lamb chop
3 oz (90 g) peas
3 oz (90 g) green beans
3 oz (90 g) boiled potatoes
1 teaspoon margarine
5 oz (150 g) strawberries

**SNACKS OR DRINKS
AT PLANNED TIMES** 15 fl oz (450 ml) skim milk

DAY3

MORNING MEAL 4 fl oz (120 ml) orange juice
1 egg, scrambled in 1 teaspoon low-fat
spread
1 slice (1 oz/30 g) bread, toasted

MIDDAY MEAL **Parsley Soup** (page 285)
3 oz (90 g) cooked chicken
mixed salad
2 teaspoons salad dressing
2 cream crackers
2 medium plums

EVENING MEAL 4 oz (120 g) grilled haddock dotted with 1
teaspoon low-fat spread
3 oz (90 g) cauliflower
green salad with **Russian Dressing** (page
292)
5 oz (150 g) strawberries
4 fl oz (120 ml) wine

**SNACKS OR DRINKS
AT PLANNED TIMES** 5 fl oz (150 ml) low-fat natural yogurt, ½ pint
(300 ml) skim milk

DAY4

MORNING MEAL **Oatmeal with Spiced Fruit Ambrosia** (page 285)

MIDDAY MEAL
4 oz (120 g) grilled liver
3 oz (90 g) poached mushrooms
3 oz (90 g) peas
2 oz (60 g) boiled rice
1 teaspoon margarine
sliced tomatoes and onion rings
4 oz (120 g) pear

EVENING MEAL
4 oz (120 g) grilled veal
3 oz (90 g) green beans
3 oz (90 g) carrots
3 oz (90 g) boiled potatoes
4 teaspoons low-fat spread
1 medium orange

SNACKS OR DRINKS AT PLANNED TIMES
15 fl oz (450 ml) skim milk

DAY5

MORNING MEAL
4 fl oz (120 ml) orange juice
1 oz (30 g) Cheddar cheese
grilled on 1 slice (1 oz/30 g) bread, toasted

MIDDAY MEAL
Salmon Salad (page 265) on shredded lettuce
3 oz (90 g) sweet corn
1 medium peach

EVENING MEAL
3 oz (90 g) grilled lamb fillet
3 oz (90 g) broccoli
1 teaspoon margarine
mixed salad with shredded lettuce, sliced tomatoes, green pepper and onion rings
Vinaigrette Dressing (page 293)
5 oz (150 g) blackcurrants, stewed
½ pint (300 ml) beer or cider

SNACKS OR DRINKS AT PLANNED TIMES
5 fl oz (150 ml) low-fat natural yogurt, ½ pint (300 ml) skim milk

DAY 6

MORNING MEAL
1 medium peach, sliced
¾ oz (20 g) wheat flakes
5 fl oz (150 ml) skim milk

MIDDAY MEAL
3 tablespoons peanut butter on 2 slices (1
    oz/30 g each) wholemeal bread, toasted,
    with 3 oz (90 g) cucumber, cut into sticks
1 medium orange

EVENING MEAL
4 oz (120 g) cooked chicken
1 hard-boiled egg
mixed salad with low-calorie salad dressing,
    up to 50 calories
Baked Apple (page 295)

**SNACKS OR DRINKS
AT PLANNED TIMES**
15 fl oz (450 ml) skim milk

DAY 7

MORNING MEAL
Honey-Stewed Prunes (page 298)
1 egg, cooked in 1 teaspoon oil on 1 slice
    (1 oz/30 g) bread, toasted with 1 tomato,
    halved and grilled

MIDDAY MEAL
3 oz (90 g) roast beef
3 oz (90 g) boiled potatoes
3 oz (90 g) cabbage
3 oz (90 g) carrots and turnips, dotted with 1
    teaspoon margarine
5 oz (150 g) gooseberries

EVENING MEAL
8 fl oz (240 ml) tomato juice
4 oz (120 g) canned sardines with mixed salad
3 oz (90 g) beetroot
2 teaspoons salad cream
1 portion rhubarb

**SNACKS OR DRINKS
AT PLANNED TIMES**
5 fl oz (150 ml) low-fat natural yogurt, ½ pint
    (300 ml) skim milk

WEEK 32

Liver is a budget meat with no waste and no fat. For a change, try chicken livers.

DAY 1

MORNING MEAL
1 medium orange
1 oz (30 g) Edam cheese
1 slice (1 oz/30 g) wholemeal bread, toasted

MIDDAY MEAL
3 oz (90 g) roast chicken
1 tomato, sliced on lettuce with radishes and spring onion
2 teaspoons salad cream
1 slice (1 oz/30 g) wholemeal bread
5 oz (150 g) gooseberries, stewed with 1½ teaspoons honey

EVENING MEAL
5 oz (150 g) uncooked chicken livers sauteed in 1 teaspoon oil with 2 oz (60 g) sliced onion
3 oz (90 g) carrots dotted with 1 teaspoon margarine
4 oz (120 g) fruit salad

SNACKS OR DRINKS AT PLANNED TIMES
5 fl oz (150 ml) low-fat natural yogurt, ½ pint (300 ml) skim milk

DAY 2

MORNING MEAL
4 fl oz (120 ml) orange juice
1 boiled egg
1 slice (1 oz/30 g) wholemeal bread, toasted
1 teaspoon margarine

MIDDAY MEAL
3 oz (90 g) canned tuna with mixed salad
3 oz (90 g) beetroot
2 teaspoons salad cream
2 water biscuits
5 oz (150 g) blackberries with 5 fl oz (150 ml) low-fat natural yogurt

EVENING MEAL
8 fl oz (240 ml) tomato juice
Sesame Chicken with Green Beans (page 239)
3 oz (90 g) marrow

SNACKS OR DRINKS AT PLANNED TIMES
½ pint (300 ml) skim milk

DAY 3

MORNING MEAL
1 medium orange
Cinnamon-Cheese Toast (page 234)

MIDDAY MEAL
4 oz (120 g) liver sausage with mixed salad
3 oz (90 g) sweet corn
2 teaspoons salad cream
2 medium plums

EVENING MEAL
3 oz (90 g) Pacific prawns brushed with 1 teaspoon vegetable oil and grilled
3 oz (90 g) peas
1 tomato, halved and grilled
3 oz (90 g) poached mushrooms dotted with 1 teaspoon margarine
4 oz (120 g) fruit salad

SNACKS OR DRINKS AT PLANNED TIMES
5 fl oz (150 ml) low-fat natural yogurt, ½ pint (300 ml) skim milk

DAY4

MORNING MEAL
1 medium orange
1 egg, scrambled in 1 teaspoon margarine
1 slice (1 oz/30 g) bread, toasted

MIDDAY MEAL
sardine open sandwich made with 3 oz (90 g)
  sardines on 1 slice (1 oz/30 g) wholemeal
  bread, topped with tomato and cucumber
  slices with 2 teaspoons low-calorie
  mayonnaise
1 medium plum

EVENING MEAL
Sweet and Sour Chicken Stir-Fry (page
  240)
3 oz (90 g) courgettes
3 oz (90 g) cauliflower
4 oz (120 g) stewed apple

**SNACKS OR DRINKS
AT PLANNED TIMES**
½ pint (300 ml) skim milk, 5 fl oz (150 ml)
  low-fat natural yogurt

DAY5

MORNING MEAL
4 fl oz (120 ml) orange juice
2½ oz (75 g) cottage cheese
melba toast, up to 80 calories

MIDDAY MEAL
2 hard-boiled eggs
green salad with 2 teaspoons mayonnaise
melba toast, up to 80 calories
4 oz (120 g) fruit salad

EVENING MEAL
5 oz (150 g) grilled mackerel
1 tomato, grilled
3 oz (90 g) green beans
1 teaspoon margarine
5 oz (150 g) strawberries
2 oz (60 g) vanilla ice cream

**SNACKS OR DRINKS
AT PLANNED TIMES**
5 fl oz (150 ml) low-fat natural yogurt, ½ pint
  (300 ml) skim milk

DAY6

MORNING MEAL
4 fl oz (120 ml) orange juice
¾ oz (20 g) cornflakes
5 fl oz (150 ml) skim milk

MIDDAY MEAL
4 oz (120 g) canned pilchards
mixed salad
3 oz (90 g) beetroot
4 teaspoons salad cream
5 oz (150 g) blackcurrants with 3 tablespoons
(45 ml) single cream

EVENING MEAL
4 oz (120 g) grilled beefburgers
3 oz (90 g) courgettes
3 oz (90 g) carrots
1 tomato, sliced, sprinkled with 1 teaspoon
oil and wine vinegar
3 oz (90 g) boiled potatoes
4 oz (120 g) fruit salad

**SNACKS OR DRINKS
AT PLANNED TIMES**
5 fl oz (150 ml) low-fat natural yogurt, 5 fl oz
(150 ml) skim milk

DAY7

MORNING MEAL
4 fl oz (120 ml) orange juice
¾ oz (20 g) wheat flakes
5 fl oz (150 ml) skim milk

MIDDAY MEAL
4 oz (120 g) grilled beef steak
1 tomato, halved and grilled
3 oz (90 g) green beans
3 oz (90 g) boiled potatoes
1 teaspoon margarine
1 medium peach

EVENING MEAL
8 fl oz (240 ml) tomato juice
Fish and Rice Salad (page 262)
mixed salad with 2 oz (60 g) beetroot
2 teaspoons salad cream
1 portion stewed rhubarb

**SNACKS OR DRINKS
AT PLANNED TIMES**
15 fl oz (450 ml) skim milk

WEEK 33

Cold soups don't readily come to mind in our cool climate, but the Spanish Gazpacho is perfect on a hot summer's day. It's very satisfying, too.

DAY 1

MORNING MEAL
5 oz (150 g) strawberries
1 oz (30 g) Cheddar cheese, grated and grilled on 1 slice (1 oz/30 g) bread, toasted

MIDDAY MEAL
Ginger-Grilled Chicken (page 238)
3 oz (90 g) peas
3 oz (90 g) green beans
green salad with red pepper rings
2 teaspoons mayonnaise
1 medium orange, peeled and diced
Custard (page 297)

EVENING MEAL
cheese omelette made with 2 eggs and 1 oz (30 g) Cheddar cheese, cooked in 1 teaspoon vegetable oil
3 oz (90 g) baked beans
3 oz (90 g) spinach
5 oz (150 g) blackcurrants

SNACKS OR DRINKS AT PLANNED TIMES
15 fl oz (450 ml) skim milk

DAY 2

MORNING MEAL
½ medium grapefruit
¾ oz (20 g) cereal
5 fl oz (150 ml) skim milk

MIDDAY MEAL
5 oz (150 g) cottage cheese
1 tomato, sliced onto lettuce with cucumber
and radishes
Vinaigrette Dressing (page 293)
1 slice (1 oz/30 g) wholemeal bread
1 teaspoon margarine
4 oz (120 g) apricots

EVENING MEAL
Frankfurter Stir-Fry (page 255)
6 oz (180 g) courgettes

SNACKS OR DRINKS
AT PLANNED TIMES
15 fl oz (450 ml) skim milk, 2 oz (60 g) corned
beef, 1 slice (1 oz/30 g) bread

DAY 3

MORNING MEAL
5 oz (150 g) strawberries
¾ oz (20 g) muesli
5 fl oz (150 ml) skim milk

MIDDAY MEAL
2 hard-boiled eggs, chopped, and 1 oz (30 g)
Cheddar cheese grated, lettuce with 1
tomato, and cucumber, sliced
2 teaspoons salad cream
3 oz (90 g) baked beans
1 medium apple

EVENING MEAL
5 oz (150 g) grilled sole with 2 teaspoons
mayonnaise
2 oz (60 g) cooked rice
3 oz (90 g) carrots
3 oz (90 g) turnips
Baked Apple (page 295) with 2 oz (60 g)
vanilla ice cream

SNACKS OR DRINKS
AT PLANNED TIMES
15 fl oz (450 ml) skim milk

DAY4

MORNING MEAL
1 medium orange
2½ oz (75 g) cottage cheese
crispbread, up to 80 calories

MIDDAY MEAL
4 oz (120 g) grilled liver
3 oz (90 g) diced onion, sauteed in 1 teaspoon
    margarine
3 oz (90 g) broccoli
3 oz (90 g) poached mushrooms
2 oz (60 g) cooked pasta shells
4 oz (120 g) peaches and 2½ fl oz (75 ml)
    low-fat natural yogurt

EVENING MEAL
3 oz (90 g) grilled chicken
3 oz (90 g) cauliflower
3 oz (90 g) green beans dotted with 2
    teaspoons margarine
4 oz (120 g) mandarin oranges

**SNACKS OR DRINKS
AT PLANNED TIMES**
15 fl oz (450 ml) skim milk

DAY5

MORNING MEAL
4 fl oz (120 ml) orange juice
1 oz (30 g) Edam cheese sliced on melba
    toast, up to 80 calories

MIDDAY MEAL
Gazpacho (page 217)
3 oz (90 g) canned tuna
mixed salad
3 teaspoons salad cream
1 medium plum

EVENING MEAL
4 oz (120 g) grilled pork chop
2 oz (60 g) cooked noodles
3 oz (90 g) cabbage
3 oz (90 g) carrots
2 teaspoons tomato relish
4 oz (120 g) fruit salad

**SNACKS OR DRINKS
AT PLANNED TIMES**
½ pint (300 ml) skim milk, 5 fl oz (150 ml)
    low-fat natural yogurt

DAY 6

MORNING MEAL
5 oz (150 g) strawberries sliced on ¾ oz (20 g) cereal
5 fl oz (150 ml) skim milk

MIDDAY MEAL
4 oz (120 g) roast turkey
mixed salad
Vinaigrette Dressing (page 293)
3 oz (90 g) baked beans
2 inch (5 cm) wedge honeydew melon

EVENING MEAL
4 oz (120 g) grilled mackerel
2 teaspoons cucumber relish
1 tomato, halved and grilled
3 oz (90 g) mushrooms, sauteed in 2 teaspoons vegetable oil
3 oz (90 g) boiled potatoes
2 oz (60 g) apple stewed with 2½ oz (75 g) blackberries

SNACKS OR DRINKS AT PLANNED TIMES
15 fl oz (450 ml) skim milk

DAY 7

MORNING MEAL
4 fl oz (120 ml) orange juice
2 oz (60 g) smoked salmon with lemon wedge
1 slice (1 oz/30 g) wholemeal bread
1 teaspoon margarine

MIDDAY MEAL
4 oz (120 g) dressed crab with mixed salad
3 oz (90 g) beetroot
2 teaspoons low-calorie mayonnaise
Baked Apple (page 295)
Custard (page 297)

EVENING MEAL
2 inch (5 cm) wedge honeydew melon
tomato omelette made with 2 eggs and 3 oz (90 g) tomatoes, skinned and chopped, cooked in 1 teaspoon vegetable oil
3 oz (90 g) baked beans
green salad with lemon juice
4 fl oz (120 ml) white wine

SNACKS OR DRINKS AT PLANNED TIMES
15 fl oz (450 ml) skim milk

WEEK 34

Forget the wrinkled prunes of childhood memories. Stewing them gently in honey-sweet liquid makes them very palatable indeed!

DAY 1

MORNING MEAL
½ medium banana, sliced
6 oz (180 g) baked beans
1 slice (1 oz/30 g) bread, toasted

MIDDAY MEAL
5 oz (150 g) cottage cheese, tomato and
  lettuce salad with 1 teaspoon salad
  dressing
2 cream crackers
1 teaspoon low-fat spread
1 medium orange

EVENING MEAL
Sole Veronique (page 266)
3 oz (90 g) carrots
2 oz (60 g) boiled rice dotted with 1 teaspoon
  low-fat spread
1 portion rhubarb

**SNACKS OR DRINKS
AT PLANNED TIMES**
17½ fl oz (525 ml) skim milk

DAY 2

MORNING MEAL
4 fl oz (120 ml) grapefruit juice
1 boiled egg
1 slice (1 oz/30 g) bread
1 teaspoon margarine

MIDDAY MEAL
3 oz (90 g) grilled haddock
1 teaspoon margarine
3 oz (90 g) spinach
1 tomato, halved and grilled
2 oz (60 g) cooked noodles dotted with 1
    teaspoon margarine
½ medium banana, sliced with 5 fl oz (150 ml)
    low-fat natural yogurt

EVENING MEAL
4 oz (120 g) grilled ham, with 2 slices (4 oz/
    120 g) pineapple
3 oz (90 g) peas
mixed green salad with lemon juice and
    seasoning salt

**SNACKS OR DRINKS
AT PLANNED TIMES**
½ pint (300 ml) skim milk

DAY 3

MORNING MEAL
Honey-Stewed Prunes (page 298)
2½ oz (75 g) cottage cheese
crispbread, up to 80 calories

MIDDAY MEAL
Mushroom Omelette (page 230)
mixed salad
1 teaspoon mayonnaise
5 oz (150 g) damsons, stewed with 1
    teaspoon honey

EVENING MEAL
5 oz (150 g) grilled mackerel with lemon
    slices
3 oz (90 g) broccoli
3 oz (90 g) carrots
3 oz (90 g) boiled potatoes
1 teaspoon margarine
5 oz (150 g) strawberries with 3 tablespoons
    single cream

**SNACKS OR DRINKS
AT PLANNED TIMES**
5 fl oz (150 ml) low-fat natural yogurt, ½ pint
    (300 ml) skim milk

DAY4

MORNING MEAL
4 fl oz (120 ml) grapefruit juice
1 oz (30 g) Cheddar cheese
crispbread, up to 80 calories

MIDDAY MEAL
3 oz (90 g) diced cooked chicken, 1 tomato,
diced, chopped watercress and 1
teaspoon mayonnaise with 1 slice (1 oz/30
g) wholemeal bread
2 medium plums

EVENING MEAL
5 oz (150 g) uncooked chicken livers sauteed
in 2 teaspoons vegetable oil with 3 oz (90
g) diced onion
3 oz (90 g) peas
5 oz (150 g) gooseberries stewed with 1 ½
teaspoons honey

SNACKS OR DRINKS AT PLANNED TIMES
5 fl oz (150 ml) low-fat natural yogurt, ½ pint
(300 ml) skim milk

DAY5

MORNING MEAL
2½ fl oz (75 ml) pineapple juice
1 egg, scrambled in 1 teaspoon margarine
1 slice (1 oz/30 g) wholemeal bread, toasted

MIDDAY MEAL
3 oz (90 g) tuna
mixed salad
2 oz (60 g) beetroot
1 slice (1 oz/30 g) wholemeal bread
2 teaspoons margarine
1 medium orange

EVENING MEAL
4 oz (120 g) grilled pork fillet
3 oz (90 g) cooked carrots
3 oz (90 g) green beans
4 oz (120 g) fruit salad
4 fl oz (120 ml) wine

SNACKS OR DRINKS AT PLANNED TIMES
1 pint (600 ml) skim milk

DAY6

MORNING MEAL

1 medium orange
1 oz (30 g) Cheddar cheese
1 slice (1 oz/30 g) wholemeal bread

MIDDAY MEAL

3 oz (90 g) cooked chicken and mixed salad
    with **Vinaigrette Dressing** (page 293)
3 oz (90 g) sweet corn
5 oz (150 g) blackberries

EVENING MEAL

Trout with Mushroom Stuffing (page 259)
3 oz (90 g) spinach
3 oz (90 g) carrots dotted with 1 teaspoon
    margarine
1 medium peach

SNACKS OR DRINKS AT PLANNED TIMES

5 fl oz (150 ml) low-fat natural yogurt, ½ pint
    (300 ml) skim milk

DAY7

MORNING MEAL

4 oz (120 g) fruit salad
¾ oz (20 g) cornflakes
5 fl oz (150 ml) skim milk

MIDDAY MEAL

4 oz (120 g) roast lamb with **Mint Sauce**
    (page 291)
3 oz (90 g) boiled potatoes
3 oz (90 g) green beans
3 oz (90 g) courgettes
3 teaspoons margarine
5 oz (150 g) strawberries with 2½ fl oz (75 ml)
    low-fat natural yogurt

EVENING MEAL

9 oz (270 g) baked beans, heated and served
    on 1 slice (1 oz/30 g) wholemeal bread,
    toasted and topped with 1 oz (30 g) grated
    Cheddar cheese
1 tomato, halved and grilled
3 oz (90 g) poached mushrooms
3 oz (90 g) grapes

SNACKS OR DRINKS AT PLANNED TIMES

½ pint (300 ml) skim milk

WEEK 35

Barbecuing is a method of cooking outdoors on a rack over hot charcoal. The food to be cooked is often improved by being marinaded first to tenderise and improve flavour.

DAY 1

MORNING MEAL
4 oz (120 g) grapefruit sections
¾ oz (20 g) wheat flakes
5 fl oz (150 ml) skim milk

MIDDAY MEAL
4 oz (120 g) fresh sardines, barbecued or grilled
1 oz (30 g) French bread
1 teaspoon margarine
1 tomato with onion rings
Apple Slaw (page 290)
3 oz (90 g) cherries with 2½ fl oz (75 ml) low-fat natural yogurt

EVENING MEAL
Barbecued Pork (page 252)
3 oz (90 g) peas
3 oz (90 g) baked jacket potato
mixed salad with **Vinaigrette Dressing** (page 293)
4 oz (120 g) fruit salad
2 oz (60 g) vanilla ice cream

SNACKS OR DRINKS AT PLANNED TIMES
½ pint (300 ml) skim milk

DAY 2

MORNING MEAL
2½ fl oz (75 ml) apple juice
1 boiled egg
1 slice (1 oz/30 g) wholemeal bread, toasted
2 teaspoons low-fat spread

MIDDAY MEAL
4 oz (120 g) smoked mackerel fillets
1 tomato, sliced with onion rings on lettuce
   with 1 teaspoon mayonnaise
1 oz (30 g) French bread
1 teaspoon margarine
5 oz (150 g) strawberries

EVENING MEAL
3 oz (90 g) grilled chicken
2 grilled tomatoes
3 oz (90 g) baked beans
Pineapple Sorbet (page 301)

SNACKS OR DRINKS AT PLANNED TIMES
½ pint (300 ml) skim milk

DAY 3

MORNING MEAL
4 fl oz (120 ml) orange juice
Cinnamon-Cheese Toast (page 234)

MIDDAY MEAL
2 poached eggs on 6 oz (180 g) spinach
1 oz (30 g) wholemeal bread roll
2 teaspoons low-fat spread
2 medium plums

EVENING MEAL
5 oz (150 g) scampi, brushed with 1 teaspoon
   oil and grilled
2 oz (60 g) cooked rice
Chinese Cabbage and Tomato Medley
   (page 280)

SNACKS OR DRINKS AT PLANNED TIMES
1 medium peach, sliced with 5 fl oz (150 ml)
   low-fat natural yogurt, ½ pint (300 ml)
   skim milk

DAY4

MORNING MEAL
5 oz (150 g) strawberries
¾ oz (20 g) cornflakes
5 fl oz (150 ml) low-fat natural yogurt

MIDDAY MEAL
5 oz (150 g) uncooked lamb's liver sauteed in
  2 teaspoons olive oil
Courgette Basil (page 278)
watercress and lettuce
1 medium peach

EVENING MEAL
4 oz (120 g) roast turkey breast
3 oz (90 g) carrots with 2 teaspoons low-fat
  spread
3 oz (90 g) green beans
6 oz (180 g) baked jacket potato

SNACKS OR DRINKS AT PLANNED TIMES
½ pint (300 ml) skim milk, 8 fl oz (240 ml)
  tomato juice

DAY5

MORNING MEAL
8 fl oz (240 ml) tomato juice
1 poached egg
1 slice (1 oz/30 g) wholemeal bread, toasted
1 teaspoon margarine

MIDDAY MEAL
3 oz (90 g) cold roast turkey
1 tomato, 3 oz (90 g) beetroot with lettuce
1 slice (1 oz/30 g) wholemeal bread
2 teaspoons low-fat spread

EVENING MEAL
2 inch (5 cm) wedge honeydew melon
4 oz (120 g) grilled rump steak
3 oz (90 g) marrow
3 oz (90 g) celery hearts
1 grilled tomato
2 oz (60 g) cooked noodles
2 teaspoons low-fat spread
5 oz (150 g) damsons

SNACKS OR DRINKS AT PLANNED TIMES
½ pint (300 ml) skim milk, 5 fl oz (150 g)
  low-fat natural yogurt

DAY6

MORNING MEAL
2 inch (5 cm) wedge honeydew melon
2½ oz (75 g) cottage cheese on 1 slice (1 oz/ 30 g) wholemeal bread, toasted

MIDDAY MEAL
Chilli-Cheese Rarebit (page 231)
mixed green salad with lemon juice
3 oz (90 g) baked beans

EVENING MEAL
Chicken Kebabs (page 237)
mushroom and beansprout salad with 1 teaspoon vegetable oil and wine vinegar
1 oz (30 g) French bread
1 teaspoon margarine
4 fl oz (120 ml) white wine
1 medium orange

SNACKS OR DRINKS AT PLANNED TIMES
5 fl oz (150 ml) skim milk, 5 fl oz (150 ml) low-fat natural yogurt with 5 oz (150 g) stewed blackberries, **Coconut-Coffee Mounds** (page 300)

DAY7

MORNING MEAL
4 fl oz (120 ml) orange juice
¾ oz (20 g) wheat flakes
5 fl oz (150 ml) skim milk

MIDDAY MEAL
Lemon-Minted Lamb (page 248)
3 oz (90 g) green beans
3 oz (90 g) courgettes
3 oz (90 g) baked jacket potato
1 teaspoon low-fat spread
2½ oz (75 g) blackberries, cooked with 2 oz (60 g) sliced apple
2½ fl oz (75 ml) low-fat natural yogurt

EVENING MEAL
1 medium corn-on-the-cob, cooked
1 teaspoon low-fat spread
4 oz (120 g) grilled lemon sole
mixed salad with **Vinaigrette Dressing** (page 293)
1 medium peach

SNACKS OR DRINKS AT PLANNED TIMES
½ pint (300 ml) skim milk

WEEK 36

Steaming is a good way to cook vegetables. They stay whole and firm in the steamer fitted over a pan of gently boiling water. Be sure to fit the lid on tightly to keep the steam in.

DAY 1

MORNING MEAL
½ medium cantaloupe melon
2½ oz (75 g) quark or cottage cheese
2 water biscuits
1 teaspoon margarine

MIDDAY MEAL
open sandwich made with
    1 slice (1 oz/30 g) wholemeal bread with 1 teaspoon margarine, shredded lettuce topped with 3 oz (90 g) canned sardines, sliced tomatoes and 2 teaspoons low-calorie mayonnaise
1 medium apple

EVENING MEAL
4 oz (120 g) grilled plaice with lemon juice
3 oz (90 g) broccoli
3 oz (90 g) carrots
Curried Cole Slaw (page 288)
5 oz (150 g) strawberries

SNACKS OR DRINKS AT PLANNED TIMES
5 fl oz (150 ml) low-fat natural yogurt, ½ pint (300 ml) skim milk

DAY 2

MORNING MEAL 4 fl oz (120 ml) orange juice
¾ oz (20 g) oatmeal cooked with water
5 fl oz (150 ml) skim milk

MIDDAY MEAL 4 oz (120 g) liver sausage
mixed salad
Vinaigrette Dressing (page 293)
1 slice (1 oz/30 g) wholemeal bread
5 oz (150 g) raspberries

EVENING MEAL 4 oz (120 g) grilled chicken
1 oz (90 g) back bacon, grilled
3 oz (90 g) peas
3 oz (90 g) green beans
2 oz (60 g) boiled rice dotted with 2 teaspoons
margarine

SNACKS OR DRINKS AT PLANNED TIMES 15 fl oz (450 ml) skim milk, 1 medium orange

DAY 3

MORNING MEAL ½ medium grapefruit
¾ oz (20 g) cornflakes
5 fl oz (150 ml) skim milk

MIDDAY MEAL 4 oz (120 g) salmon with mixed salad
2 teaspoons mayonnaise
1 slice (1 oz/30 g) bread
1 teaspoon margarine
1 medium pear

EVENING MEAL 4 oz (120 g) grilled herring
3 oz (90 g) mashed potato
3 oz (90 g) spinach
3 oz (90 g) courgettes
4 oz (120 g) fruit salad

SNACKS OR DRINKS AT PLANNED TIMES 15 fl oz (450 ml) skim milk

DAY 4

MORNING MEAL
2½ fl oz (75 ml) apple juice
1 egg, scrambled in 1 teaspoon margarine
1 slice (1 oz/30 g) wholemeal bread, toasted

MIDDAY MEAL
open cheese sandwich made
    with 1 slice (1 oz/30 g) wholemeal bread,
    2 oz (60 g) grated Cheddar cheese, sliced
    tomatoes and watercress
1 medium orange

EVENING MEAL
5 oz (150 g) roast chicken
3 oz (90 g) swede
3 oz (90 g) cabbage, dotted with 2 teaspoons
    margarine
4 oz (120 g) peaches

SNACKS OR DRINKS AT PLANNED TIMES
5 fl oz (150 ml) low-fat natural yogurt, ½ pint
(300 ml) skim milk

DAY 5

MORNING MEAL
½ medium cantaloupe melon
2 boiled eggs
1 slice (1 oz/30 g) bread
1 teaspoon margarine

MIDDAY MEAL
5 oz (150 g) cottage cheese mixed with 3 oz
    (90 g) diced green pepper and 1
    tablespoon diced onion
green salad with **Vinaigrette Dressing** (page
    293)
melba toast, up to 80 calories
1 medium peach

EVENING MEAL
Chicken Livers Sauteed in Wine (page 257)
2 oz (60 g) cooked rice
3 oz (90 g) asparagus
3 oz (90 g) red pepper rings
1 medium orange

SNACKS OR DRINKS AT PLANNED TIMES
1 pint (600 ml) skim milk

DAY 6

MORNING MEAL
½ medium grapefruit
1 tablespoon crunchy peanut butter
crispbread, up to 80 calories

MIDDAY MEAL
cheese omelette made with 2 eggs and 1 oz
    (30 g) Cheddar cheese
1 tomato, sliced
green salad with 2 teaspoons salad dressing
1 slice (1 oz/30 g) bread
4 oz (120 g) peaches

EVENING MEAL
Cod-Vegetable Bake (page 260)
3 oz (90 g) green beans
1 medium kiwi fruit

SNACKS OR DRINKS AT PLANNED TIMES
5 fl oz (150 ml) low-fat natural yogurt, ½ pint
    (300 ml) skim milk

DAY 7

MORNING MEAL
½ medium grapefruit
1 egg, poached
1 slice (1 oz/30 g) brown bread, toasted
1 teaspoon margarine

MIDDAY MEAL
4 oz (120 g) roast beef
3 oz (90 g) baked jacket potato
3 oz (90 g) parsnips and 2 small onions, baked
    in 2 teaspoons oil
4 oz (120 g) fruit salad with 3 tablespoons
    single cream

EVENING MEAL
3 oz (90 g) canned tuna with mixed salad
low-calorie dressing, up to 50 calories
1 medium pear

SNACKS OR DRINKS AT PLANNED TIMES
5 fl oz (150 ml) low-fat natural yogurt, ½ pint
    (300 ml) skim milk

WEEK 37

A fresh apple – preferably from an English orchard – makes a marvellous end to a meal. It cleanses the teeth and is said to kill unhealthy germs in the stomach. Hence the old saying, 'an apple a day keeps the doctor away'.

DAY 1

MORNING MEAL	2 inch (5 cm) wedge honeydew melon 1 boiled egg 1 slice (1 oz/30 g) wholemeal bread, toasted 1 teaspoon margarine
MIDDAY MEAL	prawn cocktail salad made with 3 oz (90 g) peeled prawns, shredded lettuce, sliced cucumber and 1 medium tomato, cut into quarters 4 teaspoons salad cream mixed with 1 teaspoon tomato ketchup and a dash of Worcestershire sauce 1 slice (1 oz/30 g) wholemeal bread 3 oz (90 g) grapes
EVENING MEAL	**Tomato Soup** (page 218) 4 oz (120 g) grilled chicken breast 3 oz (90 g) whole green beans 4 oz (120 g) orange sections
SNACKS OR DRINKS AT PLANNED TIMES	5 fl oz (150 ml) low-fat natural yogurt, ½ pint (300 ml) skim milk

DAY 2

MORNING MEAL
4 fl oz (120 ml) grapefruit juice
¾ oz (20 g) porridge oats cooked with water
5 fl oz (150 ml) skim milk

MIDDAY MEAL
4 oz (120 g) grilled lamb's liver
3 oz (90 g) green beans
salad of sliced red pepper and shredded
    lettuce with 2 teaspoons mayonnaise
2 oz (60 g) cooked rice
1 medium apple

EVENING MEAL
4 oz (120 g) grilled turkey breast
3 oz (90 g) courgettes
green salad with 1 teaspoon mayonnaise
4 oz (120 g) fruit salad

SNACKS OR DRINKS AT PLANNED TIMES
15 fl oz (450 ml) skim milk, 1 digestive biscuit

DAY 3

MORNING MEAL
4 oz (120 g) fruit salad
1 tablespoon peanut butter
crispbread, up to 80 calories

MIDDAY MEAL
Split Pea Soup (page 275)
2 water biscuits
1 teaspoon margarine
1 medium orange
2 oz (60 g) vanilla ice cream

EVENING MEAL
5 oz (150 g) grilled pork chop with 1 medium
    apple, peeled, cored and sliced in rings,
    sprinkled with lemon juice and grilled until
    tender
3 oz (90 g) peas
1 tomato, halved and grilled
3 oz (90 g) broccoli

SNACKS OR DRINKS AT PLANNED TIMES
17½ fl oz (525 ml) skim milk

DAY4

MORNING MEAL
½ medium grapefruit
¾ oz (20 g) cornflakes
5 fl oz (150 ml) skim milk

MIDDAY MEAL
Tuna-Potato Cakes (page 263)
mixed salad with 2 teaspoons salad dressing
Baked Apple (page 295)

EVENING MEAL
5 oz (150 g) grilled chicken
3 oz (90 g) green beans
2 oz (60 g) cooked rice
Cole Slaw Vinaigrette (page 288)
4 oz (120 g) peaches

SNACKS OR DRINKS AT PLANNED TIMES
15 fl oz (450 ml) skim milk

DAY5

MORNING MEAL
2½ fl oz (75 ml) apple juice
Cinnamon-Cheese Toast (page 234)

MIDDAY MEAL
Curried Beef (page 251)
3 oz (90 g) peas
3 oz (90 g) carrots mashed with 3 oz (90 g) potato
5 fl oz (150 ml) low-fat natural yogurt
4 fl oz (120 ml) tomato juice

EVENING MEAL
Fillet of Sole Florentine (page 270)
3 oz (90 g) green beans
1½ teaspoons margarine
5 oz (150 g) strawberries

SNACKS OR DRINKS AT PLANNED TIMES
½ pint (300 ml) skim milk

DAY6

MORNING MEAL	2 inch (5 cm) wedge honeydew melon 2 poached eggs 1 slice (1 oz/30 g) bread, toasted 1 teaspoon margarine
MIDDAY MEAL	4 oz (120 g) grilled veal 1 tomato, halved and grilled 3 oz (90 g) broccoli 3 oz (90 g) carrots dotted with 1 teaspoon margarine 1 medium orange

EVENING MEAL	cheese salad made with shredded lettuce,
	    sliced tomatoes and cucumber, spring
	    onion and 2 oz (60 g) grated cheese
	3 oz (90 g) beetroot
	3 oz (90 g) sweet corn
	2 teaspoons salad cream
	4 oz (120 g) fruit salad

SNACKS OR DRINKS AT PLANNED TIMES	5 fl oz (150 ml) low-fat natural yogurt, ½ pint (300 ml) skim milk

---

DAY7

MORNING MEAL	**Honey-Stewed Prunes** (page 298) ¾ oz (20 g) wheat flakes 5 fl oz (150 ml) skim milk
MIDDAY MEAL	4 oz (120 g) roast lamb 3 oz (90 g) peas 3 oz (90 g) Brussels sprouts 3 oz (90 g) baked jacket potato 2 teaspoons margarine 5 oz (150 g) strawberries
EVENING MEAL	4 oz (120 g) grilled plaice dotted with 1 teaspoon margarine 3 oz (90 g) broccoli 3 oz (90 g) swede 2 oz (60 g) cooked rice 4 oz (120 g) pineapple
SNACKS OR DRINKS AT PLANNED TIMES	15 fl oz (450 ml) skim milk

WEEK 38

Dried peas, beans and lentils (pulses) are a good source of nourishment, supplying protein, iron and other minerals. They are inexpensive and satisfying. Most of them require an overnight soak and long, gentle cooking without salt.

DAY 1

MORNING MEAL
½ medium grapefruit
¾ oz (20 g) porridge oats cooked with water, served with 5 fl oz (150 ml) skim milk

MIDDAY MEAL
6 oz (180 g) canned tuna
mixed salad
3 oz (90 g) beetroot
3 oz (90 g) sweet corn
1 tablespoon mayonnaise
1 medium apple

EVENING MEAL
Chick Peas Croquettes (page 273)
1 medium pear

SNACKS OR DRINKS AT PLANNED TIMES
5 fl oz (150 ml) skim milk

DAY 2

MORNING MEAL
4 fl oz (120 ml) orange juice
3 oz (90 g) baked beans
1 slice (1 oz/30 g) bread
2 teaspoons low-fat spread

MIDDAY MEAL
Bean Soup (page 273)
4 oz (120 g) peaches

EVENING MEAL
6 oz (180 g) uncooked liver, sauteed in 2
   teaspoons olive oil
3 oz (90 g) cauliflower
3 oz (90 g) boiled potatoes
3 oz (90 g) carrots
1 medium apple

SNACKS OR DRINKS
AT PLANNED TIMES
1 portion rhubarb, 5 fl oz (150 ml) low-fat
   natural yogurt, ½ pint (300 ml) skim milk

DAY 3

MORNING MEAL
1 medium banana
1 boiled egg
1 slice (1 oz/30 g) brown bread
1 teaspoon margarine

MIDDAY MEAL
4 oz (120 g) grilled lamb chop
3 oz (90 g) cabbage
3 oz (90 g) cooked potatoes
4 fl oz (120 ml) orange juice

EVENING MEAL
9 oz (270 g) baked beans
1 oz (30 g) French bread
2 teaspoons margarine
5 fl oz (150 ml) low-fat natural yogurt

SNACKS OR DRINKS
AT PLANNED TIMES
½ pint (300 ml) skim milk

DAY4

MORNING MEAL
½ medium grapefruit
2 oz (60 g) smoked salmon
1 slice (1 oz/30 g) wholemeal bread

MIDDAY MEAL
Mushroom and Lentil Pate (page 274)
green salad with lemon juice
1 oz (30 g) dried apricots chopped, mixed
    with 5 fl oz (150 ml) low-fat natural yogurt

EVENING MEAL
3-egg omelette cooked in 1 teaspoon
    vegetable oil
2 grilled tomatoes
3 oz (90 g) broccoli

SNACKS OR DRINKS AT PLANNED TIMES
½ pint (300 ml) skim milk, 1 medium apple,
    2 digestive biscuits

DAY5

MORNING MEAL
4 oz (120 g) peaches
¾ oz (20 g) cornflakes with 5 fl oz (150 ml)
    skim milk

MIDDAY MEAL
5 oz (150 g) peeled prawns
green salad
1 teaspoon mayonnaise
3 oz (90 g) beetroot
1 slice (1 oz/30 g) wholemeal bread
2 teaspoons low-fat spread
1 medium orange
5 fl oz (150 ml) low-fat natural yogurt

EVENING MEAL
'Re-Fried' Beans (page 272)
2 oz (60 g) cooked rice
3 oz (90 g) green beans
¼ pint (150 ml) orange-flavoured jelly

SNACKS OR DRINKS AT PLANNED TIMES
5 fl oz (150 ml) skim milk

DAY6

MORNING MEAL

4 oz (120 g) pineapple
2½ oz (75 g) cottage cheese
crispbread, up to 80 calories
1 teaspoon margarine

MIDDAY MEAL

3 oz (90 g) grilled beef sausages
3 oz (90 g) baked beans
1 grilled tomato
1 oz (30 g) pitta bread
2 teaspoons margarine
1 medium orange

EVENING MEAL

4 oz (120 g) roast chicken
3 oz (90 g) carrots
3 oz (90 g) spring greens
5 oz (150 g) blackcurrants

SNACKS OR DRINKS AT PLANNED TIMES

½ pint (300 ml) skim milk, 5 fl oz (150 ml)
  low-fat natural yogurt

DAY7

MORNING MEAL

4 fl oz (120 ml) orange juice
2 poached eggs
1 oz (30 g) grilled back bacon
1 slice (1 oz/30 g) wholemeal bread
2 teaspoons low-fat spread

MIDDAY MEAL

4 oz (120 g) grilled halibut
3 oz (90 g) cauliflower
3 oz (90 g) carrots
3 oz (90 g) celery hearts
2 teaspoons margarine
2 pear halves with 2½ fl oz (75 ml) low-fat
  natural yogurt and 1 teaspoon chocolate
  sauce

EVENING MEAL

Bean and Cheese Potatoes (page 276)
8 fl oz (240 ml) tomato juice

SNACKS OR DRINKS AT PLANNED TIMES

7½ fl oz (225 ml) skim milk, 2½ fl oz (75 ml)
  low-fat natural yogurt

WEEK 39

Homemade bread is one of life's simple pleasures. Use a standard cookbook recipe – you can then go on to make other varieties. They can all be slotted into menus with careful planning.

DAY 1

MORNING MEAL
4 fl oz (120 ml) grapefruit juice
1 poached egg
1 slice (1 oz/30 g) homemade bread
2 teaspoons margarine

MIDDAY MEAL
5 oz (150 g) cottage cheese with mixed salad
2 teaspoons salad cream
crispbread, up to 80 calories
1 medium apple

EVENING MEAL
Fresh Mushroom Soup (page 219)
5 oz (150 g) grilled cod
3 oz (90 g) sweet corn
2 inch (5 cm) wedge honeydew melon

SNACKS OR DRINKS AT PLANNED TIMES
5 fl oz (150 ml) low-fat natural yogurt, ½ pint (300 ml) skim milk

DAY 2

MORNING MEAL	4 fl oz (120 ml) grapefruit juice ¾ oz (20 g) cornflakes 5 fl oz (150 ml) skim milk
MIDDAY MEAL	**Baked Cheese Souffle** (page 226) 3 oz (90 g) green beans 4 oz (120 g) orange sections
EVENING MEAL	6 oz (180 g) grilled steak green salad with 2 teaspoons low-calorie mayonnaise 3 oz (90 g) cooked potatoes 2 teaspoons margarine **Baked Apple** (page 295)
SNACKS OR DRINKS AT PLANNED TIMES	½ pint (300 ml) skim milk

DAY 3

MORNING MEAL	1 medium peach 2½ oz (75 g) cottage cheese 1 slice (1 oz/30 g) bread
MIDDAY MEAL	3 oz (90 g) grilled fillet of sole 3 oz (90 g) cauliflower 3 oz (90 g) carrots dotted with 1 teaspoon margarine 4 oz (120 g) fruit cocktail
EVENING MEAL	4 oz (120 g) grilled chicken livers 3 oz (90 g) onion rings 3 oz (90 g) broccoli 4 oz (120 g) cooked noodles dotted with 2 teaspoons margarine 1 medium orange with **Custard** (page 297)
SNACKS OR DRINKS AT PLANNED TIMES	15 fl oz (450 ml) skim milk

DAY4

MORNING MEAL
4 fl oz (120 ml) orange juice
¾ oz (20 g) porridge oats, cooked with water
5 fl oz (150 ml) skim milk

MIDDAY MEAL
Vegetable-Cheese Platter (page 233)
melba toast, up to 80 calories
2 teaspoons margarine
4 oz (120 g) stewed apple with 3 tablespoons
　　single cream

EVENING MEAL
6 oz (180 g) grilled chicken
3 oz (90 g) peas
3 oz (90 g) green beans
1 teaspoon margarine
2 oz (60 g) cooked rice
1 medium pear

SNACKS OR DRINKS AT PLANNED TIMES
12½ fl oz (375 ml) skim milk

DAY5

MORNING MEAL
½ medium grapefruit
1 oz (30 g) Cheddar cheese
1 slice (1 oz/30 g) homemade bread

MIDDAY MEAL
Salmon Salad (page 265)
sliced tomatoes and chicory with 1 teaspoon
　　vegetable oil plus cider vinegar
1 slice (1 oz/30 g) homemade bread
2 medium plums
sparkling mineral water with lemon slice

EVENING MEAL
3 oz (90 g) grilled beef sausages
2 oz (60 g) sliced mushrooms sauteed in 1
　　teaspoon vegetable oil
3 oz (90 g) grilled onion rings
3 oz (90 g) boiled potatoes
5 fl oz (150 ml) low-fat natural yogurt with ½
　　medium banana, sliced

SNACKS OR DRINKS AT PLANNED TIMES
½ pint (300 ml) skim milk

DAY 6

MORNING MEAL
½ medium grapefruit
1 boiled egg
1 slice (1 oz/30 g) homemade bread
1 teaspoon margarine

MIDDAY MEAL
9 oz (270 g) baked beans
1 oz (30 g) back bacon, grilled
1 tomato, halved and grilled
1 slice (1 oz/30 g) bread
1 teaspoon margarine
4 oz (120 g) fruit salad

EVENING MEAL
4 oz (120 g) grilled mackerel
3 oz (90 g) green beans
3 oz (90 g) carrots and swede, mashed with 1
    teaspoon margarine
5 oz (150 g) gooseberries, stewed with 1½
    teaspoons honey, and 2½ fl oz (75 ml)
    low-fat natural yogurt

SNACKS OR DRINKS AT PLANNED TIMES
15 fl oz (450 ml) skim milk

DAY 7

MORNING MEAL
½ medium banana
¾ oz (20 g) wheat flakes
5 fl oz (150 ml) skim milk

MIDDAY MEAL
5 oz (150 g) roast chicken
3 oz (90 g) marrow
3 oz (90 g) peas
3 oz (90 g) baked jacket potato with 2
    teaspoons margarine
4 oz (120 g) peaches with 2½ fl oz (75 ml)
    low-fat natural yogurt

EVENING MEAL
3 oz (90 g) grilled pork chop
3 oz (90 g) leeks
3 oz (90 g) carrots
2 oz (60 g) cooked noodles dotted with 1
    teaspoon margarine
8 fl oz (240 ml) tomato juice

SNACKS OR DRINKS AT PLANNED TIMES
½ pint (300 ml) skim milk

Yogurt appears often on these pages. It fits so well into a slimmer's food plan. You may like to substitute it for milk or to use it in sauces and dressings both sweet and savoury.

DAY 1

MORNING MEAL
½ medium grapefruit
1 boiled egg
1 slice (1 oz/30 g) wholemeal bread
1 teaspoon margarine

MIDDAY MEAL
3 oz (90 g) roast chicken
green salad
2 oz (60 g) cooked rice mixed with 2 tablespoons chopped onion and red pepper and 1½ teaspoons mayonnaise
1 medium pear

EVENING MEAL
Lamb Stew (page 253)
3 oz (90 g) carrots
3 oz (90 g) swede

SNACKS OR DRINKS AT PLANNED TIMES
½ pint (300 ml) skim milk, 5 fl oz (150 ml) low-fat natural yogurt with 1 oz (30 g) raisins and rum flavouring

DAY 2

MORNING MEAL
4 fl oz (120 ml) orange juice
¾ oz (20 g) bran flakes
5 fl oz (150 ml) low-fat natural yogurt

MIDDAY MEAL
5 oz (150 g) cottage cheese
mixed salad
melba toast, up to 80 calories
2 teaspoons low-fat spread
1 medium apple

EVENING MEAL
6 oz (180 g) grilled plaice with lemon wedge
3 oz (90 g) green beans
3 oz (90 g) boiled potatoes
2 teaspoons margarine
4 oz (120 g) pineapple

SNACKS OR DRINKS AT PLANNED TIMES
½ pint (300 ml) skim milk

DAY 3

MORNING MEAL
8 fl oz (240 ml) tomato juice
1 oz (30 g) Cheddar cheese
1 slice (1 oz/30 g) wholemeal bread

MIDDAY MEAL
3 oz (90 g) canned pilchards served on
    chopped cucumber, green pepper, onion
    and tomato tossed with 2½ fl oz (75 ml)
    low-fat natural yogurt
3 oz (90 g) beetroot
1 medium apple

EVENING MEAL
Shredded Chicken with Peanut Sauce
    (page 236)
4 oz (120 g) boiled rice
3 oz (90 g) broccoli
4 oz (120 g) pineapple with 2½ fl oz (75 ml)
    low-fat natural yogurt

SNACKS OR DRINKS AT PLANNED TIMES
½ pint (300 ml) skim milk

DAY4

MORNING MEAL
5 oz (150 g) strawberries
¾ oz (20 g) instant cereal with 5 fl oz (150 ml)
    hot skim milk

MIDDAY MEAL
2 oz (60 g) Edam cheese
2 sticks celery
1 tomato
crispbread, up to 80 calories
2 teaspoons margarine
1 medium pear

EVENING MEAL
6 oz (180 g) grilled liver dotted with 1
    teaspoon margarine
3 oz (90 g) carrots
3 oz (90 g) broccoli

SNACKS OR DRINKS AT PLANNED TIMES
5 fl oz (150 ml) skim milk, 5 fl oz (150 ml)
    low-fat natural yogurt, mixed with 1 oz
    (30 g) chopped dried apricots

DAY5

MORNING MEAL
4 fl oz (120 ml) orange juice
1 poached egg
1 slice (1 oz/30 g) bread
1 teaspoon low-fat spread

MIDDAY MEAL
Stir-Fry Tuna (page 271)
green salad with lemon juice
1 teaspoon low-fat spread
1 slice (1 oz/30 g) wholemeal bread

EVENING MEAL
3 oz (90 g) grilled steak
3 oz (90 g) cauliflower
3 oz (90 g) potato
1 grilled tomato
2 teaspoons low-fat spread
½ medium apple, chopped and ½ oz (15 g)
    raisins with 5 fl oz (150 ml) low-fat natural
    yogurt

SNACKS OR DRINKS AT PLANNED TIMES
½ pint (300 ml) skim milk

DAY6

MORNING MEAL
½ medium grapefruit
1 oz (30 g) Cheddar cheese
1 slice (1 oz/30 g) bread

MIDDAY MEAL
3 eggs scrambled in 1 teaspoon vegetable oil
1 slice (1 oz/30 g) bread, toasted
1 teaspoon margarine
3 oz (90 g) grilled tomatoes
3 oz (90 g) poached mushrooms
5 fl oz (150 ml) low-fat natural yogurt
4 oz (120 g) peaches

EVENING MEAL
1 portion boil-in-the-bag fish with sauce (any
    type)
3 oz (90 g) broccoli
3 oz (90 g) carrots
1 teaspoon low-fat spread
green salad
1 teaspoon salad cream
2 small clementines

**SNACKS OR DRINKS
AT PLANNED TIMES**
½ pint (300 ml) skim milk

DAY7

MORNING MEAL
½ medium banana
¾ oz (20 g) cornflakes
5 fl oz (150 ml) low-fat natural yogurt
crispbread, up to 80 calories
2 teaspoons low-fat spread

MIDDAY MEAL
4 oz (120 g) roast lamb
3 oz (90 g) spring greens
3 oz (90 g) baked onion
1 teaspoon low-fat spread
1 medium orange
4 fl oz (120 ml) red wine

EVENING MEAL
Chicken Hotpot (page 241)
3 oz (90 g) green beans
3 oz (90 g) carrots
4 oz (120 g) pineapple

**SNACKS OR DRINKS
AT PLANNED TIMES**
½ pint (300 ml) skim milk

WEEK 41

Many of us look forward to the 'sweet conclusion' of a meal. If you think that the sweet course shouldn't feature in a weight loss programme, just look at the delights in this week's plan.

DAY 1

MORNING MEAL
½ medium grapefruit
¾ oz (20 g) muesli
5 fl oz (150 ml) skim milk

MIDDAY MEAL
toss together 5 oz (150 g) cottage cheese with 2 oz (60 g) chopped chicken breast and serve on bed of lettuce
2 oz (60 g) bap with 3 teaspoons low-fat spread
1 medium apple

EVENING MEAL
2 inch (5 cm) wedge honeydew melon
1 portion boil-in-the-bag fish in sauce (any type)
3 oz (90 g) peas
3 oz (90 g) carrots
3 teaspoons low-fat spread

SNACKS OR DRINKS AT PLANNED TIMES
15 fl oz (450 ml) skim milk

DAY 2

MORNING MEAL
½ medium grapefruit
1 tablespoon peanut butter on 1 slice (1 oz/30 g) wholemeal bread, toasted

MIDDAY MEAL
2 oz (60 g) canned mackerel, mixed with chopped tomato, cucumber, green pepper and onion, dressed with wine vinegar and pinch garlic salt
Pineapple Cheesecake (page 296)

EVENING MEAL
4 oz (120 g) grapefruit sections
4 oz (120 g) grilled lamb's liver
3 oz (90 g) broad beans
3 oz (90 g) cauliflower
1 grilled tomato
1 small diced satsuma with 5 fl oz (150 ml) low-fat natural yogurt

SNACKS OR DRINKS AT PLANNED TIMES
5 fl oz (150 ml) skim milk

DAY 3

MORNING MEAL
½ medium grapefruit
¾ oz (20 g) cornflakes
5 fl oz (150 ml) skim milk

MIDDAY MEAL
2 hard-boiled eggs, sliced and served with 2 teaspoons mayonnaise and mixed green salad
1 medium apple
1 digestive biscuit

EVENING MEAL
5 oz (150 g) roast chicken
3 oz (90 g) mashed swede
3 oz (90 g) sliced carrots
2 teaspoons low-fat spread
Rice Pudding (page 302)

SNACKS OR DRINKS AT PLANNED TIMES
11 fl oz (330 ml) skim milk

DAY4

MORNING MEAL
1 medium orange
2½ oz (75 g) cottage cheese, lightly grilled on
  1 slice (1 oz/30 g) wholemeal bread,
  toasted

MIDDAY MEAL
toss together, 3 oz (90 g) diced cooked
  chicken, 3 oz (90 g) canned red kidney
  beans, 1 diced celery stick, 1 grated
  carrot, 1 grated medium apple sprinkled
  with lemon juice, 4 teaspoons low-calorie
  mayonnaise

EVENING MEAL
4 oz (120 g) grilled lamb chop
3 oz (90 g) mushrooms
3 oz (90 g) cauliflower
3 oz (90 g) peas with 2 teaspoons low-fat
  spread
Knickerbocker Glory (page 301)

**SNACKS OR DRINKS
AT PLANNED TIMES**
5 fl oz (150 ml) low-fat natural yogurt, ½ pint
  (300 ml) skim milk

DAY5

MORNING MEAL
1 oz (30 g) raisins mixed with ¾ oz (20 g)
  porridge oats cooked with water
5 fl oz (150 ml) skim milk

MIDDAY MEAL
4 oz (120 g) sardines
6 oz (180 g, tomato and onion salad dressed
  with 2 teaspoons mayonnaise
1 slice (1 oz/30 g) wholemeal bread

EVENING MEAL
4 oz (120 g) grapefruit sections
4 oz (120 g) grilled trout
3 oz (90 g) braised celery
3 oz (90 g) Brussels sprouts
1 teaspoon margarine

**SNACKS OR DRINKS
AT PLANNED TIMES**
15 fl oz (450 ml) skim milk, 1 digestive biscuit

DAY6

MORNING MEAL
4 oz (120 g) peaches sliced on to 2½ oz (75 g)
    quark or cottage cheese
crispbread, up to 80 calories
2 teaspoons low-fat spread

MIDDAY MEAL
8 fl oz (240 ml) tomato juice
3 oz (90 g) grilled beefburger
2 oz (60 g) bap
2 teaspoons low-fat spread
2 teaspoons relish or tomato ketchup

EVENING MEAL
4 oz (120 g) grilled plaice
3 oz (90 g) green beans
3 oz (90 g) courgettes
1 teaspoon margarine
Strawberry 'Cream' (page 296)

SNACKS OR DRINKS AT PLANNED TIMES
½ pint (300 ml) skim milk

DAY7

MORNING MEAL
½ medium grapefruit
1 oz (30 g) grated Cheddar cheese, grilled on
    1 slice (1 oz/30 g) wholemeal bread,
    toasted
1 grilled tomato

MIDDAY MEAL
3 oz (90 g) roast turkey breast
3 oz (90 g) parsnips
3 oz (90 g) spinach
3 oz (90 g) baked jacket potato
1 teaspoon low-fat spread
Rich Fruit Pudding (page 298)
2 oz (60 g) vanilla ice cream

EVENING MEAL
4 oz (120 g) canned tuna
mixed salad
2 teaspoons mayonnaise
5 oz (150 g) raspberries with 5 fl oz (150 ml)
    low-fat natural yogurt

SNACKS OR DRINKS AT PLANNED TIMES
9 fl oz (270 ml) skim milk

WEEK 42

The pub lunch is a great British tradition. Of course, you don't always have to eat it in pubs! This satisfying meal can be enjoyed in your own garden or on a picnic outing, too.

DAY 1

MORNING MEAL
5 oz (150 g) strawberries
2½ oz (75 g) cottage cheese
1 slice (1 oz/30 g) brown bread, toasted
1 teaspoon margarine
1 teaspoon honey

MIDDAY MEAL
3 oz (90 g) cooked chicken
mixed salad with **Vinaigrette Dressing** (page 293)
crispbread, up to 80 calories
1 teaspoon margarine
1 medium apple

EVENING MEAL
4 oz (120 g) grilled chicken livers
3 oz (90 g) onion rings
3 oz (90 g) green beans
2 medium plums

SNACKS OR DRINKS AT PLANNED TIMES
5 fl oz (150 ml) low-fat natural yogurt, ½ pint (300 ml) skim milk

DAY 2

MORNING MEAL
1 medium orange
1 poached egg
1 slice (1 oz/30 g) brown bread, toasted
1 teaspoon margarine

MIDDAY MEAL
3 oz (90 g) baked mackerel
3 oz (90 g) courgettes
3 oz (90 g) carrots

EVENING MEAL
Turkey Oriental (page 238)
2 oz (60 g) cooked rice dotted with 1
  teaspoon margarine
shredded Chinese cabbage topped with
  grated carrot and **Vinaigrette Dressing**
  (page 293)

**SNACKS OR DRINKS
AT PLANNED TIMES**
5 oz (150 g) blackberries with 5 fl oz (150 ml)
  low-fat natural yogurt, ½ pint (300 ml)
  skim milk

DAY 3

MORNING MEAL
½ medium grapefruit
¾ oz (20 g) cornflakes
5 fl oz (150 ml) skim milk

MIDDAY MEAL
4 oz (120 g) grilled beefburger
2 oz (60 g) bap
1 tomato
2 pickled cucumbers
carrot and celery salad with 2 teaspoons
  mayonnaise
3 oz (90 g) black grapes

EVENING MEAL
4 oz (120 g) grilled plaice dotted with 2
  teaspoons low-fat spread
3 oz (90 g) peas
3 oz (90 g) spinach
5 oz (150 g) blackcurrants
4 fl oz (120 ml) white wine

**SNACKS OR DRINKS
AT PLANNED TIMES**
15 fl oz (450 ml) skim milk

DAY4

MORNING MEAL
4 fl oz (120 ml) orange juice
¾ oz (20 g) porridge oats cooked with water
5 fl oz (150 ml) skim milk

MIDDAY MEAL
3 oz (90 g) canned salmon
Apple Slaw (page 290)
1 slice (1 oz/30 g) wholemeal bread
2 teaspoons low-fat spread
1 oz (30 g) dried apricots cooked with water
    and 1 teaspoon honey

EVENING MEAL
chicken and egg salad made with 4 oz (120 g)
    chopped cooked chicken, 1 chopped hard-
    boiled egg on mixed salad with 1 teaspoon
    vegetable oil and cider vinegar
2 oz (60 g) cooked rice
3 oz (90 g) fruit cocktail

**SNACKS OR DRINKS
AT PLANNED TIMES**
15 fl oz (450 ml) skim milk

DAY5

MORNING MEAL
4 fl oz (120 ml) orange juice
1 scrambled egg on 1 slice (1 oz/30 g) bread,
    toasted

MIDDAY MEAL
3 tablespoons crunchy peanut butter on
    crispbread, up to 80 calories, topped with
    diced cucumber, radishes and green
    pepper
3 oz (90 g) green grapes

EVENING MEAL
Ham and Turkey Casserole (page 245)
3 oz (90 g) Brussels sprouts
3 oz (90 g) broad beans
½ medium banana on 2 oz (60 g) vanilla ice
    cream

**SNACKS OR DRINKS
AT PLANNED TIMES**
15 fl oz (450 ml) skim milk

DAY6

MORNING MEAL ½ medium grapefruit
Cinnamon-Cheese Toast (page 234)

MIDDAY MEAL 3 oz (90 g) grilled veal
3 oz (90 g) carrots
1 tomato, halved and grilled
green salad with 1 teaspoon vegetable oil and
cider vinegar
3 oz (90 g) boiled potato
1 medium pear

EVENING MEAL 4 oz (120 g) grilled trout
3 oz (90 g) courgettes
mixed salad with 2 teaspoons mayonnaise
4 oz (120 g) peaches

**SNACKS OR DRINKS
AT PLANNED TIMES** 5 fl oz (150 ml) low-fat natural yogurt, ½ pint
(300 ml) skim milk

DAY7

MORNING MEAL 4 fl oz (120 ml) orange juice
1 boiled egg
1 slice (1 oz/30 g) bread, toasted
1 teaspoon margarine

MIDDAY MEAL **'Pub Lunch'**
3 oz (90 g) Cheddar cheese
2 oz (60 g) French bread
mixed salad
1 teaspoon mayonnaise
2 teaspoons relish
1 medium apple

EVENING MEAL **Lemon-Minted Lamb** (page 248)
3 oz (90 g) poached mushrooms
3 oz (90 g) peas
2 medium plums

**SNACKS OR DRINKS
AT PLANNED TIMES** 5 fl oz (150 ml) low-fat natural yogurt, ½ pint
(300 ml) skim milk

WEEK 43

The most popular British cheese is Cheddar – equally good cooked or fresh. Its protein value is almost double that of meat. Be careful to stay within the limits we give you.

DAY 1

MORNING MEAL
½ medium banana
¾ oz (20 g) muesli
5 fl oz (150 ml) skim milk

MIDDAY MEAL
4 oz (120 g) cooked chicken
1 tomato
2-3 sticks celery
1 slice (1 oz/30 g) bread
1 teaspoon margarine
1 medium orange

EVENING MEAL
4 oz (120 g) grilled salmon
3 oz (90 g) green beans
3 oz (90 g) broccoli
2 oz (60 g) cooked rice dotted with 2 teaspoons margarine
1 medium pear

SNACKS OR DRINKS AT PLANNED TIMES
15 fl oz (450 ml) skim milk

Cream of
Asparagus and
Leek Soup

Hot Mushroom
Turnovers

Baked Cheese
Souffle

Broccoli Quiche

Chicken Kebabs

Irish Stew

Beef and
Corn Casserole

Sauteed Prawns
and Corn

Knickerbocker
Glory

DAY 2

MORNING MEAL
4 fl oz (120 ml) orange juice
1 boiled egg
1 slice (1 oz/30 g) bread, toasted
1 teaspoon margarine

MIDDAY MEAL
2 oz (60 g) Cheddar cheese, sliced onto
crispbread, up to 80 calories, with 3-4
celery sticks
1 tablespoon relish
1 medium orange

EVENING MEAL
4 oz (120 g) grilled steak
1 tomato, halved and grilled
3 oz (90 g) baked beans
3 oz (90 g) mushrooms, sauteed in 2
teaspoons margarine
4 oz (120 g) fruit salad

SNACKS OR DRINKS
AT PLANNED TIMES
5 fl oz (150 ml) low-fat natural yogurt, ½ pint
(300 ml) skim milk

DAY 3

MORNING MEAL
2½ fl oz (75 ml) pineapple juice
2½ oz (75 g) curd cheese
melba toast, up to 80 calories

MIDDAY MEAL
3 oz (90 g) canned pilchards with mixed salad,
with 2 teaspoons salad cream
1 slice (1 oz/30 g) wholemeal bread
1 teaspoon margarine
1 medium peach

EVENING MEAL
4 oz (120 g) grilled haddock dotted with 1
teaspoon margarine
3 oz (90 g) carrots
3 oz (90 g) peas
4 oz (120 g) orange sections

SNACKS OR DRINKS
AT PLANNED TIMES
5 fl oz (150 ml) low-fat natural yogurt, ½ pint
(300 ml) skim milk

DAY4

MORNING MEAL
2½ fl oz (75 ml) pineapple juice
¾ oz (20 g) cornflakes
5 fl oz (150 ml) skim milk

MIDDAY MEAL
4 oz (120 g) cooked chicken
mixed salad with 3 teaspoons salad dressing
3 oz (90 g) sweet corn
1 medium orange

EVENING MEAL
5 oz (150 g) uncooked lamb's liver sauteed in
    1 teaspoon oil with 3 oz (90 g) sliced onion
3 oz (90 g) poached mushrooms
2 oz (60 g) cooked rice dotted with 1
    teaspoon low-fat spread
4 oz (120 g) fruit salad with 2 oz (60 g) vanilla
    ice cream

**SNACKS OR DRINKS
AT PLANNED TIMES**
15 fl oz (450 ml) skim milk

DAY5

MORNING MEAL
4 fl oz (120 ml) orange juice
1 egg, cooked in 1 teaspoon margarine
1 slice (1 oz/30 g) bread, toasted

MIDDAY MEAL
Cheese and Butter Bean Peppers (page
    277)
3 oz (90 g) carrots
green salad with 1 teaspoon vegetable oil and
    wine vinegar
4 oz (120 g) fruit salad

EVENING MEAL
5 oz (150 g) grilled lamb chop
3 oz (90 g) peas
3 oz (90 g) cauliflower
6 oz (180 g) baked jacket potato
1 teaspoon margarine
2 medium plums

**SNACKS OR DRINKS
AT PLANNED TIMES**
5 fl oz (150 ml) low-fat natural yogurt, ½ pint
    (300 ml) skim milk

DAY6

MORNING MEAL
4 fl oz (120 ml) orange juice
¾ oz (20 g) porridge oats cooked with water
5 fl oz (150 ml) skim milk

MIDDAY MEAL
egg and cheese salad made with 2 hard-boiled eggs, 2½ oz (75 g) cottage cheese, shredded lettuce, 1 tomato, sliced, cucumber, sliced and 2 teaspoons salad dressing
4 oz (120 g) peaches

EVENING MEAL
5 oz (150 g) grilled veal
3 oz (90 g) green beans
3 oz (90 g) swede
6 oz (180 g) baked jacket potato
2 teaspoons margarine
4 oz (120 g) pineapple

SNACKS OR DRINKS AT PLANNED TIMES
15 fl oz (450 ml) skim milk

DAY7

MORNING MEAL
1 medium orange
1 egg, scrambled in 1 teaspoon margarine
1 slice (1 oz/30 g) bread, toasted

MIDDAY MEAL
3 oz (90 g) roast lamb
3 oz (90 g) carrots
3 oz (90 g) parsnips
2 oz (60 g) cooked rice dotted with 1 teaspoon margarine
1 medium pear

EVENING MEAL
4 oz (120 g) grilled lemon sole dotted with 1 teaspoon margarine
3 oz (90 g) broccoli
3 oz (90 g) courgettes
3 oz (90 g) grapes
4 fl oz (120 ml) white wine

SNACKS OR DRINKS AT PLANNED TIMES
5 fl oz (150 ml) low-fat natural yogurt, ½ pint (300 ml) skim milk

WEEK 44

Cheese with fruit – a delicious combination – can be made with any of the available soft cheeses and fruit.

DAY 1

MORNING MEAL
½ medium banana
¾ oz (20 g) muesli
5 fl oz (150 ml) skim milk

MIDDAY MEAL
3 tablespoons (45 ml) peanut butter
crispbread, up to 80 calories
1 tablespoon jam
1 medium orange

EVENING MEAL
5 oz (150 g) grilled mackerel
3 oz (90 g) baked jacket potato with 2½ fl oz (75 ml) low-fat natural yogurt and chopped chives
3 oz (90 g) peas
3 oz (90 g) carrots
mixed salad with lemon juice

SNACKS OR DRINKS AT PLANNED TIMES
1 medium orange sliced into 2½ fl oz (75 ml) low-fat natural yogurt, 5 fl oz (150 ml) skim milk

DAY 2

MORNING MEAL
4 fl oz (120 ml) orange juice
1 egg, scrambled in 1 teaspoon margarine on
  1 slice (1 oz/30 g) bread, toasted

MIDDAY MEAL
Fruited Cheese Delight (page 227)
watercress salad
2 teaspoons low-calorie mayonnaise
1 slice (1 oz/30 g) rye bread
½ medium banana

EVENING MEAL
4 oz (120 g) grilled beefburger with 2
  teaspoons tomato ketchup or relish
3 oz (90 g) baked beans
3 oz (90 g) sweet corn
sliced tomato and onion with 1 teaspoon
  olive oil, wine vinegar and pinch oregano

SNACKS OR DRINKS
AT PLANNED TIMES
5 fl oz (150 ml) low-fat natural yogurt, ½ pint
  (300 ml) skim milk

DAY 3

MORNING MEAL
½ medium grapefruit
¾ oz (20 g) cornflakes
5 fl oz (150 ml) skim milk

MIDDAY MEAL
5 oz (150 g) cottage cheese
1 hard-boiled egg with mixed salad
3 teaspoons low-calorie mayonnaise
3 oz (90 g) cooked potato, chilled and cubed,
  tossed with chopped onion and 2½ fl oz
  (75 ml) low-fat natural yogurt
1 medium pear

EVENING MEAL
5 oz (150 g) roast chicken
2 oz (60 g) cooked rice
3 oz (90 g) Brussels sprouts
½ pint (300 ml) beer or cider

SNACKS OR DRINKS
AT PLANNED TIMES
1 medium orange, ½ pint (300 ml) skim milk

DAY4

MORNING MEAL
4 fl oz (120 ml) orange juice
2½ oz (75 g) cottage cheese lightly grilled on
    1 slice (1 oz/30 g) rye bread, toasted

MIDDAY MEAL
3 poached eggs on 6 oz (180 g) spinach
1 slice (1 oz/30 g) bread
1 teaspoon margarine
4 oz (120 g) pineapple
5 fl oz (150 ml) low-fat natural yogurt

EVENING MEAL
½ medium grapefruit
Salmon Salad (page 265)
1 tomato, sliced
3 oz (90 g) baked jacket potato
2 teaspoons low-fat spread

SNACKS OR DRINKS AT PLANNED TIMES
½ pint (300 ml) skim milk

DAY5

MORNING MEAL
1 medium orange
¾ oz (20 g) cereal
5 fl oz (150 ml) skim milk

MIDDAY MEAL
Lamb's Liver Creole (page 254)
3 oz (90 g) onion rings, sauteed 3-4 minutes in
    1 teaspoon vegetable oil
crispbread, up to 80 calories, with 2
    teaspoons low-fat spread and 2
    teaspoons grated Parmesan cheese
2½ fl oz (75 ml) apple juice

EVENING MEAL
4 oz (120 g) roast lamb
3 oz (90 g) carrots
3 oz (90 g) parsnips
3 oz (90 g) baked jacket potato
2 teaspoons low-fat spread
2 oz (60 g) vanilla ice cream
1 medium pear

SNACKS OR DRINKS AT PLANNED TIMES
5 fl oz (150 ml) low-fat natural yogurt, 5 fl oz
    (150 ml) skim milk

DAY6

MORNING MEAL
½ medium grapefruit
3 oz (90 g) baked beans
1 slice (1 oz/30 g) wholemeal bread
1 teaspoon low-fat spread

MIDDAY MEAL
3 oz (90 g) grilled plaice
3 oz (90 g) broccoli
sliced cucumber on lettuce with **Vinaigrette Dressing** (page 293)
1 medium apple

EVENING MEAL
4 oz (120 g) grilled steak
3 oz (90 g) braised celery
3 oz (90 g) Brussels sprouts
3 oz (90 g) sweet corn
2 teaspoons low-fat spread
Strawberry 'Cream' (page 296)

SNACKS OR DRINKS AT PLANNED TIMES
crispbread, up to 80 calories, 1 teaspoon low-fat spread, 1 tablespoon jam, ½ pint (300 ml) skim milk

---

DAY7

MORNING MEAL
1 medium orange
1 oz (30 g) Edam cheese
1 oz (30 g) wholemeal roll
1 teaspoon low-fat spread

MIDDAY MEAL
3 oz (90 g) roast chicken
3 oz (90 g) mashed swede with 2 teaspoons low-fat spread and black pepper
3 oz (90 g) boiled potatoes mashed with 1 teaspoon low-fat spread
1 portion rhubarb

EVENING MEAL
4 oz (120 g) canned sardines
mixed salad
1 slice (1 oz/30 g) wholemeal bread
1 teaspoon margarine
1 medium pear

SNACKS OR DRINKS AT PLANNED TIMES
1 medium orange, 5 fl oz (150 ml) low-fat natural yogurt, ½ pint (300 ml) skim milk

WEEK 45

Cold weather seems to call for a hot and nourishing soup. We provide several soup recipes this week, all based on easily available vegetables.

DAY 1

MORNING MEAL
½ medium banana, sliced on ¾ oz (20 g) cornflakes
5 fl oz (150 ml) skim milk
1 slice (1 oz/30 g) bread with 1 teaspoon margarine and 1 teaspoon honey

MIDDAY MEAL
Tomato and Marrow Soup (page 218)
3 oz (90 g) Cheddar cheese, grated with mixed salad
5 fl oz (150 ml) low-fat natural yogurt with 2 oz (60 g) peaches

EVENING MEAL
5 oz (150 g) trout, grilled with sliced onion rings and lemon juice
3 oz (90 g) green beans
3 oz (90 g) baked jacket potato with 2 teaspoons margarine
1 medium orange

SNACKS OR DRINKS AT PLANNED TIMES
5 fl oz (150 ml) skim milk

DAY 2

MORNING MEAL 4 fl oz (120 ml) orange juice
1 oz (30 g) Cheddar cheese toasted on 1 slice
(1 oz/30 g) wholemeal bread

MIDDAY MEAL 3 tablespoons peanut butter
crispbread, up to 80 calories
cucumber and tomato slices
5 fl oz (150 ml) low-fat natural yogurt with 4 oz
(120 g) peaches

EVENING MEAL 4 oz (120 g) roast chicken with herbs and
lemon juice
3 oz (90 g) peas
2 oz (60 g) cooked noodles
1 medium pear

SNACKS OR DRINKS ½ pint (300 ml) skim milk, 1 portion rhubarb
AT PLANNED TIMES

DAY 3

MORNING MEAL ½ medium grapefruit
¾ oz (20 g) bran flakes
5 fl oz (150 ml) skim milk

MIDDAY MEAL 9 oz (270 g) baked beans
1 slice (1 oz/30 g) bread, toasted
2 teaspoons margarine
3 oz (90 g) poached mushrooms
1 medium apple

EVENING MEAL **Minestrone** (page 221)
5 oz (150 g) liver sausage
tomato and onion salad with 1 teaspoon olive
oil and wine vinegar
3 oz (90 g) grapes

SNACKS OR DRINKS 5 fl oz (150 ml) skim milk, 5 fl oz (150 ml)
AT PLANNED TIMES low-fat natural yogurt

DAY4

MORNING MEAL
3 oz (90 g) grapes
2½ oz (75 g) cottage cheese
1 slice (1 oz/30 g) currant bread

MIDDAY MEAL
Fresh Mushroom Soup (page 219)
3 eggs, poached
2 slices (1 oz/30 g each) bread, toasted with 4
    teaspoons low-fat spread

EVENING MEAL
4 oz (120 g) grilled lamb's liver
3 oz (90 g) broccoli
3 oz (90 g) carrots
2 teaspoons low-fat spread
5 fl oz (150 ml) low-fat natural yogurt with 1 oz
    (30 g) raisins

SNACKS OR DRINKS
AT PLANNED TIMES
½ pint (300 ml) skim milk, 1 medium orange

DAY5

MORNING MEAL
½ medium grapefruit
1 boiled egg
crispbread, up to 80 calories
2 teaspoons low-fat spread
1 teaspoon honey

MIDDAY MEAL
5 oz (150 g) cottage cheese mixed with 3 oz
    (90 g) sweet corn
2 tablespoons green pepper, chopped
2 tablespoons onion, chopped
1 oz (30 g) sultanas and 2 teaspoons salad
    cream
2 cream crackers

EVENING MEAL
Broccoli Soup (page 217)
5 oz (150 g) grilled plaice with 1 teaspoon
    margarine and lemon juice
3 oz (90 g) cauliflower
3 oz (90 g) broad beans
5 oz (150 g) blackcurrants

SNACKS OR DRINKS
AT PLANNED TIMES
5 fl oz (150 ml) low-fat natural yogurt, 5 fl oz
    (150 ml) skim milk

DAY6

MORNING MEAL
½ medium banana
¾ oz (20 g) muesli
5 fl oz (150 ml) skim milk

MIDDAY MEAL
Garden Pea Soup (page 216)
3 oz (90 g) cooked ham
3 oz (90 g) baked jacket potato
3 oz (90 g) cooked asparagus tips with 2
    teaspoons margarine
1 medium orange

EVENING MEAL
5 oz (150 g) canned sardines grilled on 1 slice
    (1 oz/30 g) wholmeal bread, toasted and
    spread with 2 teaspoons low-fat spread
2 grilled tomatoes
4 oz (120 g) pineapple

**SNACKS OR DRINKS
AT PLANNED TIMES**
15 fl oz (450 ml) skim milk

DAY7

MORNING MEAL
4 fl oz (120 ml) orange juice
1 egg, cooked in 1 teaspoon vegetable oil
1 oz (30 g) grilled back bacon
1 grilled tomato
1 slice (1 oz/30 g) bread

MIDDAY MEAL
Cream of Asparagus and Leek Soup (page
    220)
4 oz (120 g) roast beef with fresh horseradish
3 oz (90 g) cabbage
3 oz (90 g) parsnips
3 oz (90 g) cooked potato
4 oz (120 g) fresh fruit salad

EVENING MEAL
5 oz (150 g) cottage cheese with 1 hard-
    boiled egg
mixed salad with 1 teaspoon salad cream
crispbread, up to 80 calories, with 1 teaspoon
    low-fat spread
4 oz (120 g) pineapple

**SNACKS OR DRINKS
AT PLANNED TIMES**
5 fl oz (150 ml) low-fat natural yogurt, 9 fl oz
    (270 ml) skim milk

WEEK 46

Only six weeks to Christmas now, so it's time to start planning and shopping. We suggest simple meals this week to give you some spare time for your preparations. The Sauteed Prawns and Corn is particularly easy and tasty.

DAY 1

MORNING MEAL
½ medium banana, sliced
¾ oz (20 g) muesli
2½ fl oz (75 ml) low-fat natural yogurt

MIDDAY MEAL
5 oz (150 g) cottage cheese with mixed salad
2 teaspoons salad cream
1 slice (1 oz/30 g) wholemeal bread
1 medium orange

EVENING MEAL
6 oz (180 g) grilled haddock
3 oz (90 g) carrots
1 slice (1 oz/30 g) wholemeal bread
2 teaspoons margarine
4 oz (120 g) stewed apple

SNACKS OR DRINKS AT PLANNED TIMES
15 fl oz (450 ml) skim milk

DAY 2

MORNING MEAL
½ medium grapefruit
1 poached egg
1 slice (1 oz/30 g) wholemeal bread
1 teaspoon low-fat spread

MIDDAY MEAL
3 oz (90 g) canned salmon
sliced tomatoes and cucumber
2 teaspoons low-calorie mayonnaise
1 oz (30 g) bread roll
2 small satsumas

EVENING MEAL
4 oz (120 g) roast beef
1 tablespoon horseradish relish
3 oz (90 g) peas
3 oz (90 g) baked jacket potato
3 teaspoons low-fat spread
4 oz (120 g) fruit salad

SNACKS OR DRINKS AT PLANNED TIMES
5 fl oz (150 ml) low-fat natural yogurt, ½ pint (300 ml) skim milk

---

DAY 3

MORNING MEAL
1 medium apple
1 oz (30 g) Cheddar cheese
1 slice (1 oz/30 g) wholemeal bread

MIDDAY MEAL
2 hard-boiled eggs, sliced onto shredded lettuce with 1 tomato, 2-3 spring onions and 2 teaspoons mayonnaise
3 oz (90 g) sweet corn
Baked Apple (page 295)
Custard (page 297)

EVENING MEAL
5 oz (150 g) grilled plaice with lemon juice
3 oz (90 g) Brussels sprouts
3 oz (90 g) green beans dotted with 1 teaspoon margarine
1 medium orange

SNACKS OR DRINKS AT PLANNED TIMES
5 fl oz (150 ml) skim milk, 5 fl oz (150 ml) low-fat natural yogurt

DAY4

MORNING MEAL
4 oz (120 g) fruit cocktail
¾ oz (20 g) cornflakes
5 fl oz (150 ml) skim milk

MIDDAY MEAL
4 oz (120 g) grilled liver
3 oz (90 g) courgettes
3 oz (90 g) cauliflower
1 slice (1 oz/30 g) wholemeal bread
2 teaspoons margarine
1 medium orange

EVENING MEAL
4 oz (120 g) grilled pork chop
1 teaspoon horseradish relish
3 oz (90 g) broccoli
3 oz (90 g) carrots dotted with 1 teaspoon
    margarine
4 oz (120 g) pineapple

**SNACKS OR DRINKS
AT PLANNED TIMES**
15 fl oz (450 ml) skim milk

DAY5

MORNING MEAL
1 medium orange
2½ oz (75 g) cottage cheese
1 slice (1 oz/30 g) wholemeal bread

MIDDAY MEAL
3 oz (90 g) canned sardines on mixed salad
2 teaspoons low-calorie mayonnaise
1 slice (1 oz/30 g) wholemeal bread
2 teaspoons low-fat spread
1 medium apple

EVENING MEAL
4 oz (120 g) grilled herring with 1 tablespoon
    mustard relish
3 oz (90 g) spinach
3 oz (90 g) carrots dotted with 1 teaspoon
    margarine
4 oz (120 g) mandarin oranges
4 fl oz (120 ml) white wine

**SNACKS OR DRINKS
AT PLANNED TIMES**
5 fl oz (150 ml) low-fat natural yogurt, ½ pint
    (300 ml) skim milk

DAY6

MORNING MEAL
2½ fl oz (75 ml) apple juice
1 oz (30 g) Cheshire cheese grilled on 1 slice
(1 oz/30 g) bread, toasted

MIDDAY MEAL
open sandwich made with 3 oz (90 g) sliced
chicken, shredded lettuce, sliced
tomatoes on 1 slice (1 oz/30 g) wholemeal
bread, spread with 1 teaspoon margarine
and topped with 2 teaspoons low-calorie
mayonnaise
4 oz (120 g) orange sections

EVENING MEAL
Sauteed Prawns and Corn (page 265)
3 oz (90 g) broccoli
3 oz (90 g) peas
2 medium plums

**SNACKS OR DRINKS
AT PLANNED TIMES**
½ pint (300 ml) skim milk, 5 fl oz (150 ml)
low-fat natural yogurt

DAY7

MORNING MEAL
4 fl oz (120 ml) orange juice
¾ oz (20 g) porridge oats cooked with water
5 fl oz (150 ml) skim milk

MIDDAY MEAL
Cheese Omelette (page 230)
3 oz (90 g) baked beans
1 slice (1 oz/30 g) rye bread
1 teaspoon margarine
4 oz (120 g) pineapple
2 oz (60 g) vanilla ice cream

EVENING MEAL
4 oz (120 g) grilled rump steak
1 tomato, halved and grilled
3 oz (90 g) green beans
3 oz (90 g) boiled potatoes
1 teaspoon margarine
½ medium banana, sliced into **Custard** (page
297)

**SNACKS OR DRINKS
AT PLANNED TIMES**
½ pint (300 ml) skim milk

WEEK 47

The wok is essential in Chinese cooking.
Treat yourself to one. You'll find it very
useful for the quick cooking of
vegetables and small pieces of meat, fish
or chicken.

DAY 1

MORNING MEAL
Honey-Stewed Prunes (page 298)
¾ oz (20 g) porridge oats, cooked in water
5 fl oz (150 ml) skim milk

MIDDAY MEAL
Soused Herring (page 264)
tomato and onion salad
1 medium orange

EVENING MEAL
Chinese Salad (page 287)
1½ oz (45 g) pitta bread
2 teaspoons margarine
1 medium orange

**SNACKS OR DRINKS
AT PLANNED TIMES**
5 fl oz (150 ml) low-fat natural yogurt, 5 fl oz
(150 ml) skim milk

DAY 2

MORNING MEAL
½ medium grapefruit
1 boiled egg
1 slice (1 oz/30 g) granary bread
1 teaspoon margarine

MIDDAY MEAL
8 fl oz (240 ml) tomato juice
3 oz (90 g) peeled prawns
mixed salad with 1 teaspoon mayonnaise
4 oz (120 g) pineapple

EVENING MEAL
4 oz (120 g) grilled rump steak
bean sprouts and mushroom salad with
    lemon juice
4 oz (120 g) cooked rice, dotted with 1
    teaspoon margarine

SNACKS OR DRINKS AT PLANNED TIMES
1 pint (600 ml) skim milk

DAY 3

MORNING MEAL
½ medium banana, sliced over ¾ oz (20 g)
    muesli with 5 fl oz (150 ml) skim milk

MIDDAY MEAL
4 oz (120 g) grilled chicken
mixed salad with 2 teaspoons salad dressing
1 slice (1 oz/30 g) granary bread
1 teaspoon margarine

EVENING MEAL
8 fl oz (240 ml) tomato juice
4 oz (120 g) grilled calf's liver
2 oz (60 g) cooked noodles
3 oz (90 g) peas
green salad with 1 teaspoon oil with wine
    vinegar
8 fresh lychees

SNACKS OR DRINKS AT PLANNED TIMES
5 fl oz (150 ml) low-fat natural yogurt, 5 fl oz
    (150 ml) skim milk

DAY4

MORNING MEAL
4 oz (120 g) grapefruit sections
1 oz (30 g) Cheddar cheese
1 slice (1 oz/30 g) bread

MIDDAY MEAL
3 oz (90 g) steamed lemon sole
3 oz (90 g) courgettes
3 oz (90 g) cauliflower
2 oz (60 g) cooked noodles
2 teaspoons margarine
4 oz (120 g) pineapple with 2 oz (60 g) vanilla
    ice cream

EVENING MEAL
4 oz (120 g) grilled pork chop
3 oz (90 g) broccoli
3 oz (90 g) carrots dotted with 1 teaspoon
    margarine
4 oz (120 g) peaches

SNACKS OR DRINKS AT PLANNED TIMES
5 fl oz (150 ml) low-fat natural yogurt with 1
    teaspoon honey, ½ pint (300 ml) skim milk

DAY5

MORNING MEAL
4 fl oz (120 ml) grapefruit juice
¾ oz (20 g) puffed rice
5 fl oz (150 ml) skim milk

MIDDAY MEAL
Chinese-Style Pancakes (page 225)
3 oz (90 g) bean sprouts
3 oz (90 g) poached mushrooms
1 medium pear

EVENING MEAL
6 oz (240 g) roast chicken
6 oz (180 g) Chinese leaves, shredded and
    sauteed in 1 teaspoon margarine
3 oz (90 g) celery hearts
2 inch (5 cm) wedge honeydew melon with
    pinch ground ginger

SNACKS OR DRINKS AT PLANNED TIMES
5 fl oz (150 ml) low-fat natural yogurt, 5 fl oz
    (150 ml) skim milk, 1 digestive biscuit with
    1 teaspoon margarine and 1 tablespoon
    jam

DAY6

MORNING MEAL 4 fl oz (120 ml) grapefruit juice
2½ oz (75 g) cottage cheese
2 cream crackers

MIDDAY MEAL 3 oz (90 g) grilled plaice dotted with 1
teaspoon margarine
3 oz (90 g) carrots
3 oz (90 g) potatoes
green salad with **Vinaigrette Dressing** (page
293)
8 fresh lychees

EVENING MEAL **Sweet and Sour Pork Fillet** (page 244)
2 oz (60 g) cooked rice

SNACKS OR DRINKS AT PLANNED TIMES 5 fl oz (150 ml) low-fat natural yogurt with 1
teaspoon honey, ½ pint (300 ml) skim milk

DAY7

MORNING MEAL 2½ fl oz (75 ml) pineapple juice
1 egg, scrambled in 1 teaspoon margarine
with 1 slice (1 oz/30 g) bread, toasted
1 teaspoon margarine

MIDDAY MEAL 3 oz (90 g) roast chicken
3 oz (90 g) poached mushrooms
3 oz (90 g) peas
2 oz (60 g) cooked rice
green salad with lemon juice
1 medium orange
4 fl oz (120 ml) white wine

EVENING MEAL 2½ oz (75 g) cottage cheese
3 oz (90 g) peeled prawns
1 teaspoon mayonnaise
mixed salad
4 oz (120 g) peaches

SNACKS OR DRINKS AT PLANNED TIMES 5 fl oz (150 ml) low-fat natural yogurt, ½ pint
(300 ml) skim milk

WEEK 48

On Day 6 we give you kidneys cooked in red wine. Wine makes all the difference to an inexpensive meal.

DAY 1

MORNING MEAL
½ medium banana
¾ oz (20 g) muesli with 5 fl oz (150 ml) low-fat natural yogurt

MIDDAY MEAL
4 oz (120 g) canned tuna
mixed salad
3 oz (90 g) beetroot
2 teaspoons low-calorie mayonnaise
2 cream crackers
1 medium orange

EVENING MEAL
4 oz (120 g) grilled cod steak dotted with 2 teaspoons margarine
1 grilled tomato
3 oz (90 g) green beans
2 small clementines

SNACKS OR DRINKS AT PLANNED TIMES
½ pint (300 ml) skim milk, 1 digestive biscuit

DAY 2

MORNING MEAL
4 fl oz (120 ml) orange juice
1 oz (30 g) Cheddar cheese, grilled on 1 slice
(1 oz/30 g) bread, toasted
1 grilled tomato

MIDDAY MEAL
1 hard-boiled egg, chopped
2½ oz (75 g) cottage cheese mixed with 1 oz
(30 g) sultanas and sprinkling of curry powder
celery, cucumber and green pepper salad,
mixed with 2 teaspoons mayonnaise
crispbread, up to 80 calories, with 1 teaspoon
low-fat spread

EVENING MEAL
5 oz (150 g) roast chicken
3 oz (90 g) Brussels sprouts
3 oz (90 g) swede
3 oz (90 g) boiled potatoes with 1 teaspoon
low-fat spread
¼ pint (150 ml) raspberry jelly with 5 oz (150
g) raspberries

SNACKS OR DRINKS AT PLANNED TIMES
5 fl oz (150 ml) low-fat natural yogurt, ½ pint
(300 ml) skim milk

DAY 3

MORNING MEAL
¾ oz (20 g) porridge oats cooked with water
5 fl oz (150 ml) skim milk
1 oz (30 g) raisins

MIDDAY MEAL
4 oz (120 g) grilled plaice, dotted with 1
teaspoon margarine
3 oz (90 g) green beans
3 oz (90 g) carrots
5 fl oz (150 ml) low-fat natural yogurt with 1 oz
(30 g) dried apricots, chopped

EVENING MEAL
4 oz (120 g) grilled chicken livers, dotted with
2 teaspoons margarine
3 oz (90 g) peas
4 oz (120 g) cooked noodles
1 medium orange

SNACKS OR DRINKS AT PLANNED TIMES
5 fl oz (150 ml) skim milk

DAY4

MORNING MEAL
½ medium grapefruit
¾ oz (20 g) cornflakes
5 fl oz (150 ml) skim milk

MIDDAY MEAL
Meatball and Vegetable Stir-Fry (page 249)
¼ small pineapple

EVENING MEAL
9 oz (270 g) baked beans
1 poached egg
3 oz (90 g) mushrooms, sauteed in 1
   teaspoon margarine
2 grilled tomatoes
3 oz (90 g) grapes

SNACKS OR DRINKS
AT PLANNED TIMES
5 fl oz (150 ml) low-fat natural yogurt with 1
   portion rhubarb, 5 fl oz (150 ml) skim milk

DAY5

MORNING MEAL
4 fl oz (120 ml) orange juice
1 boiled egg
1 slice (1 oz/30 g) wholemeal bread

MIDDAY MEAL
3 tablespoons peanut butter
crispbread, up to 80 calories
tomato and cucumber salad
3 oz (90 g) grapes

EVENING MEAL
1 portion boil-in-the-bag fish in sauce (any
   type)
3 oz (90 g) boiled potatoes
3 oz (90 g) leeks
3 oz (90 g) peas
2 small clementines

SNACKS OR DRINKS
AT PLANNED TIMES
5 fl oz (150 ml) low-fat natural yogurt, ½ pint
   (300 ml) skim milk

DAY 6

MORNING MEAL
1 medium orange
6 oz (180 g) baked beans
1 slice (1 oz/30 g) bread, toasted

MIDDAY MEAL
5 oz (150 g) cottage cheese with chopped
    celery, cucumber, tomato and watercress
2 teaspoons salad dressing
5 fl oz (150 ml) low-fat natural yogurt with ½
    medium banana, sliced

EVENING MEAL
Kidneys in Red Wine (page 256)
¼ small pineapple

**SNACKS OR DRINKS
AT PLANNED TIMES**
½ pint (300 ml) skim milk

DAY 7

MORNING MEAL
2½ oz (75 g) cottage cheese with 4 oz (120 g)
    peaches
1 slice (1 oz/30 g) wholemeal bread
2 teaspoons low-fat spread

MIDDAY MEAL
4 oz (120 g) roast lamb
3 oz (90 g) cabbage
3 oz (90 g) carrots
3 oz (90 g) potato
2 teaspoons low-fat spread
4 oz (120 g) fruit salad
5 fl oz (150 ml) low-fat natural yogurt
4 fl oz (120 ml) red wine

EVENING MEAL
3-egg omelette with pinch mixed herbs
green salad with 1 tomato
1 oz (30 g) Scotch pancake with 1 teaspoon
    margarine and 1 teaspoon honey
1 medium orange

**SNACKS OR DRINKS
AT PLANNED TIMES**
½ pint (300 ml) skim milk

WEEK 49

This week's menu plan contains home-produced fast food to give you time for your Christmas shopping. It's varied, quick and nourishing and you're sure to enjoy it.

DAY 1

MORNING MEAL
4 fl oz (120 ml) orange juice
¾ oz (20 g) porridge oats, cooked with water and served with 5 fl oz (150 ml) skim milk

MIDDAY MEAL
4 oz (120 g) corned beef with 2 teaspoons relish
mixed salad with 2 teaspoons salad cream
crispbread, up to 80 calories
2 teaspoons low-fat spread
1 medium apple

EVENING MEAL
1 portion boil-in-the-bag fish in sauce (any type)
3 oz (90 g) carrots
3 oz (90 g) courgettes
3 oz (90 g) boiled potatoes, mashed with 2 teaspoons low-fat spread
2 small tangerines with 5 fl oz (150 ml) low-fat natural yogurt

SNACKS OR DRINKS AT PLANNED TIMES
5 fl oz (150 ml) skim milk

DAY 2

MORNING MEAL
4 fl oz (120 ml) orange juice
1 boiled egg
1 oz (30 g) bread roll
1 teaspoon low-fat spread

MIDDAY MEAL
2½ oz (75 g) cottage cheese, mixed with 1 teaspoon salad cream and pinch curry powder, with mixed salad
Pancakes with Orange Sauce (page 224)

EVENING MEAL
5 oz (150 g) grilled fillet of plaice
3 oz (90 g) carrots
3 oz (90 g) peas
3 oz (90 g) sweet corn
4 oz (120 g) pineapple

SNACKS OR DRINKS AT PLANNED TIMES
9 fl oz (270 ml) skim milk, 5 fl oz (150 ml) low-fat natural yogurt

---

DAY 3

MORNING MEAL
½ medium grapefruit
1 oz (30 g) Cheddar cheese
1 slice (1 oz/30 g) bread

MIDDAY MEAL
3 oz (90 g) canned tuna
mixed salad with lemon juice
1 slice (1 oz/30 g) bread
1 teaspoon margarine
½ medium banana with 5 fl oz (150 ml) low-fat natural yogurt

EVENING MEAL
5 oz (150 g) uncooked lamb's liver, sauteed in 2 teaspoons vegetable oil
3 oz (90 g) cauliflower
3 oz (90 g) leeks
1 medium pear

SNACKS OR DRINKS AT PLANNED TIMES
½ pint (300 ml) skim milk

DAY4

MORNING MEAL
½ medium grapefruit
¾ oz (20 g) cornflakes with 5 fl oz (150 ml)
    skim milk

MIDDAY MEAL
3-egg omelette with mixed salad, with 2
    teaspoons salad dressing
1 slice (1 oz/30 g) bread
3 oz (90 g) grapes

EVENING MEAL
5 oz (150 g) grilled haddock
3 oz (90 g) peas
3 oz (90 g) swede, mashed with 3 oz (90 g)
    boiled potato
2 teaspoons margarine
½ medium banana with 2 oz (60 g) vanilla ice
    cream

SNACKS OR DRINKS AT PLANNED TIMES
15 fl oz (450 ml) skim milk

DAY5

MORNING MEAL
4 fl oz (120 ml) grapefruit juice
2½ oz (75 g) cottage cheese
1 slice (1 oz/30 g) currant bread
1 teaspoon margarine

MIDDAY MEAL
3 oz (90 g) canned sardines
cucumber, onion and lettuce salad with 1
    teaspoon mayonnaise
1 tomato
1 slice (1 oz/30 g) bread
1 teaspoon margarine
1 medium apple

EVENING MEAL
4 oz (120 g) grilled lamb chop
3 oz (90 g) spinach
3 oz (90 g) parsnips
1 medium pear

SNACKS OR DRINKS AT PLANNED TIMES
½ pint (300 ml) skim milk, 5 fl oz (150 ml)
    low-fat natural yogurt

DAY 6

MORNING MEAL
4 fl oz (120 ml) grapefruit juice
1 oz (30 g) Edam cheese
1 slice (1 oz/30 g) bread, toasted
1 teaspoon margarine

MIDDAY MEAL
9 oz (270 g) baked beans served on 1 slice
(1 oz/30 g) bread, toasted, spread with 1
teaspoon margarine
1 grilled tomato
3 oz (90 g) poached mushrooms
4 oz (120 g) fruit salad

EVENING MEAL
4 oz (120 g) grilled kipper
3 oz (90 g) beetroot
tomato, lettuce and onion salad with wine
vinegar
1 slice (1 oz/30 g) bread, spread with 1
teaspoon margarine
1 medium orange

SNACKS OR DRINKS AT PLANNED TIMES
½ pint (300 ml) skim milk, 5 fl oz (150 ml)
low-fat natural yogurt

DAY 7

MORNING MEAL
4 fl oz (120 ml) grapefruit juice
¾ oz (20 g) puffed rice with 5 fl oz (150 ml)
skim milk

MIDDAY MEAL
4 oz (120 g) roast lamb
3 oz (90 g) baked jacket potato with 2
teaspoons low-fat spread
3 oz (90 g) leeks
3 oz (90 g) carrots
4 oz (120 g) peaches

EVENING MEAL
Chicken Stir-Fry (page 239)
2 oz (60 g) cooked noodles
spring onion, celery, cucumber and lettuce
salad with lemon juice
1 medium apple

SNACKS OR DRINKS AT PLANNED TIMES
15 fl oz (450 ml) skim milk

WEEK 50

The food processor adds a whole new dimension to kitchen help. It will grind, mince, blend, mix, slice, grate, shred and extract juice. What about putting one on your list for Father Christmas.

DAY 1

MORNING MEAL
4 fl oz (120 ml) grapefruit juice
3 oz (90 g) baked beans
1 slice (1 oz/30 g) wholemeal bread, toasted

MIDDAY MEAL
5 oz (150 g) uncooked chicken livers and 2 oz
   (60 g) onion, sliced, sauteed with 2
   teaspoons vegetable oil
3 oz (90 g) green beans
mixed salad with lemon juice

EVENING MEAL
8 fl oz (240 ml) tomato juice
Fillet of Sole Florentine (page 270)
3 oz (90 g) cabbage
3 oz (90 g) baked jacket potato

**SNACKS OR DRINKS
AT PLANNED TIMES**
1 medium apple with 5 fl oz (150 ml) low-fat
   natural yogurt, ½ pint (300 ml) skim milk

DAY2

MORNING MEAL
4 fl oz (120 ml) grapefruit juice
¾ oz (20 g) cornflakes
5 fl oz (150 ml) skim milk

MIDDAY MEAL
Tomato Stuffed with Herb Cheese (page 226)
2 oz (60 g) slice French bread
2 teaspoons margarine

EVENING MEAL
4 oz (120 g) boiled ham
3 oz (90 g) green beans
6 oz (180 g) baked beans
2 teaspoons low-fat spread
1 medium apple
2 oz (60 g) vanilla ice cream

SNACKS OR DRINKS AT PLANNED TIMES
1 medium orange, 5 fl oz (150 ml) skim milk, 5 fl oz (150 ml) low-fat natural yogurt

---

DAY3

MORNING MEAL
4 fl oz (120 ml) grapefruit juice
1 oz (30 g) Cheddar cheese, grated
1 oz (30 g) toasted muffin

MIDDAY MEAL
3 oz (90 g) baked cod
1 grilled tomato
3 oz (90 g) Brussels sprouts
tossed salad with **Vinaigrette Dressing** (page 293)
1 slice (1 oz/30 g) rye bread, toasted
1 teaspoon margarine

EVENING MEAL
4 oz (120 g) roast chicken
3 oz (90 g) cabbage
3 oz (90 g) sweet corn
mixed salad
2 teaspoons low-calorie mayonnaise
1 portion rhubarb
5 fl oz (150 ml) low-fat natural yogurt

SNACKS OR DRINKS AT PLANNED TIMES
2 small satsumas, 1 medium apple, ½ pint (300 ml) skim milk

DAY4

MORNING MEAL
4 fl oz (120 ml) orange juice
6 oz (180 g) baked beans
1 slice (1 oz/30 g) bread, toasted

MIDDAY MEAL
Cheese Souffle (page 232)
3 oz (90 g) peas
1 grilled tomato
4 oz (120 g) orange sections

EVENING MEAL
2 inch (5 cm) wedge melon
Chicken and Pork Meatballs (page 245)
3 oz (90 g) cabbage
3 oz (90 g) cauliflower
3 oz (90 g) boiled potatoes
2 teaspoons low-fat spread
4 fl oz (120 ml) white wine

SNACKS OR DRINKS AT PLANNED TIMES
15 fl oz (450 ml) skim milk

DAY5

MORNING MEAL
2 inch (5 cm) wedge melon
1 boiled egg
1 slice (1 oz/30 g) wholemeal bread
2 teaspoons low-fat spread

MIDDAY MEAL
2½ oz (75 g) cottage cheese mixed with 2 oz (60 g) canned tuna
mixed salad
2 water biscuits
2 teaspoons low-fat spread

EVENING MEAL
½ medium grapefruit
4 oz (120 g) grilled chicken with herbs and lemon juice
Fennel with Parmesan Cheese (page 278)
3 oz (90 g) carrots
3 oz (90 g) mashed swede
2 teaspoons low-fat spread

SNACKS OR DRINKS AT PLANNED TIMES
½ medium banana, with 5 fl oz (150 ml) low-fat natural yogurt, ½ pint (300 ml) skim milk

DAY6

MORNING MEAL
½ medium banana
¾ oz (20 g) muesli
5 fl oz (150 ml) low-fat natural yogurt

MIDDAY MEAL
5 oz (150 g) cottage cheese mixed with 1 oz
(30 g) raisins and pinch curry powder
tomato, cucumber and celery, sliced on
lettuce with 2 teaspoons low-calorie
mayonnaise
melba toast, up to 80 calories

EVENING MEAL
½ medium grapefruit
6 oz (180 g) steamed smoked haddock
2 teaspoons low-fat spread
2 oz (60 g) steamed mushrooms
3 oz (90 g) spinach
1 oz (30 g) wholemeal roll
2 teaspoons low-fat spread

**SNACKS OR DRINKS
AT PLANNED TIMES**
½ pint (300 ml) skim milk

DAY7

MORNING MEAL
1 medium orange, peeled and sliced
2 tablespoons peanut butter
crispbread, up to 80 calories

MIDDAY MEAL
4 oz (120 g) roast beef
3 oz (90 g) boiled potatoes
3 oz (90 g) parsnips
3 oz (90 g) carrots
1 medium baked onion
1 medium baked apple topped with 5 oz
(150 g) stewed blackberries and 3
tablespoons single cream

EVENING MEAL
Mushroom Omelette (page 230)
tomato and chicory salad with lemon juice

**SNACKS OR DRINKS
AT PLANNED TIMES**
5 fl oz (150 ml) low-fat natural yogurt, 1
teaspoon honey, ½ pint (300 ml) skim milk

WEEK 51

The blandest and most innocuous dish can be 'rescued' by a good dressing. Use our standard vinaigrette dressing with a pinch of herbs and different spices to add interest to meals.

DAY 1

MORNING MEAL
½ medium banana
2 eggs scrambled in 1 teaspoon margarine
1 slice (1 oz/30 g) wholemeal bread, toasted

MIDDAY MEAL
Cream of Cauliflower Soup (page 216)
2 oz (60 g) Brie cheese
1 slice (1 oz/30 g) wholemeal bread
1 teaspoon margarine
1 medium orange

EVENING MEAL
4 oz (120 g) frankfurters
3 oz (90 g) canned sauerkraut
3 oz (90 g) boiled potato, mashed with 2 teaspoons low-fat spread

SNACKS OR DRINKS AT PLANNED TIMES
2 small satsumas, 17½ fl oz (525 ml) skim milk

DAY 2

MORNING MEAL
½ medium banana
1 boiled egg
1 slice (1 oz/30 g) wholemeal bread, toasted
1 teaspoon low-fat spread

MIDDAY MEAL
3 oz (90 g) grilled haddock
3 oz (90 g) green beans
grated carrot and white cabbage, mixed with
    3 teaspoons low-calorie mayonnaise

EVENING MEAL
4 oz (120 g) grilled ham
3 oz (90 g) parsnips
2 teaspoons low-fat spread
2 oz (60 g) cooked pasta shells
5 fl oz (150 ml) low-fat natural yogurt
4 oz (120 g) apricots

SNACKS OR DRINKS AT PLANNED TIMES
½ pint (300 ml) skim milk, 1 medium orange

DAY 3

MORNING MEAL
½ medium grapefruit
2½ oz (75 g) curd cheese
1 tablespoon jam
1 slice (1 oz/30 g) wholemeal bread, toasted

MIDDAY MEAL
3 poached eggs on 6 oz (180 g) steamed
    spinach
2 teaspoons margarine
1 grilled tomato

EVENING MEAL
4 oz (120 g) canned tuna, flaked and mixed
    with 4 oz (120 g) cooked rice
mixed salad with **Vinaigrette Dressing**
    (page 293)
1 medium apple

SNACKS OR DRINKS AT PLANNED TIMES
2 dried dates chopped into 5 fl oz (150 ml)
    low-fat natural yogurt, ½ pint (300 ml)
    skim milk

DAY4

MORNING MEAL
1 oz (30 g) raisins
¾ oz (20 g) muesli
5 fl oz (150 ml) low-fat natural yogurt

MIDDAY MEAL
9 oz (270 g) baked beans
1 slice (1 oz/30 g) wholemeal bread, toasted
1 teaspoon margarine
mixed salad with **Vinaigrette Dressing**
    (page 293)

EVENING MEAL
4 oz (120 g) grilled lamb chop
3 oz (90 g) Brussels sprouts
3 oz (90 g) carrots
3 oz (90 g) boiled potato mashed with 2
    teaspoons low-fat spread
1 medium baked apple with **Custard** (page
    297)

SNACKS OR DRINKS
AT PLANNED TIMES
5 fl oz (150 ml) skim milk, 1 medium orange,
    2½ oz (75 g) cottage cheese

DAY5

MORNING MEAL
2½ fl oz (75 ml) pineapple juice
1 boiled egg
1 slice (1 oz/30 g) wholemeal bread, toasted

MIDDAY MEAL
3 tablespoons peanut butter
crispbread, up to 80 calories, with sliced
    cucumber
1 medium orange

EVENING MEAL
4 breadcrumbed fish fingers, grilled
3 oz (90 g) poached mushrooms
3 oz (90 g) peas
2 teaspoons tomato ketchup
4 oz (120 g) pear

SNACKS OR DRINKS
AT PLANNED TIMES
½ pint (300 ml) skim milk, 5 fl oz (150 ml)
    low-fat natural yogurt

DAY6

MORNING MEAL
1 medium apple
2½ oz (75 g) cottage cheese
crispbread, up to 80 calories
2 teaspoons low-fat spread

MIDDAY MEAL
5 oz (150 g) uncooked chicken livers, sauteed
    in 2 teaspoons margarine
1 oz (30 g) grilled back bacon
1 grilled tomato
3 oz (90 g) peas
2 oz (60 g) cooked rice

EVENING MEAL
3 oz (90 g) grilled veal
3 oz (90 g) courgettes
2 oz (60 g) cooked pasta shells
4 oz (120 g) peaches with 5 fl oz (150 ml)
    low-fat natural yogurt

**SNACKS OR DRINKS
AT PLANNED TIMES**
8 fl oz (240 ml) tomato juice with dash
    Worcestershire sauce, ½ pint (300 ml)
    skim milk

DAY7

MORNING MEAL
1 oz (30 g) dried apricots, chopped
¾ oz (20 g) wheat flakes
5 fl oz (150 ml) skim milk
1 oz (30 g) toasted muffin with 1 teaspoon
    margarine
1 tablespoon marmalade

MIDDAY MEAL
6 oz (180 g) roast chicken
3 oz (90 g) cauliflower
3 oz (90 g) mashed swede
2 teaspoons low-fat spread
¼ fresh pineapple
5 fl oz (150 ml) low-fat natural yogurt
4 fl oz (120 ml) white wine

EVENING MEAL
½ medium grapefruit
2 oz (60 g) grated Cheddar cheese grilled on 1
    slice (1 oz/30 g) wholemeal bread, toasted
sliced tomato and onion rings with
    Vinaigrette Dressing (page 293)

**SNACKS OR DRINKS
AT PLANNED TIMES**
5 fl oz (150 ml) skim milk

WEEK 52

Enjoy Christmas. Put food in its proper place – a pleasure but not an obsession. This week's menus include traditional dishes and unusual treats. Follow the plan and enjoy the festive season.

DAY 1

MORNING MEAL
4 fl oz (120 ml) grapefruit juice
2½ oz (75 g) curd cheese
1 slice (1 oz/30 g) wholemeal bread, toasted
1 teaspoon margarine

MIDDAY MEAL
3 oz (90 g) cooked chicken
mixed salad with 3 oz (90 g) beetroot
1 water biscuit
Vinaigrette Dressing (page 293)

Christmas Eve Cocktail Party
Hot Mushroom Turnovers (page 220)
cucumber and celery sticks with **Curry Dip**
   (page 293)
8 fl oz (240 ml) tomato juice

EVENING MEAL
1 portion boil-in-the-bag fish in sauce (any type)
3 oz (90 g) spinach
3 oz (90 g) sliced carrots
3 oz (90 g) cooked potatoes
5 fl oz (150 ml) low-fat natural yogurt with 1
   dried fig, diced

SNACKS OR DRINKS
AT PLANNED TIMES
7 fl oz (210 ml) skim milk

DAY 2

MORNING MEAL
4 fl oz (120 ml) grapefruit juice
1 oz (30 g) grated Cheddar cheese grilled on 1 slice (1 oz/30 g) wholemeal bread, toasted

MIDDAY MEAL
4 oz (120 g) roast turkey with **Spicy Plum Sauce** (page 292)
3 oz (90 g) baked jacket potato
3 oz (90 g) parsnips
3 oz (90 g) carrots
3 oz (90 g) Brussels sprouts
1 teaspoon margarine
Rich Fruit Pudding (page 298)
2½ fl oz (75 ml) low-fat natural yogurt
4 fl oz (120 ml) white wine

EVENING MEAL
3 oz (90 g) canned crabmeat
1 wedge iceberg lettuce, shredded
3 oz (90 g) sliced cucumber
3 teaspoons low-calorie mayonnaise

SNACKS OR DRINKS AT PLANNED TIMES
14 fl oz (420 ml) skim milk

DAY 3

MORNING MEAL
5 oz (150 g) canned strawberries
¾ oz (20 g) cornflakes
5 fl oz (150 ml) skim milk

MIDDAY MEAL
4 oz (120 g) roast loin of pork with 2 oz (60 g) pureed cooked apple
3 oz (90 g) mashed swede
3 oz (90 g) courgettes
3 oz (90 g) baked jacket potato
2 teaspoons low-fat spread
4 fl oz (120 ml) white wine
Pineapple-Orange 'Cream' (page 299)

EVENING MEAL
1 medium corn-on-the-cob
1 teaspoon low-fat spread
Salmon Mousse (page 268)
1 sliced tomato
lettuce and onion rings

SNACKS OR DRINKS AT PLANNED TIMES
5 fl oz (150 ml) skim milk, 4 fl oz (120 ml) tomato juice

DAY4

MORNING MEAL
8 fl oz (240 ml) tomato juice
1 poached egg
1 slice (1 oz/30 g) bread, toasted
1 teaspoon margarine

MIDDAY MEAL
4 oz (120 g) liver sausage
mixed salad
3 oz (90 g) beetroot
crispbread, up to 80 calories
2 teaspoons margarine
4 oz (120 g) fruit cocktail
5 fl oz (150 ml) low-fat natural yogurt

EVENING MEAL
Cream of Cauliflower Soup (page 216)
3 oz (90 g) grilled haddock
3 oz (90 g) courgettes
3 oz (90 g) mashed swede
¼ small fresh pineapple

SNACKS OR DRINKS AT PLANNED TIMES
7½ fl oz (225 ml) skim milk, 1 digestive biscuit

DAY5

MORNING MEAL
½ medium grapefruit
1 boiled egg
1 slice (1 oz/30 g) bread, toasted
1 teaspoon low-fat spread

MIDDAY MEAL
4 oz (120 g) mackerel fillets, 3 oz (90 g) shredded white cabbage, 1 grated carrot and onion rings, with **Creamy Yogurt Dressing** (page 292)
1 medium orange

EVENING MEAL
3 oz (90 g) turkey
3 oz (90 g) steamed mushrooms
3 oz (90 g) broccoli
6 oz (180 g) baked jacket potato
3 teaspoons low-fat spread
4 oz (120 g) pears

SNACKS OR DRINKS AT PLANNED TIMES
15 fl oz (450 ml) skim milk

DAY6

MORNING MEAL
1 medium orange
1 tablespoon peanut butter
crispbread, up to 80 calories

MIDDAY MEAL
1 oz (30 g) Cheddar cheese grilled on 1 slice
(1 oz/30 g) wholemeal bread, toasted,
topped with 1 poached egg
1 grilled tomato
2 small clementines

EVENING MEAL
2-inch (5-cm) wedge honeydew melon
6 oz (180 g) uncooked lamb's liver sauteed in
2 teaspoons vegetable oil with onion rings
3 oz (90 g) green beans
3 oz (90 g) peas
2 oz (60 g) cooked noodles tossed in 2
teaspoons Parmesan cheese

SNACKS OR DRINKS AT PLANNED TIMES
5 fl oz (150 ml) low-fat natural yogurt, ½ pint
(300 ml) skim milk

DAY7

MORNING MEAL
4 fl oz (120 ml) orange juice
¾ oz (20 g) cornflakes
5 fl oz (150 ml) skim milk

MIDDAY MEAL
4 oz (120 g) roast veal
3 oz (90 g) carrots
3 oz (90 g) turnips
Sweet and Sour Cabbage (page 280)
3 medium dessert plums

EVENING MEAL
4 oz (120 g) grilled trout
3 oz (90 g) spinach
3 oz (90 g) cooked potato, diced and chilled,
tossed with 4 teaspoons low-calorie
mayonnaise
5 fl oz (150 ml) low-fat natural yogurt

SNACKS OR DRINKS AT PLANNED TIMES
2 cream crackers, 2 teaspoons grated
Parmesan cheese, 5 fl oz (150 ml) skim
milk

Starters

The 'starter' of a meal should be the foretaste of the delights to come, and the delicious inspirations in this section will be music to your palate.

Garden Pea Soup
See Menu Plan for Week 45.

6 oz (180 g) peas, fresh or frozen
1 pint (600 ml) water
1 chicken stock cube
2–3 sprigs mint
salt and pepper to taste

Combine peas, water, stock cube, mint, salt and pepper in a saucepan. Bring to the boil, cover and simmer until peas are soft. Transfer to blender container and puree until smooth. Reheat, adjust seasoning.
Makes 2 servings.   *Per serving: 45 calories.*

Cream of Cauliflower Soup
See Menu Plans for Weeks 5, 17, 51 and 52.

1 lb (480 g) cauliflower florets
1½ pints (900 ml) water
2 chicken stock cubes
2 teaspoons arrowroot
½ pint (300 ml) skim milk
2 tablespoons chopped parsley
pinch white pepper

Place cauliflower in saucepan. Add water and stock cubes, bring to the boil. Cover and simmer for 15–20 minutes or until cauliflower is soft. Transfer mixture in 3 batches to blender container and puree. Return puree to saucepan and heat. Combine arrowroot with milk and pour into cauliflower mixture; cook, stirring constantly, until thickened. Stir in parsley and pepper and serve.

Makes 4 servings.   *Per serving: 60 calories.*

Broccoli Soup
See Menu Plan for Week 45.

6 oz (180 g) broccoli
1 pint (600 ml) chicken stock made with 1 cube
1 oz (30 g) low-fat dry milk
salt and pepper to taste

Wash broccoli and cook in chicken stock until tender. Transfer to blender and puree until smooth. Add dry milk, puree for a further few seconds. Season and reheat before serving, but do not allow to boil.

Makes 2 servings.   *Per serving: 75 calories.*

Gazpacho
See Menu Plan for Week 33.

16 fl oz (480 ml) tomato juice
3 oz (90 g) cucumber, peeled, seeded and finely chopped
2 oz (60 g) celery, finely chopped
2 oz (60 g) green pepper, finely chopped
2 tablespoons chopped spring onion
2 tablespoons olive oil
1 teaspoon Worcestershire sauce
1 teaspoon chopped parsley
½ teaspoon salt
pinch freshly ground pepper
1 clove garlic, finely chopped

Combine all ingredients in medium bowl. Cover and chill overnight. Stir just before serving.

Makes 4 servings.   *Per serving: 95 calories.*

Tomato and Marrow Soup

See Menu Plan for Week 45.

1½ chicken stock cubes

4 fl oz (120 ml) boiling water

12 fl oz (360 ml) tomato juice

1 medium onion, chopped

12 oz (360 g) marrow, peeled, cored and diced

1 teaspoon basil

salt and pepper to taste

1 teaspoon brown sugar

Dissolve stock cubes in boiling water. Place in large saucepan, add tomato juice, chopped onion, marrow and basil. Bring to the boil, cover and simmer gently for about 10 minutes or until marrow is very tender. Pour soup into blender container and puree until smooth. Return soup to pan and reheat. Taste and adjust seasoning. Serve piping hot.

Makes 3 servings.   *Per serving: 80 calories.*

Tomato Soup

See Menu Plan for Week 37.

2 × 15 oz (450 g) cans whole tomatoes, chopped

4 medium celery sticks, thinly sliced

3 oz (90 g) onion, finely chopped

½ small clove garlic, chopped

½ teaspoon honey

¼ teaspoon salt

pinch white pepper

Pour tomatoes and juice into large saucepan; add celery and garlic; cover and bring to the boil. Reduce heat to low and simmer for 45 minutes. Puree in blender container. Reheat. Stir in honey, salt, and pepper to taste.

Makes 2 servings.   *Per serving: 86 calories.*

Cock-a-Leekie
See Menu Plan for Week 4.

8 fl oz (240 ml) chicken stock, made with ½ stock cube

3 oz (90 g) leek, thinly sliced

2 oz (60 g) onion, chopped

¾ oz (20 g) rice

pinch salt

pinch pepper

1 teaspoon chopped parsley

Place all ingredients together in a saucepan and simmer gently for half an hour.
Makes 1 serving.   *Per serving: 150 calories.*

Fresh Mushroom Soup
See Menu Plans for Weeks 39 and 45.

6 oz (180 g) mushrooms, sliced

2 oz (60 g) onion, finely chopped

4 teaspoons flour

16 fl oz (480 ml) water

1 chicken stock cube, crumbled

pinch thyme

pinch each salt and pepper

2 teaspoons chopped parsley

Heat non-stick frying pan on low heat. Add mushrooms and onion; cook over low heat, stirring, about 2 minutes or until softened. Stir in flour and cook until mixture is lightly browned. Gradually stir in water, stock cube and thyme. Bring mixture to the boil, stirring; reduce heat and simmer 10 minutes or until slightly thickened. Season with salt and pepper. Just before serving, sprinkle with parsley.
Makes 2 servings.   *Per serving: 50 calories.*

Cream of Asparagus and Leek Soup
See Menu Plans for Weeks 9 and 45.

6 medium canned asparagus spears

2 tablespoons margarine

6 oz (180 g) leeks, chopped

1 tablespoon flour

1 pint (600 ml) chicken stock, made with 2 stock cubes

6 fl oz (180 ml) skim milk

pinch each salt, white pepper, and ground nutmeg

Cut off stems of asparagus, reserving tips. Puree stems in blender container or bowl of food processor. Melt margarine in saucepan; add leeks and saute until soft. Stir in flour, cook for 1–2 minutes. Gradually stir in stock and pureed asparagus. Bring to the boil, stirring; cover and simmer for 10 minutes. Add asparagus tips, milk, and seasonings. Heat but do not allow to boil.

Makes 6 servings.   *Per serving: 70 calories.*

Hot Mushroom Turnovers
See Menu Plan for Week 52.

3 oz (90 g) flour

¼ teaspoon salt

8 teaspoons margarine

2 fl oz (60 ml) low-fat natural yogurt

4 oz (120 g) mushrooms, finely chopped

1 small onion, finely chopped

1 tablespoon chopped parsley

¼ teaspoon Worcestershire sauce

1 clove garlic, crushed

pinch each thyme, salt and pepper

Mix flour and salt in a bowl. Rub in margarine until mixture resembles fine breadcrumbs. Add yogurt and mix thoroughly; form into a ball and chill about 1 hour. Combine remaining ingredients in non-stick pan; cook until mushrooms are soft and all the moisture has evaporated. Remove from heat. Preheat oven to 375°F, 190°C, Gas Mark 5. Roll out dough to about ⅛-inch (0.3-cm) thickness. With a pastry wheel, cut lengthwise strips 2½ inches (6.5 cm) apart; then cut crosswise, making 2½ inch (6.5 cm) squares. Re-roll scraps of dough and continue cutting until all dough is used. Place an equal amount of mushroom mixture on each square (about 1 teaspoon) and fold in half to enclose filling and form a triangle; seal well by pressing edges together with prongs of a fork. Bake on non-stick baking sheet about 15 minutes or until lightly browned.

Makes 8 servings, about 3 turnovers each　　　*Per serving: 80 calories.*

Minestrone
See Menu Plan for Week 45.

1 pint (600 ml) beef stock made with 1 stock cube
1 tablespoon tomato puree
4 oz (120 g) onion, chopped
3 oz (90 g) carrots, sliced
3 oz (90 g) courgettes, sliced
1 sachet bouquet garni
salt and pepper to taste
garlic powder to taste
1 tablespoon cornflour
4 oz (120 g) cooked pasta rings
chopped parsley to garnish

Place stock, tomato puree, onion, carrots, courgettes and bouquet garni in large saucepan. Season with salt, pepper and garlic powder. Bring to the boil, cover and simmer for 15–20 minutes, or until vegetables are soft. Mix cornflour with 1 tablespoon cold water, add to soup and bring to the boil, stirring constantly. Add pasta rings and allow to simmer for a further 5 minutes. Serve piping hot sprinkled with parsley.

Makes 2 servings.　　　*Per serving: 140 calories.*

Vegetable Medley Soup
See Menu Plan for Week 10.

4 teaspoons vegetable oil

8 oz (240 g) courgettes, chopped

4 oz (120 g) mushrooms, sliced

6 oz (180 g) green beans, chopped

4 oz (120 g) carrots, chopped

4 oz (120 g) onions, chopped

2 oz (60 g) celery, chopped

3 oz (90 g) green pepper, seeded and chopped

1 pint (600 ml) chicken stock made with 2 stock cubes

4 tablespoons tomato puree

1–2 teaspoons Worcestershire sauce

½ teaspoon thyme

dash chilli sauce (optional)

10 fl oz (300 ml) skim milk

1 tablespoon chopped parsley

Heat oil in large pan; add next 7 ingredients and saute, stirring occasionally, for 10 minutes. Add remaining ingredients except milk and parsley; bring to the boil, cover and simmer 30–40 minutes, stirring occasionally. Stir in milk; heat but do not boil. Garnish with parsley.

Makes 4 servings.   _Per serving: 125 calories._

Eggs and Cheese

Eggs and cheese may be two of the most versatile foods around. Each can stand on its own as the basis for a meal or do a delicious disappearing act in conjunction with other ingredients. Used together, cheese and eggs are a winning combination in omelettes and quiches, while fluffy beaten egg whites help your souffles rise to new heights.

Macaroni-Cheese Salad

See Menu Plan for Week 20.

4 oz (120 g) hot cooked short-cut macaroni
4 oz (120 g) strong Cheddar cheese, coarsely grated
2½ fl oz (75 ml) low-fat natural yogurt
4 teaspoons low-calorie mayonnaise
1 teaspoon French-style mustard
2 tablespoons celery, chopped
2 tablespoons red pepper, chopped
2 tablespoons green pepper, chopped
salt and pepper
4 green pepper strips

Combine macaroni with half of the cheese; toss until cheese is melted. Combine remaining cheese with yogurt, mayonnaise and mustard; add to macaroni mixture and stir well. Add celery and diced peppers. Toss well and season to taste. Serve at once garnished with pepper strips.

Makes 2 servings.

Per serving: 340 calories.

Matzo Brei

See Menu Plan for Week 15.

2 eggs

2 fl oz (60 ml) water

¼ teaspoon ground cinnamon

¼ teaspoon salt

1½ oz (45g) matzo board, broken into pieces

2 teaspoons margarine

In a medium bowl beat eggs lightly. Stir in water, cinnamon and salt; add matzo and let stand 15 minutes. Melt margarine in a non-stick pan; add matzo mixture, cover and cook over medium heat until browned on bottom. With a spatula, loosen sides of matzo mixture, slide on to a dish and invert into pan to brown other side.

Makes 2 servings.   *Per serving: 150 calories.*

Pancakes with Orange Sauce

See Menu Plan for Week 49.

Pancake

1 egg

2 tablespoons skim milk

¾ oz (20 g) flour

2 teaspoons oil

Sauce

4 fl oz (120 ml) orange juice

2 teaspoons arrowroot

½ teaspoon honey

Beat egg and milk together. Gradually beat into flour to make a smooth batter. Heat 1 teaspoon of oil in non-stick frying pan. Pour half the pancake mixture in and cook, turning once, until both sides are golden brown. Place on plate and keep warm.

Repeat the process with the rest of the mixture.

Mix orange juice and arrowroot together thoroughly in a small saucepan and slowly bring to the boil. Cook for one minute, add honey and mix thoroughly. Pour some over each pancake; roll up and serve.

Makes 1 serving.　　　　　　　　　　　*Per serving: 345 calories.*

Chinese-Style Pancakes

See Menu Plans for Weeks 21 and 47.

4 oz (120 g) white cabbage, shredded
4 oz (120 g) cooked brown rice
2 oz (60 g) carrot, grated
2 oz (60 g) spring onion, sliced
1 teaspoon sesame seeds, toasted
1 clove garlic, finely chopped
½ teaspoon finely chopped fresh ginger root
pinch pepper
4 eggs, beaten
4 teaspoons soy sauce
2 teaspoons vegetable oil
6 fl oz (180 ml) chicken stock made with ½ stock cube
2 teaspoons cornflour blended with 1 tablespoon water

Combine cabbage, rice, carrot, 1 oz (30 g) spring onion, sesame seeds, garlic, ginger and pepper. In separate bowl beat eggs with 3 teaspoons soy sauce; stir into vegetable mixture. Heat ½ teaspoon oil in non-stick pan. Pour in quarter of mixture; cook, turning once, until pancakes are brown on each side and vegetables are tender. Remove from pan and keep warm. Repeat until all batter is used. In small saucepan combine stock, remaining teaspoon soy sauce, and 1 oz (30 g) spring onion. Bring to the boil; stir in blended cornflour and cook, stirring constantly, until thickened. Serve sauce over pancakes.

Makes 2 servings.　　　　　　　　　　*Per serving: 345 calories.*

Tomato Stuffed with Herb Cheese
See Menu Plans for Weeks 2, 26 and 50.

10 oz (300 g) cottage cheese
1 oz (30 g) spring onion, finely chopped
1 tablespoon chopped parsley
1 small clove garlic, finely chopped
pinch each salt and white pepper
6 oz (180 g) tomatoes
2 parsley sprigs

Combine cottage cheese with spring onion, parsley, garlic, salt and pepper. With pointed knife, remove stem end of each tomato. Make 4 vertical intersecting cuts through top of each tomato, almost to the base, dividing tomatoes into eighths; spread tomatoes open. Fill centre of each tomato with half the herb cheese; garnish each with one parsley sprig.

Makes 2 servings. *Per serving: 150 calories.*

Baked Cheese Souffle
See Menu Plans for Weeks 10, 23 and 39.

4 slices (1 oz/30 g each) white bread, toasted
4 oz (120 g) Cheddar cheese, sliced
4 eggs, size 4 to 5, separated
1 teaspoon French mustard
2 teaspoons grated Parmesan cheese
pinch each salt and pepper

Preheat oven to 350°F, 180°C, Gas Mark 4. Arrange toast on non-stick baking tin; top with cheese. Using an electric mixer, beat egg yolks for 3–4 minutes or until thick and pale. Beat in mustard, Parmesan cheese, salt and pepper. Using clean beaters, whisk egg whites until stiff but not dry. Carefully fold into the yolk mixture. Gently spoon egg mixture over. Bake for 20 minutes.

Makes 4 servings. *Per serving: 275 calories.*

Welsh Rarebit
See Menu Plan for Week 9.

1 oz (30 g) Caerphilly cheese, finely grated
1 teaspoon margarine
½ teaspoon prepared mustard
dash Worcestershire sauce
1 slice (1 oz/30 g) bread, toasted

Preheat grill. Combine cheese, margarine, mustard and Worcestershire sauce and stir until smooth. Spread mixture on to hot toast and place under grill until cheese has melted. Serve at once.

Makes 1 serving.   *Per serving: 230 calories.*

Fruited Cheese Delight
See Menu Plan for Week 44.

10 oz (300 g) cottage cheese
1 teaspoon each honey and lemon juice
1 teaspoon sugar
drop vanilla flavouring
pinch salt
3 oz (90 g) grapes, cut into halves and deseeded
1½ oz (45 g) carrots, finely chopped
¾ teaspoon unflavoured gelatine
2½ fl oz (75 ml) apple juice

Combine cheese, honey, lemon juice, sweetener, vanilla and salt in blender container; puree until very smooth. Transfer to bowl; stir in grapes and carrots. Sprinkle gelatine over apple juice in small bowl and let stand to soften. Place bowl over pan of heated water and stir juice until gelatine is dissolved; cool slightly. Add dissolved gelatine to cheese mixture; stir to combine. Spoon into 2 individual dishes; cover and refrigerate until firm, about 3–4 hours.

Makes 2 servings.   *Per serving: 190 calories.*

Pitta Bread Sandwich

See Menu Plan for Week 10.

1 tablespoon vegetable oil

1 tablespoon wine vinegar

1 tablespoon water

pinch dill

pinch oregano

pinch pepper

4 oz (120 g) Edam cheese, chopped

1 inch (2.5 cm) cucumber, chopped

4 radishes, sliced

1 tablespoon chopped spring onion

2 pitta breads, 1 oz (30 g) each

Combine first 6 ingredients in bowl. Add remaining ingredients except pitta breads; stir to coat cheese and vegetables. Cover and marinate in refrigerator for at least 1 hour. Cut each pitta bread halfway around edge and open to form a pocket. Spoon half of salad mixture into each pitta pocket.

Makes 2 servings.   *Per serving: 315 calories.*

Swiss Cheese Bake

See Menu Plan for Week 24

3 oz (90 g) leeks

1 teaspoon margarine

2 teaspoons flour

¼ teaspoon ground nutmeg

2 oz (60 g) boiled ham, thinly sliced

3 oz (90 g) potato, baked or boiled in skin, sliced

1 oz (30 g) Emmenthal Cheese, grated

Wash leeks thoroughly, cut into 4–5-inch (10–12.5-cm) lengths. Boil in salted water for about 5 minutes, or until tender. Drain and reserve liquid. Melt margarine in pan; stir in flour, cook 1 minute. Remove from heat and gradually stir in 6 fl oz (180 ml) cooking liquid from the leeks and cook until thickened, stirring occasionally. Add nutmeg. Wrap ham round leeks and place in ovenproof dish. Cover with potatoes, then with sauce and sprinkle with grated cheese. Bake at 350°F, 180°C, Gas Mark 4 for 15–20 minutes.

Makes 1 serving.   _Per serving: 380 calories._

Broccoli Quiche

See Menu Plan for Week 21.

3 oz (90 g) flour
¾ teaspoon salt
8 teaspoons margarine
2 fl oz (60 ml) low-fat natural yogurt
5 oz (150 g) cooked broccoli, well drained and chopped
1 oz (30 g) spring onion, finely chopped
4 teaspoons imitation bacon bits, optional
8 oz (240 g) Emmenthal cheese, grated
4 eggs, lightly beaten
2 oz (60 g) low-fat dry milk
8 fl oz (240 ml) water
pinch pepper

Mix flour and ¼ teaspoon salt in mixing bowl. Rub margarine in until mixture resembles fine breadcrumbs. Add yogurt and mix thoroughly; form into a ball. Roll dough out to approximately ⅛-inch (0.3-cm) thickness. Fit into a 9-inch (23-cm) pie plate; flute edges and put aside. Combine vegetables and bacon bits. Cover bottom of pastry shell with 4 oz (120 g) cheese; add entire vegetable mixture. Combine eggs, dry milk and water, ½ teaspoon salt and pepper. Pour egg mixture over vegetables; top evenly with remaining cheese. Bake at 325°F, 160°C, Gas Mark 3, for 50–60 minutes or until knife, when inserted in centre, comes out clean. Remove from oven and let stand 10 minutes before serving.

Makes 8 servings.   _Per serving: 285 calories._

Mushroom Omelette

See Menu Plans for Weeks 1, 4, 26 and various other weeks.

6 oz (180 g) mushrooms, sliced

1 stick celery, chopped

½ teaspoon salt

2 eggs

pinch freshly ground pepper

1 teaspoon margarine

Heat non-stick pan over medium heat; add mushrooms, celery and salt. Cover and cook until mushrooms are tender. Set aside and keep warm. Beat together eggs and pepper. Melt margarine in 7-inch (18-cm) non-stick frying pan; when pan is hot pour in eggs and cook over medium heat. As eggs begin to set, using a fork carefully lift cooked edges of omelette and tilt pan so that uncooked portion flows underneath. When bottom of omelette is lightly browned and top surface is still moist, spread mushroom mixture over half the omelette. Fold other half over mushroom mixture. Invert omelette on to plate.

Makes 1 serving.   *Per serving: 240 calories.*

Cheese Omelette

See Menu Plan for Week 46.

1 teaspoon margarine

2 eggs

1 tablespoon water

pinch salt

1 oz (30 g) Cheddar cheese, grated

Melt margarine until hot in a 6½-inch (16.5-cm) non-stick frying or omelette pan. Mix eggs, water and salt and beat with wire whisk. Pour egg mixture into pan and cook until bottom is lightly browned and firm. Sprinkle grated cheese over egg. Place under grill as close to heat source as possible; grill until top puffs and turns light brown. Remove from grill and fold omelette in half. Slide out of pan onto heated plate.

Makes 1 serving.   *Per serving: 335 calories.*

Chilli-Cheese Rarebit
See Menu Plans for Weeks 5 and 35.

2 teaspoons margarine

1 tablespoon chopped onion

2 tablespoons chopped green pepper

8 oz (240 g) canned tomatoes, chopped

¾ teaspoon chilli powder, or to taste

4 oz (120 g) strong Cheddar cheese, grated

1 teaspoon cornflour, blended with 1 tablespoon water

2 slices (1 oz/30 g each) rye bread, toasted

Melt margarine in saucepan; add onion and saute until softened. Add green pepper and saute about 3 minutes longer. Add tomatoes and chilli powder and simmer mixture 10 minutes or until some of the liquid has evaporated. Add cheese and stir until it is melted. Stir in blended cornflour and simmer, stirring constantly until thickened. Remove from heat, serve over toast.

Makes 2 servings.   *Per serving: 360 calories.*

Pancakes with Lemon Juice
See Menu Plan for Week 7.

¾ oz (20 g) flour

pinch salt

1 egg white

2½ fl oz (75 ml) skim milk

1 teaspoon vegetable oil

1 teaspoon sugar

juice of ½ lemon

Sift flour and salt into a bowl. Beat in egg and milk. Heat ½ teaspoon oil in a small non-stick frying pan. Pour in half of mixture and and cook over moderate heat until golden underneath. Turn and cook second side. Repeat process with remainder of batter. Serve sprinkled with sugar and lemon juice.

Makes 1 serving.   *Per serving: 255 calories.*

Spinach Frittata
See Menu Plan for Week 20.

4 eggs, well beaten

6 oz (180 g) cooked, well-drained spinach, chopped

2 tablespoons chopped parsley

¼ teaspoon salt

¼ clove garlic, finely chopped

pinch each pepper and grated nutmeg

1 tablespoon margarine

2 tablespoons chopped spring onion

1 teaspoon sesame seeds

Combine eggs, spinach, parsley, salt, garlic, pepper and nutmeg. Mix well. Melt margarine in 12-inch (30.5-cm) non-stick frying pan with flameproof handle. Add spring onion and saute 2 minutes. Pour in egg-spinach mixture. Cook over moderately high heat, briskly shaking pan back and forth to prevent sticking. When underside is lightly browned, grill for a few minutes until frittata is set. Sprinkle with sesame seeds.
Makes 2 servings.   *Per serving: 275 calories.*

Cheese Souffle
See Menu Plan for Week 50.

1 tablespoon margarine

1 tablespoon finely chopped onion

2 tablespoons flour

½ pint (300 ml) buttermilk

2 oz (60 g) strong Cheddar cheese, coarsely grated

¼ teaspoon each powdered mustard and salt

2 eggs, separated

pinch ground red pepper

2 teaspoons chopped chives

Preheat oven to 375°F, 190°C, Gas Mark 5. Melt margarine in saucepan; add onion and saute until softened. Stir in flour and cook over low heat for 2 minutes. Remove pan from heat and gradually stir in buttermilk. Return to heat and bring to the boil, stirring. Remove from heat; add cheese, mustard and salt; stir until cheese is melted. Beat in egg yolks, one at a time; add red pepper. Whisk egg whites until stiff peaks form. Gently fold whites and chives into yolk mixture. Turn souffle into a 2-pint (1.2-litre) souffle dish. Bake 25 minutes. Serve immediately.

Makes 2 servings. _Per serving: 395 calories._

Vegetable-Cheese Platter

See Menu Plans for Weeks 15 and 39.

5 oz (150 g) curd cheese
2½ fl oz (75 ml) low-fat natural yogurt
½ teaspoon prepared mustard
¼ teaspoon salt
½ clove garlic, crushed
pinch white pepper
2 tablespoons grated carrot
2 tablespoons chopped green pepper
2 tablespoons chopped celery
6 oz (180 g) cucumber, peeled and cut lengthwise into quarters
2 eggs, hard-boiled and cut lengthwise into quarters
8 small celery sticks
2 medium tomatoes, cut into 8 wedges
chopped parsley to garnish

Combine cheese with yogurt, mustard, salt, garlic, and pepper. Add carrot, green pepper and chopped celery; mix well and chill for 1 hour. Spoon cheese mixture on to centre of serving plate. Cut each cucumber quarter in half crosswise. Arrange cucumber spears, eggs, celery sticks and tomato wedges alternately around edge of plate. Garnish with parsley.

Makes 2 servings. _Per serving: 255 calories._

Cinnamon-Cheese Toast
See Menu Plans for Weeks 5, 20, 32 and various other weeks.

2½ oz (75 g) cottage cheese

artificial sweetener to equal 1 teaspoon sugar

pinch ground cinnamon

1 slice (1 oz/30 g) brown bread, toasted

1 teaspoon desiccated coconut

Mix cottage cheese with sweetener and cinnamon. Spread on toast. Sprinkle with coconut; grill for 2–3 minutes or until bubbly.

Makes 1 serving.   *Per serving: 160 calories.*

Cheese and Vegetable Risotto
See Menu Plan for Week 24.

1½ oz (45 g) carrots, chopped

1½ oz (45 g) peas

1½ oz (45 g) turnips, chopped

1½ oz (45 g) swede, chopped

1 oz (30 g) onion, chopped

¾ oz (20 g) long grain rice

8 fl oz (240 ml) mixed vegetable juice

1 stock cube

3 oz (90 g) Cheddar cheese, grated

Put carrots, peas, turnips, swede and onion in a saucepan; add rice, mixed vegetable juice and stock cube. Bring to the boil; stir, reduce heat, cover pan and simmer gently for about 20 minutes until vegetables are tender and liquid absorbed. Place on warmed plate, sprinkle with grated cheese and serve at once.

Makes 1 serving.   *Per serving: 510 calories.*

Poultry and Veal

The delicate flavours of chicken and veal lend themselves to a variety of sauces, seasonings and accompaniments. We have created some delicious recipes with an international flair.

Chicken Capri with Potatoes
See Menu Plan for Week 15.

2 teaspoons margarine	
3 oz (90 g) red pepper, seeded and cut into 1-inch (2.5-cm) pieces	
6 oz (180 g) cooked potatoes, cut into large cubes	
8 oz (240 g) skinned, cooked chicken, cut into ½-inch (1-cm) cubes	
½ small clove garlic	
¼ teaspoon salt	
8 oz (240 g) canned tomatoes, pureed	
½ teaspoon oregano	
¼ teaspoon basil	
pinch thyme	

Melt margarine in small pan. Add red pepper; cover and cook over low heat about 5 minutes – pepper should still be crisp. Combine pepper, potatoes and chicken in deep 3-pint (1.75-litre) casserole. Chop garlic with salt. Using flat side of knife, mash garlic and salt together to form a paste. Combine garlic paste with pureed tomatoes, oregano, basil and thyme. Add to casserole and stir to combine. Cover and bake 25–30 minutes at 350°F, 180°C, Gas Mark 4, or until heated through.

Makes 2 servings. *Per serving: 295 calories.*

Chicken Provencale

See Menu Plans for Weeks 8 and 25.

2 teaspoons olive oil

1 lb (480 g) skinned chicken portions

6 oz (180 g) mushrooms, sliced

6 oz (180 g) tomatoes, skinned, seeded and chopped

6 oz (180 g) green or red peppers, sliced

4 oz (120 g) onion, sliced

1 clove garlic, crushed

1 teaspoon oregano

pinch salt and pepper

4 teaspoons white wine

8 black olives, stoned and sliced

Heat oil in non-stick frying pan, add chicken portions and saute gently until lightly browned. Remove chicken and set aside. In same pan saute all vegetables with garlic until tender. Add oregano, salt and pepper. Arrange chicken and vegetables in small casserole; add wine. Cover and bake at 375°F, 190°C, Gas Mark 5, for 45 minutes. Garnish with black olives.
Makes 2 servings.   *Per serving: 290 calories.*

Shredded Chicken with Peanut Sauce

See Menu Plan for Week 40.

1 teaspoon vegetable oil

3 oz (90 g) skinned and boned chicken breast, cut into thin strips

1 oz (30 g) onion, finely chopped

1 clove garlic, crushed

2 tablespoons crunchy-style peanut butter

2 tablespoons each lemon juice and soy sauce

artificial sweetener to taste

dash chilli sauce

Heat vegetable oil in wok or non-stick frying pan until hot. Stir-fry strips of chicken for about 3 minutes or until firm to the touch. With a slotted spoon remove chicken and reserve. Add onion to wok or non-stick pan and stir-fry 2 minutes or until onion becomes translucent. Add garlic and continue to stir-fry until garlic becomes golden. Remove wok or non-stick pan from heat, stir in remaining ingredients, including chicken, and cook until heated through.

Makes 1 serving.   *Per serving: 340 calories.*

Chicken Kebabs

See Menu Plans for Weeks 6 and 35.

2 oz (60 g) onion, sliced

2 fl oz (60 ml) cider vinegar

1 teaspoon soy sauce

5 peppercorns, crushed

1 clove garlic, split

1 bay leaf

2 fl oz (60 ml) water

10 oz (300 g) skinned and boned chicken breasts, cut into pieces

1 × 4 oz (120 g) onion, cut into 8 wedges

1 × 4 oz (120 g) green pepper, seeded and cut into 8 pieces

8 small tomatoes

¼ teaspoon salt

pinch coarsely ground pepper

lettuce and cucumber to garnish

Combine first 6 ingredients in bowl; add water and stir to combine. Add the chicken, cover and refrigerate overnight. Remove chicken and discard marinade. Thread each of four 9-inch (27-cm) skewers with 3 oz (180 g) chicken pieces, 2 onion wedges, 2 green pepper pieces, and 2 small tomatoes, alternating chicken with vegetables. Sprinkle with salt and pepper. Place on rack in grill pan and grill about 8 minutes; turn and grill 5–8 minutes longer or until chicken is tender. Serve kebabs with lettuce and cucumber.

Makes 2 servings.   *Per serving: 220 calories.*

Turkey Oriental
See Menu Plan for Week 42.

8 oz (240 g) can pineapple chunks, drained and juice reserved
2 tablespoons tomato puree
1 tablespoon cornflour blended with 3 fl oz (90 ml) water
1 tablespoon soy sauce
8 oz (240 g) skinned and boned cooked turkey, cut into 2-inch (5-cm) strips
6 oz (180 g) small tomatoes, halved
1 medium green pepper, seeded, cut into 1-inch (2.5-cm) pieces
3 oz (90 g) drained canned water chestnuts, thinly sliced
3 oz (90 g) peas

In large pan combine pineapple juice, tomato puree, cornflour, water and soy sauce. Cook over low heat, stirring constantly with wire whisk, until mixture thickens. Add pineapple chunks, turkey and vegetables; cover and cook until heated (green pepper should be tender-crisp).

Makes 2 servings.   *Per serving: 285 calories.*

Ginger-Grilled Chicken
See Menu Plans for Weeks 11 and 33

2 teaspoons soy sauce
1 teaspoon grated fresh ginger root
1 clove garlic, crushed
2 × 5 oz (150 g) skinned and boned chicken breasts

Combine soy sauce, ginger and garlic. Lift skin and brush chicken with soy mixture; turn and brush underside. Cover and let stand at room temperature 1 hour. Grill chicken on rack, skin-side down, 10 minutes. Turn and grill 8–10 minutes longer or until chicken is tender. Remove and discard skin before serving.

Makes 2 servings.   *Per serving: 165 calories.*

Chicken Stir-Fry
See Menu Plan for Week 49.

2 teaspoons vegetable oil
5 oz (150 g) skinned and boned chicken breast
1½ oz (45 g) onion, sliced
1½ oz (45 g) mushrooms, sliced
3 oz (90 g) bean sprouts
2 teaspoons soy sauce
1 teaspoon arrowroot or cornflour
4 fl oz (120 ml) chicken stock made with ¼ stock cube

Heat oil in wok or deep frying pan. Cut chicken into fine strips. Add to oil and saute for 3 minutes. Add onions and mushrooms and saute for 2–3 minutes. Add bean sprouts and saute for a further minute; sprinkle on soy sauce. Mix arrowroot or cornflour with the stock. Pour this over chicken and stir well. Cover and simmer for a further 10 minutes. Serve at once.
Makes 1 serving.   *Per serving: 295 calories.*

Sesame Chicken with Green Beans
See Menu Plans for Weeks 1, 26 and 32.

2 teaspoons olive oil
½ teaspoon sesame seeds
8 oz (240 g) skinned and boned cooked chicken, cut into ¼-inch (0.5-cm) strips
2 teaspoons desiccated coconut, toasted
½ teaspoon salt
pinch pepper
12 oz (360 g) cooked whole green beans

Heat non-stick pan. Add olive oil and sesame seeds; cook over medium heat, stirring frequently, until seeds turn light brown. Add chicken and saute until pieces are heated. Stir in coconut, salt and pepper. Serve over hot green beans.
Makes 2 servings.   *Per serving: 280 calories.*

Chicken Teriyaki

See Menu Plan for Week 12.

2½ fl oz (75 ml) apple juice

2 tablespoons soy sauce

1 tablespoon cider vinegar

1 teaspoon honey

½ teaspoon grated orange rind

¼ teaspoon fresh ginger root, finely chopped

10 oz (300 g) skinned and boned chicken breasts, cut into ½-inch (1-cm) cubes

1 teaspoon vegetable oil

Combine first 6 ingredients, add chicken. Cover and refrigerate overnight or at least 6 hours, stirring occasionally. Heat oil in medium frying pan; remove chicken from marinade and saute in heated oil 8 minutes, stirring often. Add marinade; cook 2 minutes longer.

Makes 2 servings.   *Per serving: 210 calories.*

Sweet and Sour Chicken Stir-Fry

See Menu Plan for Week 32.

2 teaspoons vegetable oil

8 oz (240 g) cooked chicken, cut into thin strips

salt and pepper

4 oz (120 g) canned crushed pineapple

1 teaspoon honey

1 teaspoon lemon juice

Heat oil in medium non-stick frying pan. Add chicken, half teaspoon salt and pinch pepper. Saute over high heat, stirring occasionally, until chicken begins to brown. Combine pineapple and honey; add to chicken and saute 3 minutes more. Remove pan from heat and stir in lemon juice; serve at once.

Makes 2 servings.   *Per serving: 245 calories.*

Chicken Hotpot
See Menu Plan for Week 40.

1½ teaspoons margarine
5 oz (150 g) skinned and boned chicken
¼ chicken stock cube dissolved in 6 fl oz (180 ml) boiling water
3 oz (90 g) tomato, seeded and sliced
1½ oz (45 g) onion, thinly sliced
1 teaspoon dry white wine
1 clove garlic, crushed
½ teaspoon sugar
3 oz (90 g) sweetcorn

Melt margarine in a thick-based or non-stick saucepan, add chicken portion and brown on all sides. Add remaining ingredients except corn; cover and cook gently for about 35 minutes or until chicken is tender. Add corn and cook for about 8–10 minutes more or until heated through, adding a little more water if contents of pan become too dry.

Makes 1 serving. *Per serving: 365 calories.*

Chicken Greek Style
See Menu Plans for Weeks 4 and 27.

6 fl oz (180 ml) chicken stock made with 1 stock cube
2 tablespoons lemon juice
2 × 5-oz (150-g) chicken breasts, skinned and boned
2 teaspoons olive oil
½ teaspoon salt
½ teaspoon oregano
pinch each garlic powder and white pepper

Pour stock and lemon juice into small ovenproof casserole. Rub each chicken breast with 1 teaspoon oil and place in casserole. Sprinkle with seasonings; cover and bake at 350°F, 180°C, Gas Mark 4 for 40 minutes or until tender.

Makes 2 servings. *Per serving: 315 calories.*

Italian Veal and Peppers

See Menu Plan for Week 25.

2 tablespoons vegetable oil
2 lb (960 g) lean stewing veal, cut into 1-inch (2.5-cm) cubes
4 tablespoons tomato puree
½ pint (300 ml) chicken stock, made with 2 stock cubes
8 oz (240 g) onions, sliced
2 cloves garlic, crushed
1 teaspoon basil
1 teaspoon oregano
freshly ground pepper to taste
1 lb (480 g) green peppers, seeded and cut into ½-inch (1-cm) strips

Heat oil in thick-based or non-stick frying pan, add veal and saute 3–4 minutes. Add all remaining ingredients except green peppers. Cover and cook over low heat for 45 minutes. Add peppers and continue cooking for 10 minutes longer or until veal and peppers are tender.

Makes 4 servings.   *Per serving: 360 calories.*

Curried Chicken Salad
See Menu Plan for Week 3.

2 oz (60 g) canned pineapple chunks

4 teaspoons low-calorie mayonnaise

1 teaspoon lemon juice

¼ teaspoon curry powder

pinch each salt and white pepper

8 oz (240 g) skinned and boned cooked chicken, cut into 1-inch (2.5-cm) pieces

4 oz (120 g) cucumber, peeled and chopped

½ medium apple, cored and diced

2 × 3-oz (90-g) green peppers, cut into halves lengthwise and seeded

lettuce leaves

Combine first 5 ingredients. Add chicken, cucumber and apple; toss to combine. Divide mixture into 4 equal portions and place 1 portion in each pepper half. Serve each person 2 stuffed pepper halves on lettuce leaves.

Makes 2 servings. *Per serving: 230 calories.*

Meats

Looking for something more interesting than plain beefburgers? Our recipes use a variety of meats and cover a range of cooking techniques that are at your fingertips.

Sweet and Sour Pork Fillet
See Menu Plan for Week 47.

10 oz (300 g) lean pork fillet
juice of 1 lemon
2 teaspoons corn oil
1 clove garlic, crushed
8 oz (240 g) beansprouts
4 oz (120 g) mushrooms, thinly sliced
3 oz (90 g) red pepper, thinly sliced
8 oz (240 g) canned pineapple chunks with 4 tablespoons juice
2 tablespoons soy sauce
1 tablespoon wine vinegar
1 teaspoon brown sugar
2 spring onions, chopped

Grill pork fillet under medium heat for 12–15 minutes, or until cooked, turning once. Moisten during cooking time with lemon juice if fillet seems dry. Slice cooked pork thinly, cover with foil and set aside in a warm place. In a large non-stick frying pan or wok, heat oil and saute garlic over a high heat. Add vegetables and saute for 30 seconds. Add the pineapple and juice, soy sauce, wine vinegar, brown sugar and remaining lemon juice. Cover and cook for 3 minutes. Arrange sliced pork fillet on top of vegetables in a serving dish and sprinkle with chopped spring onions.
Makes 2 servings.   *Per serving: 330 calories.*

Ham and Turkey Casserole
See Menu Plan for Week 42.

4 oz (120 g) skinned and boned cooked turkey, chopped
4 oz (120 g) cooked ham, chopped
4 oz (120 g) cooked tagliatelle
3 oz (90 g) green pepper, chopped, blanched
1 oz (30 g) low-fat dry milk, mixed with 4 fl oz (120 ml) water
1 tablespoon chopped parsley
2 teaspoons grated Parmesan cheese
pinch pepper

Combine all ingredients; mix thoroughly. Spoon into medium casserole; cover with foil. Bake at 400°F, 200°C, Gas Mark 6 until throughly heated, about 25–30 minutes.

Makes 2 servings.   *Per serving: 335 calories.*

Chicken and Pork Meatballs
See Menu Plan for Week 50.

5 oz (150 g) lean boned pork, cut into pieces
5 oz (150 g) skinned and boned chicken, cut into pieces
¾ teaspoon salt
½ clove garlic, finely chopped
¼ teaspoon tarragon
pinch pepper
3 oz (90 g) cooked potatoes, diced
1 teaspoon margarine

Either finely mince pork and chicken or process in bowl of food processor; add salt, garlic, tarragon and pepper, and mix well. Using a spoon, mash potatoes into meat mixture. Shape mixture into 6 or 8 equal balls; transfer to rack on baking sheet and bake at 350°F, 180°C, Gas Mark 4 for 35 minutes or until cooked through. Melt margarine in frying pan; add meatballs and brown, turning frequently.

Makes 2 servings.   *Per serving: 250 calories.*

Orange Lamb with Rosemary
See Menu Plan for Week 16.

5 oz (150 g) boneless lamb, cubed

1 small onion, chopped

1 teaspoon vegetable oil

6 fl oz (180 ml) chicken stock, made with ½ stock cube

1 medium orange, peeled and thinly sliced

1 tablespoon lemon juice

½ teaspoon crushed rosemary leaves

pinch salt and pepper

On a rack in a grill pan, cook lamb until rare, about 10 minutes; in a non-stick pan saute onion in oil until lightly browned. Add lamb and all remaining ingredients; stir to combine. Cover and cook over gentle heat for 45–50 minutes or until lamb is tender. Adjust seasoning.

Makes 1 serving.   *Per serving: 405 calories.*

Sweet and Sour Liver
See Menu Plan for Week 7.

2½ fl oz (75 ml) pineapple juice

2 teaspoons wine vinegar

1½ teaspoons soy sauce

pinch each ground ginger and ground allspice

1 teaspoon cornflour, blended with 2 teaspoons water

1 teaspoon vegetable oil

2 tablespoons finely chopped onion

10 oz (300 g) lamb's liver, cut into ¼-inch (0·5-cm) thick slices

2 teaspoons chopped parsley

salt and pepper

In small saucepan combine pineapple juice, vinegar, soy sauce, ginger and allspice. Heat. Stir in blended cornflour. Cook over medium heat, stirring constantly, until sauce comes just to the boil and begins to thicken. Keep warm. Grease frying pan with vegetable oil. Sprinkle onion over bottom of frying pan. Place liver slices over onion and sprinkle with parsley and pinch each salt and pepper. Cook about 2 minutes, then turn slices over. Sprinkle with pinch each salt and pepper and cook about 1–2 minutes longer or until liver is slightly pink inside when cut with a knife. Transfer slices to serving plate and spoon sauce over liver.

Makes 2 servings.   _Per serving: 300 calories._

Pork Goulash
See Menu Plan for Week 5.

1¼ lb (600 g) pork fillet, cut into 1½-inch (4-cm) cubes
8 oz (240 g) onions, sliced
1 tablespoon paprika
3 tablespoons tomato puree
4 fl oz (120 ml) water (optional)
1 lb (480 g) canned sauerkraut, rinsed and drained
½ teaspoon salt
pinch ground red pepper (optional)
5 fl oz (150 ml) low-fat natural yogurt
1 teaspoon cornflour
sprig of parsley to garnish

Grill pork on rack in grill pan for 6 minutes, turning to brown evenly. Cook onions in non-stick saucepan until lightly browned. Stir in paprika. Add tomato puree, pork and water; cover and simmer for 10 minutes, stirring occasionally. Place sauerkraut in separate saucepan with water to cover; bring to the boil. Boil 5 minutes; drain and add to pork mixture with salt and red pepper if desired. Stir well and heat through. Mix yogurt with cornflour, stir into pork mixture and cook, stirring constantly, until just thickened. Garnish with parsley.

Makes 4 servings.   _Per serving: 330 calories._

Lemon-Minted Lamb

See Menu Plans for Weeks 35 and 42.

2 teaspoons olive oil

2 small cloves garlic, chopped

4 fl oz (120 ml) water

1 tablespoon lemon juice

½ teaspoon salt

pinch freshly ground pepper

2 tablespoons fresh mint leaves, chopped, or 1 teaspoon dried

2 × 6 oz (180 g) lamb chops

Heat oil in small pan; add garlic and saute. Remove from heat and cool a moment. Stir in water, lemon juice, salt and pepper; sprinkle mint over mixture and simmer about 10 minutes. Place chops on rack in grill pan, under medium heat. Grill 4 minutes on each side or until done to taste. Transfer chops to serving dish and pour lemon-mint sauce over meat.

Makes 2 servings.   *Per serving: 280 calories.*

Lamb Kebabs

See Menu Plan for Week 27.

1¼ lb (600 g) boneless lamb, cut into cubes

10 fl oz (300 ml) low-fat natural yogurt

juice of 1 lemon

12 oz (360 g) small tomatoes, halved

8 oz (240 g) button mushrooms

6 oz (180 g) green pepper, cut into 8 pieces, and blanched

2 sticks celery, each stick cut into 4, and blanched

6 oz (180 g) small whole onions, peeled and blanched

garlic salt to taste

Marinate cubed lamb in yogurt and lemon juice for 6–8 hours, or overnight. Thread 4 kebab skewers with alternating pieces of meat and vegetables, reserving the remaining marinade. Season completed kebabs with garlic salt. Arrange skewers on a rack in a baking tin and cook in the oven at 375°F, 190°C, Gas Mark 5 for about 30 minutes. Heat reserved marinade gently in small pan, but do not boil. Use as a sauce to accompany the kebabs. Serve with green salad.

Makes 4 servings.   _Per serving: 305 calories._

Meatball and Vegetable Stir-Fry
See Menu Plan for Week 48.

1¼ lb (600 g) lean minced beef

8 teaspoons vegetable oil

1 slice fresh ginger root, finely chopped

1 clove garlic, finely chopped

8 oz (240 g) broccoli, broken into sprigs

8 oz (240 g) cauliflower, broken into sprigs

8 oz (240 g) green beans, sliced

8 oz (240 g) courgettes, thinly sliced

1 teaspoon sugar

½ teaspoon salt

1 tablespoon soy sauce

8 teaspoons red wine

5 fl oz (150 ml) water

2 teaspoons cornflour blended with 2 teaspoons water

1 lb (480 g) cooked rice

Form mince into small balls and cook on rack under medium grill for approximately 6–8 minutes turning to brown all sides; remove from grill and set aside. Heat oil in large non-stick pan; add ginger root and garlic; saute over low heat without colouring. Add broccoli, cauliflower, beans and courgettes. Cook, stirring, 2–3 minutes. Add sugar, salt, soy sauce, wine, water and meatballs. Cover and simmer for approximately 5 minutes; add cornflour paste; adjust seasonings. Cook, stirring until thickened. Serve at once with rice.

Makes 4 servings.   _Per serving: 585 calories._

Mexican Beef Patties

See Menu Plan for Week 26.

3 oz (90 g) button mushrooms, sliced

1 teaspoon chopped chives

2 teaspoons finely chopped celery

2 teaspoons finely chopped red pepper

5 oz (150 g) minced beef

2 oz (60 g) Cheddar cheese, grated

2 tablespoons chopped parsley

2 teaspoons Worcestershire sauce

1 teaspoon salt

pinch pepper

In small non-stick frying pan, cook mushrooms, chives, celery and red pepper until vegetables are soft and accumulated liquid evaporated. Mix with remaining ingredients. Form into 2 patties; grill on rack in grill pan, turning once, until done to taste.

Makes 2 servings.   *Per serving: 280 calories.*

Casseroled Liver

See Menu Plan for Week 29.

4 slices (4 oz/120 g) white bread, made into crumbs

4 teaspoons onion flakes

2 tablespoons chopped parsley

rind of 2 lemons, grated

8 teaspoons low-fat spread

juice of 2 lemons

1¼ lb (600 g) lamb's liver, cut into thin slices

1 pint (600 ml) beef stock, made with 2 stock cubes

2 tablespoons cornflour blended with 2 tablespoons water

Combine breadcrumbs, onion flakes, parsley and lemon rind. Melt low-fat spread in cup over hot water, add lemon juice, pour into breadcrumb mixture and mix well. Leave to cool. Lay slices of liver flat, divide stuffing evenly between each piece, roll up and secure with a cocktail stick. If using thick slices of liver, slit down centre to make pocket and fill with stuffing. Place in ovenproof casserole, pour stock over liver and bake at 425°F, 220°C, Gas Mark 7 for 30 minutes. Remove liver from stock and keep warm. Put blended cornflour into a small pan, pour in stock and bring to the boil, stirring. Adjust seasoning. Serve sauce with liver.

Makes 4 servings.   *Per serving: 390 calories.*

Curried Beef
See Menu Plan for Week 37.

8 oz (240 g) minced beef
1 teaspoon vegetable oil
2 oz (60 g) onion, diced
½ medium cooking apple, peeled, cored and chopped
½ oz (15 g) raisins
2–3 teaspoons lemon juice
1 teaspoon curry powder
pinch salt
7 fl oz (210 ml) water
1 teaspoon arrowroot

Form mince into several small flat cakes and put on rack in grill pan. Grill, turning occasionally, 5 minutes or until thoroughly browned; transfer to a bowl and mash with fork until crumbly. Heat oil in saucepan; add onion and saute until softened. Stir in grilled meat, apple, raisins, 2 teaspoons lemon juice, curry powder and salt. Add 6 fl oz (180 ml) water and mix well. Simmer partially covered, stirring occasionally, for 45 minutes or until meat is tender. Mix arrowroot with remaining water; stir into meat mixture and cook, stirring constantly, until thickened. Add additional lemon juice to taste.

Makes 2 servings.   *Per serving: 325 calories.*

Pork Chops with Orange Slices
See Menu Plan for Week 29.

8 × 3 oz (90 g) pork chops, trimmed

salt and pepper to taste

8 oz (240 g) onion, thinly sliced

4 tablespoons tomato puree mixed with 8 fl oz (240 ml) water

4 teaspoons grated lemon rind

4 medium oranges, sliced in rings

1 teaspoon marjoram

parsley to garnish

Season chops and grill on rack 4 inches (10 cm) from source of heat for 4–5 minutes on each side until brown. Turn off grill and place chops in small baking dish. Add onions, tomato puree, water and lemon rind. Arrange orange rings on top, sprinkle with marjoram and bake, covered, at 400°F, 200°C, Gas Mark 6 for 20–30 minutes or until meat is cooked through and onions are tender. Serve piping hot garnished with parsley.

Makes 4 servings.   *Per serving: 240 calories.*

Barbecued Pork
See Menu Plan for Week 35.

1¼ lb (600 g) lean pork slices without bone

8 oz (240 g) canned tomatoes, pureed

2 tablespoons chilli sauce

4 teaspoons Worcestershire sauce

4 teaspoons lemon juice

2 teaspoons prepared mustard

½ teaspoon paprika

pinch each pepper, ground cumin and salt

Trim away fat and arrange pork slices in baking pan. Combine remaining ingredients, mixing well. Pour over pork; cover and refrigerate overnight. Remove pork from pan and scrape off sauce. Transfer remaining sauce to small saucepan and set aside. Place pork on rack in baking pan; bake at 325°F, 160°C, Gas Mark 3 for 1¼ hours. While pork is baking, bring sauce to the boil; reduce heat and simmer 15 minutes. Transfer pork to serving dish and top with sauce.

Makes 4 servings.   *Per serving: 270 calories.*

Lamb Stew
See Menu Plan for Week 40.

5 oz (150 g) fillet of lamb, cubed
½ teaspoon olive oil
1 oz (30 g) onion, chopped
½ teaspoon flour
3 fl oz (90 ml) chicken stock made with ¼ stock cube
1 oz (30 g) carrots, sliced
1 oz (30 g) celery, sliced
1 clove garlic, finely chopped
½ bay leaf, crumbled
pinch thyme
2 oz (60 g) cooked pearl barley
1 tablespoon chopped parsley

Grill lamb cubes on a rack in a grill pan, 4 inches (10 cm) from source of heat until cooked through. Heat oil in a non-stick saucepan and add onion, stir and cook until golden. Sprinkle with flour and continue to cook, stirring, until onions are browned. Add lamb cubes and remaining ingredients except chopped parsley. Stir, cover and simmer about 25 minutes, or until lamb is tender. Garnish with chopped parsley.

Makes 1 serving.   *Per serving: 350 calories.*

Lamb's Liver Creole

See Menu Plans for Weeks 2, 17 and 44.

3 oz (90 g) onions, diced

1½ oz (45 g) green pepper, chopped

12 oz (360 g) canned tomatoes

¼ teaspoon salt

pinch ground cumin

10 oz (300 g) lamb's liver, sliced

Combine first 5 ingredients in saucepan; bring to the boil; cover and simmer until onion is cooked. Meanwhile grill liver about 2 minutes or until top is browned. Turn and grill for 2 minutes more. Add liver to tomato mixture. Heat 2 minutes and serve.

Makes 2 servings.   *Per serving: 290 calories.*

Liver Pate

See Menu Plans for Weeks 10 and 25.

1¼ lb (600 g) chicken livers

juice of 2 lemons

4 teaspoons Worcestershire sauce

1 teaspoon each salt and nutmeg

½ teaspoon garlic powder

4 slices (1 oz/30 g each) white bread, made into crumbs

lettuce leaves

4 medium apples, cored and sliced

1 tablespoon lemon juice

Combine first 5 ingredients in saucepan. Cover and simmer for 10 minutes. Stir in breadcrumbs. Transfer to blender container and puree until smooth. Turn into 1-lb (480-g) loaf tin lined with greaseproof or non-stick paper; smooth top; chill for 2–3 hours. Turn out on to serving plate; slice. Arrange lettuce leaves and apple slices tossed in lemon juice around pate.

Makes 4 servings.   *Per serving: 305 calories.*

Irish Stew
See Menu Plan for Week 11.

1¼ lb (600 g) lean fillet of lamb

1 pint (480 ml) chicken stock made with 1 stock cube

12 oz (360 g) potatoes, sliced

8 oz (240 g) onions, sliced

2 tablespoons chopped parsley and thyme, mixed

1 teaspoon salt

pinch pepper

Trim all visible fat from meat and cut into bite-sized pieces. Put meat on a rack in grill pan and cook, turning once, until all juices stop running. Meanwhile, put remaining ingredients in saucepan; add meat, cover and cook approximately 30–40 minutes or until meat and vegetables are tender.

Makes 4 servings.   *Per serving: 405 calories.*

Frankfurter Stir-Fry
See Menu Plan for Week 33.

2 teaspoons vegetable oil

2 oz (60 g) onion, sliced

8 oz (240 g) frankfurters, cut diagonally into 1-inch (2.5-cm) pieces

3 oz (90 g) peas, blanched

3 oz (90 g) carrot, in matchsticks, blanched

1½ oz (45 g) celery, sliced diagonally, blanched

8 oz (240 g) canned pineapple chunks

1 teaspoon soy sauce

1 teaspoon cornflour mixed with 3 tablespoons water

Heat oil in non-stick pan; add onion and saute until tender. Add frankfurters, peas, carrot and celery, and cook, stirring constantly, for 5 minutes. Add pineapple chunks and soy sauce; cook 2 minutes longer, stirring constantly. Add cornflour paste and cook until sauce thickens.

Makes 2 servings.   *Per serving: 300 calories.*

Beef and Corn Casserole
See Menu Plan for Week 1.

8 oz (240 g) cooked beef, minced

6 oz (180 g) drained canned sweet corn

3 oz (90 g) red pepper, seeded and cut into thin strips, blanched

4 fl oz (120 ml) beef stock made with ½ stock cube

pinch pepper

In a medium casserole combine beef, corn, red pepper strips, stock and pepper; toss well. Cover and bake for 30 minutes at 350°F, 180°C, Gas Mark 4.

Makes 2 servings. *Per serving: 380 calories.*

Kidneys in Red Wine
See Menu Plan for Week 48.

1¼ lb (600 g) lamb's kidneys

8 teaspoons margarine

2 medium onions, chopped

8 oz (240 g) mushrooms, sliced

1 teaspoon tarragon

2 tablespoons chopped parsley

8 tablespoons red wine

pepper to taste

1 lb (480 g) cooked rice

Remove outer membranes from kidneys; split in half lengthwise and snip out cores with scissors. Wash well. Drain. Melt margarine in non-stick frying pan and saute kidneys over high heat 3–5 minutes. Remove and keep warm. Add onions to pan, saute 5 minutes; add mushrooms and herbs; saute for further 5 mintues until onion is translucent. Add wine to pan and bring to the boil. Return kidneys to pan, season with pepper; cover and cook for 10 minutes until very hot. Serve with rice.

Makes 4 servings. *Per serving: 390 calories.*

Chicken Livers Sauteed in Wine
See Menu Plans for Weeks 12 and 36.

2 teaspoons margarine

2 oz (60 g) onion, sliced

1 clove garlic, crushed

10 oz (300 g) chicken livers

1 tablespoon red wine

pinch each salt and pepper

Melt margarine in medium frying pan; add onion and garlic and saute until tender. Add chicken livers and saute, stirring occasionally, for 5–7 minutes or until livers are cooked. Add remaining ingredients. Heat and serve.

Makes 2 servings.   *Per serving: 295 calories.*

Savoury Mince with Noodles
See Menu Plan for Week 28.

1 teaspoon sage

1 clove garlic, crushed

1 teaspoon brown sugar

½ teaspoon curry powder

1 teaspoon Worcestershire sauce

2 tablespoons tomato puree

½ pint (300 ml) water

½ beef stock cube

4 oz (120 g) onion, chopped

4 oz (120 g) cooked minced beef

2 oz (60 g) hot cooked noodles

1 teaspoon vegetable oil

Place first 9 ingredients in a saucepan and bring to the boil. Simmer until sauce is thick, add mince, mix well and simmer for a further 10 minutes. Toss noodles in oil, arrange on serving dish and serve with sauce.

Makes 1 serving.   *Per serving: 430 calories.*

Beef Pie
See Menu Plans for Weeks 9 and 25.

12 oz (360 g) cubed shin of beef
12 fl oz (360 ml) beef stock made with 1 stock cube
pinch mixed herbs
4 oz (120 g) carrots, sliced
3 oz (90 g) mushrooms, sliced
4 oz (120 g) celery, chopped
4 oz (120 g) onions, chopped
12 oz (360 g) potatoes
4 teaspoons flour
4 teaspoons margarine
4 oz (120 g) Cheddar cheese, grated
1 tablespoon chopped chives

Place beef cubes on rack in grill pan; grill until browned on all sides. Transfer beef to medium saucepan; add 10 fl oz (300 ml) stock and herbs. Cover and simmer for approximately 1½ hours. Add carrots, mushrooms, celery and onions. Simmer for further ½ hour until vegetables and meat are just tender. Meanwhile put potatoes in pan, cover with cold water, bring to the boil; cover and cook until tender; drain. In small bowl gradually add remaining stock to flour, stirring constantly to form a smooth paste; add to beef and vegetables. Bring to the boil, stirring. Cook for 2 minutes. Spoon equal amounts of mixture into 4 individual casseroles. Mash potatoes with margarine; stir in cheese and chives. Pipe or spoon potato mixture over meat in casseroles. Bake at 375°F, 190°C, Gas Mark 5 for 20 minutes, or cook under hot grill until potatoes are lightly browned.

Makes 4 servings. _Per serving: 370 calories._

Fish

Fish dishes range from the delicate to the hardy. You can be as creative as your imagination allows. Use fish in casseroles, salads and soups, or as kebabs. Fish can be poached, grilled, baked or sauteed. Serve any of our taste-tempting suggestions and you won't have to 'fish' for compliments.

Trout with Mushroom Stuffing
See Menu Plan for Week 34.

1 teaspoon margarine
1 tablespoon finely chopped spring onion
3 oz (90 g) mushrooms, chopped
2 tablespoons celery, finely chopped
1 tablespoon chopped red pepper
1 teaspoon lemon juice
¼ teaspoon salt
1 tablespoon chopped parsley
2 teaspoons low-calorie mayonnaise
1 teaspoon French mustard
2 × 6 oz (180 g) trout, filleted

Melt margarine in small non-stick pan; add spring onion and saute briefly, being careful not to burn. Add mushrooms, celery, red pepper, lemon juice and salt; saute until tender. Remove from heat and stir in parsley, mayonnaise and mustard. Arrange fish fillets in baking dish. Spread vegetable mixture over fillets; cover and bake at 400°F, 200°C, Gas Mark 6 for about 20 minutes or until fish flakes easily when tested with a fork.

Makes 2 servings.   *Per serving: 195 calories.*

Cod with Lemon

See Menu Plan for Week 11.

2 cod fillets, 5 oz (150 g) each
1 teaspoon vegetable oil
pinch salt
pinch each white pepper and paprika
4 lemon slices
1 tablespoon small capers
2 teaspoons low-fat spread
2 teaspoons chopped parsley

Place fish, skin-side up in flameproof dish; brush with half the oil. Grill under medium grill until starting to brown. Turn carefully; brush with remaining oil and sprinkle with salt and pepper. Grill for further 3–5 minutes until nearly cooked. Add lemon slices and capers and cook for 2–3 minutes to lightly brown lemon. Top each serving with 1 teaspoon low-fat spread; allow to melt. Sprinkle each with 1 teaspoon chopped parsley.

Makes 2 servings.   *Per serving: 160 calories.*

Cod-Vegetable Bake

See Menu Plans for Weeks 6 and 36.

8 oz (240 g) courgettes, sliced into ¼-inch (0.5-cm) thick slices
4 tablespoons tomato puree, mixed with 5 fl oz (150 ml) water
1 small clove garlic, finely chopped with pinch salt
pinch each summer savory, thyme and pepper
10 oz (300 g) cod fillets
6 oz (180 g) broccoli florets, blanched (optional)
1 teaspoon lemon juice
pinch salt

Blanch courgettes for 2 minutes in boiling salted water until tender-crisp. Drain; rinse with cold water and set aside. In small saucepan combine tomato puree, water, garlic, herbs and pepper. Bring to the boil; reduce heat and simmer 5 minutes. Set aside. Preheat oven to 350°F, 180°C, Gas Mark 4. Place fillets in bottom of ovenproof dish (not aluminium). If desired, place broccoli florets alongside fillets. Sprinkle fillets with lemon juice and salt. Arrange courgette slices over fish in an overlapping pattern. Be sure fish is completely covered. Spoon tomato mixture around edge of fish and vegetables. Cover with foil and bake for 20–25 minutes or until fish flakes easily. When serving, spoon tomato sauce over vegetables.

Makes 2 servings.   *Per serving: 175 calories.*

Baked Prawns Thermidor

See Menu Plan for Week 25.

4 tablespoons margarine
3 oz (90 g) mushrooms, sliced
4 tablespoons flour
½ teaspoon dry mustard
10 fl oz (300 ml) skim milk
8 oz (240 g) peeled prawns
salt and pinch ground red pepper
2 slices (2 oz/60 g) white bread, made into crumbs
2 oz (60 g) Parmesan cheese, grated
2 oz (60 g) Cheddar cheese, grated
½ teaspoon paprika
parsley sprigs to garnish

Melt margarine in non-stick saucepan; add mushrooms. Cook for 5 minutes. Blend in flour and mustard. Cook gently for 1 minute. Remove pan from heat; stir in milk. Return to heat; bring to the boil, stirring constantly. Add prawns; stir to combine. Season with salt and pepper to taste. Transfer mixture to 3-pint (1.75-litre) casserole. Combine breadcrumbs, Parmesan cheese, Cheddar cheese and paprika. sprinkle over prawn mixture. Bake at 400°F, 200°C, Gas Mark 6 for 20 minutes or until top is brown and bubbly. Garnish with parsley sprigs.

Makes 4 servings.   *Per serving: 410 calories.*

Fish and Rice Salad
See Menu Plan for Week 32.

8 oz (240 g) cooked smoked haddock

4 oz (120 g) cooked brown rice

2 tablespoons red pepper, diced

2 teaspoons olive oil

1 teaspoon lemon juice

½ teaspoon salt

pinch thyme

pinch pepper

Place fish, rice and red pepper in medium bowl. Do not combine. Combine oil, lemon juice, salt, thyme and pepper. Pour over fish rice and red pepper. Toss gently to combine, breaking fish into large chunks. Serve at once.

Makes 2 servings. *Per serving: 230 calories.*

Baked Cod
See Menu Plan for Week 29.

12 oz (360 g) tomatoes, skinned

8 oz (240 g) button mushrooms, left whole and washed

8 oz (240 g) onion, chopped

1 teaspoon salt

freshly ground black pepper to taste

4 × 7 oz (210 g) cod steaks

8 teaspoons low-fat spread

chopped parsley

Chop tomatoes and mix with mushrooms, onion and seasoning. Stand fish steaks in a large ovenproof dish. Pile tomato mixture on top, dot with low-fat spread, and cover casserole with lid or aluminium foil. Cook at 400°F, 200°C, Gas Mark 6 for about 30 minutes. Just before serving, sprinkle with chopped parsley.

Makes 4 servings. *Per serving: 225 calories.*

Tuna-Potato Cakes
See Menu Plan for Week 37.

6 oz (180 g) potatoes, finely grated and squeezed to remove excess moisture

2 tablespoons onion

2 teaspoons flour

1 teaspoon lemon juice

4 oz (120 g) drained canned tuna, roughly flaked

2 eggs, beaten

¼ teaspoon salt

¼ teaspoon allspice

pinch pepper

In medium bowl combine potatoes, onion, flour and lemon juice; stir in tuna, eggs, salt, allspice and pepper. Do not overmix (tuna should remain in small chunks). Heat medium non-stick pan over medium heat. Spoon half of potato batter into pan in two equal portions. Form each portion into round cake and brown on both sides. Repeat with remaining batter.
Makes 2 servings.   *Per serving: 295 calories.*

Tuna Boats
See Menu Plan for Week 4.

8 oz (240 g) canned tuna, finely flaked

4 teaspoons mayonnaise

2 tablespoons canned pimiento, diced

4 stoned green olives, thinly sliced

2 teaspoons lemon juice

1 teaspoon relish, any type

4 large celery sticks

Combine tuna and mayonnaise; add pimiento, olives, lemon juice and relish. Stuff each celery stick with quarter of the mixture. Wrap in plastic wrap and chill until ready to use.
Makes 2 servings.   *Per serving: 255 calories.*

Piquant Lemon Sole

See Menu Plan for Week 16.

1 teaspoon margarine, softened
1 teaspoon flour
1 teaspoon relish, any type
1 teaspoon lemon juice
¼ teaspoon Worcestershire sauce
1 × 8 oz (240 g) fillet lemon sole

Combine first 5 ingredients into a chunky paste and spread on lemon sole fillet. Place fish in ovenproof dish; cover and bake at 450°F, 230°C, Gas Mark 8 for 12–16 minutes or until fish is opaque and flakes easily when tested with a fork. Serve with juices in dish.

Makes 1 serving.   *Per serving: 250 calories.*

Soused Herring

See Menu Plans for Weeks 30 and 47.

6 × 6 oz (180 g) herrings, boned
salt and pepper
1 small onion, chopped
8 fl oz (240 ml) white wine vinegar
2 tablespoons water
1 clove garlic, crushed (optional)
1 blade mace
green salad for serving

Clean herrings, cut off heads and tails. Season well with salt and pepper and roll fish up; secure with wooden cocktail sticks. Arrange rolled herrings in shallow ovenproof dish, sprinkle with chopped onion and add vinegar, water, garlic and mace. Cover dish with foil and cook in slow oven, 300°F, 150°C, Gas Mark 2 for 1–1½ hours, or until tender. Cool; remove cocktail sticks before serving. Arrange a salad on serving plate and place fish on top.

Makes 6 servings.   *Per serving: 240 calories.*

Sauteed Prawns and Corn
See Menu Plan for Week 46.

1 teaspoon margarine

1 teaspoon vegetable oil

4 oz (120 g) spring onions, sliced

1 clove garlic, finely chopped

6 oz (180 g) drained canned sweet corn

1 teaspoon each brown sugar and salt

pinch freshly ground pepper

8 oz (240 g) peeled prawns

1 teaspoon cornflour blended with 2 fl oz (60 ml) water

parsley sprigs to garnish

Heat margarine and oil in medium pan. Add spring onions and garlic and saute briefly. Stir in sweet corn, sugar, salt and pepper; cook about 3 minutes. Add prawns and saute 1 minute longer. Add blended cornflour and cook, stirring constantly, until thickened. Serve garnished with chopped parsley.
Makes 2 servings.   *Per serving: 320 calories.*

Salmon Salad
See Menu Plans for Weeks 5, 27, 31, 39 and 44.

1 oz (30 g) onion, finely chopped

½ teaspoon lemon juice

8 oz (240 g) drained, skinned, boned and flaked canned salmon

1 oz (30 g) celery, diced

1 oz (30 g) cucumber, peeled and diced

1 oz (30 g) carrot, grated

4 teaspoons low-calorie mayonnaise

¼ teaspoon salt

pinch white pepper

Combine all ingredients. Mix well. Chill and serve.
Makes 2 servings.   *Per serving: 200 calories.*

Kipper Pate

See Menu Plan for Week 30.

8 oz (240 g) canned kipper fillets, drained

1 oz (30 g) low-fat dry milk

2 tablespoons water

4 teaspoons margarine

cayenne pepper to taste

1 tablespoon lemon juice

lemon and cucumber slices to garnish

Place all ingredients except lemon and cucumber slices in a bowl and mash or pound well until they form a paste. Transfer to a small dish, garnish with lemon and cucumber. Chill well before serving.

Makes 2 servings.   *Per serving: 395 calories.*

Sole Veronique

See Menu Plan for Week 34.

1 teaspoon lemon juice

salt

½ bay leaf

3 peppercorns

5 fl oz (150 ml) water

10 oz (300 g) sole fillets

1 tablespoon margarine

1 tablespoon flour

5 fl oz (150 ml) skim milk

4 teaspoons white wine

6 oz (180 g) small white grapes, cut into halves, deseeded

pinch white pepper

Combine lemon juice, pinch salt, bay leaf and peppercorns in medium frying pan; add water and bring to the boil. Add fillets; reduce heat, cover and simmer 5 minutes until cooked.

Using a slotted spoon, remove fillets and keep warm in serving dish. Strain liquid and reserve 2 fl oz (60 ml). Melt margarine in saucepan over medium heat. Stir in flour and cook, stirring constantly, for 2 minutes. Remove pan from heat; gradually stir in milk and reserved liquid. Return to the boil, stirring constantly, and cook until smooth and thick. Stir in wine, then 5 oz (150 g) grapes and pinch each salt and white pepper. Pour sauce over fish and serve decorated with remaining grapes.

Makes 2 servings. *Per serving: 280 calories.*

Baked Fish Casserole
See Menu Plan for Week 1.

12 oz (360 g) shredded white cabbage, lightly boiled

4 oz (120 g) sliced cooked onions

2 oz (60 g) cooked thinly-sliced carrot

12 oz (360 g) boned cooked halibut, in chunks

pinch garlic salt

2 tablespoons margarine

2 tablespoons flour

10 fl oz (300 ml) skim milk

4 oz (120 g) mature Cheddar cheese

½ teaspoon salt

pinch each white pepper and ground allspice

1 teaspoon chopped fresh parsley

Put vegetables in a large casserole. Add fish and garlic salt and stir gently to combine. Melt margarine in small saucepan; add flour and cook over low heat 2–3 minutes, stirring constantly. Add milk gradually, stirring briskly with wire whisk; continue to stir briskly until sauce is a smooth consistency. Add Cheddar cheese, salt, pepper and allspice. Continue to cook, stirring constantly until sauce has thickened and cheese is melted. Combine sauce with vegetables and fish in casserole; sprinkle with parsley. Cover and bake at 350°F, 180°C, Gas Mark 4 for 30 minutes.

Makes 4 servings. *Per serving: 350 calories.*

Salmon Mousse
See Menu Plans for Weeks 3 and 52.

2 teaspoons unflavoured gelatine
4 tablespoons water
2 tablespoons lemon juice
1 tablespoon finely chopped onion
8 oz (240 g) drained, skinned and boned canned salmon
5 fl oz (150 ml) skim milk
2½ fl oz low-fat natural yogurt
2 tablespoons low-calorie mayonnaise
2 teaspoons chopped fresh dill, or ½ teaspoon dried dill weed (optional)
½ teaspoon each white pepper and salt.

Dissolve gelatine in water in bowl over pan of hot water. Place lemon juice with onion in blender container; puree 30 seconds. Add remaining ingredients except gelatine. Puree until smooth. Finally add gelatine. Pour mixture into a 2-pint (1.2-litre) mould that has been rinsed in cold water. Chill for at least 4 hours. Unmould before serving.

Makes 2 servings.   *Per serving: 255 calories.*

Prawns with Crispy Topping
See Menu Plan for Week 1.

4 teaspoons margarine
1 oz (30 g) red pepper, diced
1 small clove garlic, finely chopped with ½ teaspoon salt
1 lb (480 g) peeled prawns
2 slices (1 oz/30 g each) bread, made into crumbs
1 teaspoon chopped parsley

Melt margarine in large non-stick frying pan; add pepper and garlic and saute over medium heat for 1 minute. Add prawns and saute, turning occasionally, until prawns are heated through; about 2–4 minutes. Using a slotted spoon, remove prawns; keep warm. Stir breadcrumbs into margarine mixture in pan; cook, stirring occasionally until breadcrumbs are golden. Stir in parsley. Divide prawns onto 4 plates. Top each portion of prawns with an equal amount of breadcrumb mixture.

Makes 4 servings. *Per serving: 195 calories.*

Skate with Lemon Sauce
See Menu Plan for Week 30.

½ teaspoon salt
10 fl oz (300 ml) water
3 tablespoons plus 1 teaspoon wine vinegar
1 sachet bouquet garni
6 peppercorns
2 × 6 oz (180 g) wings of skate
4 oz (120 g) onion, sliced
1 teaspoon vegetable oil
juice and rind of 1 lemon
salt and black pepper to taste
1 teaspoon chopped parsley
1 teaspoon thyme
2 teaspoons cornflour blended with 1 tablespoon water

Prepare a court bouillon by dissolving the salt in 8 fl oz (240 ml) water in a saucepan. Add 3 tablespoons vinegar, bouquet garni and peppercorns. Bring to the boil and boil for 5 minutes. Leave to cool. Cut the skate into 4 pieces and place it in a large saucepan. Strain the court bouillon onto the fish. Bring slowly to boiling point, cover the pan and simmer for about 10 minutes. Meanwhile prepare sauce. Saute the sliced onion gently in oil in a non-stick pan until soft. Add 2 fl oz (60 ml) water, lemon juice, 1 teaspoon vinegar, seasoning and herbs to the cooked onion. Bring to the boil, add lemon peel and simmer gently. Stir in cornflour mixture. Stir until thickened. Arrange the cooked skate in a heated serving dish. Pour the prepared sauce over the fish and serve.

Makes 2 servings. *Per serving: 190 calories.*

Fillet of Sole Florentine

See Menu Plans for Weeks 4, 23, 37 and 50.

2 teaspoons margarine
1 tablespoon lemon juice
½ teaspoon salt
½ teaspoon cornflour, blended with 2 tablespoons water
3 oz (90 g) cooked spinach, well drained and chopped
2 oz (60 g) cooked mushrooms, sliced
10 oz (300 g) fillet of sole
pinch each white pepper, garlic powder and paprika
thin lemon slices

Melt margarine in small saucepan, add lemon juice, ¼ teaspoon salt and blended cornflour. Cook, stirring constantly, until thickened. Spread spinach over bottom of shallow, oval-shaped casserole. Sprinkle with ¼ teaspoon salt. Spread mushrooms over spinach; place fish over vegetables and pour lemon sauce over fish. Sprinkle with seasonings; cover and bake at 400°F, 200°C, Gas Mark 6 for 20–30 minutes or until fish flakes when touched with a fork. Then grill for 1 minute. Garnish with lemon slices.

Makes 2 servings.   *Per serving: 175 calories.*

Stir-Fry Tuna
See Menu Plan for Week 40.

1 teaspoon vegetable oil
½ medium red apple, peeled, cored and diced
1 oz (30 g) onion, thinly sliced and separated into rings
4 oz (120 g) canned tuna, broken into chunks
1 teaspoon curry powder
pinch dry mustard
1½ oz (45 g) peas
½ oz (15 g) raisins
2 tablespoons dry white wine

Put oil in thick-based, non-stick frying pan. Add apple and onion and saute for about 1 minute. Add remaining ingredients and cook for about 5 minutes or until mixture is hot and well blended.

Makes 1 serving.   *Per serving: 415 calories.*

Dried Peas/Beans and Peanut Butter

Dried peas and beans are food plants whose pods open along two seams when the seeds within are ripe. The seeds are usually the edible part of the pod. Peas, chick peas (garbanzos), lima beans and soybeans are the best known. High in nutrition, easy to prepare and very economical, they are also delicious. That is probably why they have been cultivated and consumed for over 8,000 years.

N.B. 1 oz (30 g) dried peas/beans yields approximately 3 oz (90 g) cooked.

'Re-fried' Beans
See Menu Plan for Week 38.

2 teaspoons vegetable oil	
3 oz (90 g) onion, chopped	
1 clove garlic, chopped	
12 oz (360 g) drained canned kidney beans	
2 tablespoons tomato puree	
2 teaspoons chilli powder	
pinch ground cumin	
pinch salt	
2 oz (60 g) grated Cheddar cheese	

Heat oil in small pan; add onion and garlic and saute until tender. Add kidney beans, tomato puree, chilli powder, cumin and salt. Cook, stirring often, for 5 minutes. Turn into non-stick casserole. Top with cheese and bake at 350°F, 180°C, Gas Mark 4, for 10–15 minutes or until cheese is melted.

Makes 2 servings.   *Per serving: 300 calories.*

Chick Pea Croquettes

See Menu Plans for Weeks 9, 31 and 38.

12 oz (360 g) drained canned chick peas (garbanzos)

6 tablespoons dried breadcrumbs

½ clove garlic, finely chopped with ½ teaspoon salt

¼ teaspoon each basil, marjoram and thyme

¼ teaspoon hot pepper sauce

pinch paprika pepper

chopped parsley

10 fl oz (300 ml) low-fat natural yogurt

In blender container or bowl of food processor, puree chick peas until finely chopped. Transfer to basin. Add remaining ingredients except yogurt; mix well, making sure seasonings are well distributed. Shape mixture into 10 flat cakes. Place on non-stick baking sheet and bake at 350°F, 180°C, Gas Mark 4 for 15 minutes. Garnish with parsley and serve with yogurt.

Makes 2 servings.   *Per serving: 350 calories.*

Bean Soup

See Menu Plan for Week 38.

6 oz (180 g) potato, diced

6 oz (180 g) onion, chopped

1 pint (600 ml) water

12 oz (360 g) cooked, drained red kidney beans

2 stock cubes

2 teaspoons lemon juice

pinch salt and pepper

fresh chopped parsley

Cook potato and onion in water until soft. Add beans, stock cubes and lemon juice. Puree soup in blender container, return to pan, reheat and season to taste. Serve piping hot sprinkled with parsley.

Makes 2 servings.   *Per serving: 260 calories.*

Sauteed Chick Peas Italian Style

See Menu Plan for Week 23.

1 tablespoon olive oil
2 cloves garlic, crushed
12 oz (360 g) canned chick peas, drained
4 tablespoons tomato puree
6 fl oz (180 ml) water
½ teaspoon oregano
pinch each salt and pepper
2 teaspoons chopped parsley
2 teaspoons grated Parmesan cheese

Heat oil in medium saucepan; add garlic and saute 2 minutes.
Add remaining ingredients except parsley and cheese and cook
20 minutes, stirring frequently. Sprinkle evenly with parsley
and Parmesan cheese.

Makes 2 servings.   *Per serving: 230 calories.*

Mushroom and Lentil Pate

See Menu Plan for Week 38.

2 eggs
4 oz (120 g) lentils, any type, finely ground
8 fl oz (240 ml) water
2 tablespoons grated onion
6 oz (180 g) mushrooms, finely chopped
4 teaspoons margarine
1 large clove garlic
pinch each salt and pepper
juice and grated rind of ½ lemon
1 tablespoon chopped parsley

Hard-boil eggs. Mix ground lentils with half the water in
small, heavy-based saucepan. Cook, stirring constantly over
low heat for 10 minutes, adding more water as necessary, until

lentils cook to a thick paste. Turn out into basin to cool, and mix in grated onion. Cook mushrooms in 2 teaspoons margarine in frying pan over fairly high heat, stirring constantly until beginning to soften. Cool. Shell and chop eggs; mix mushrooms and eggs with lentil mixture and remaining margarine, melted. Rub serving dish well with cut clove of garlic. Season pate with salt, pepper, lemon juice and parsley. Add lemon rind to mixture and mix thoroughly. Spoon into serving dish; cover and refrigerate until needed.

Makes 2 servings. *Per serving: 225 calories.*

Split Pea Soup
See Menu Plan for Week 37.

4 oz (120 g) dried green split peas, soaked overnight and drained
24 fl oz (720 ml) water
½ medium onion, finely chopped
4 oz (120 g) carrots, diced
2 sticks celery, diced
pinch thyme
pinch chervil
pinch white pepper
2 teaspoons margarine
2 teaspoons flour
5 fl oz (150 ml) skim milk
½ teaspoon salt

In medium saucepan combine peas, water and onion. Bring to the boil, cover. Reduce heat and simmer until peas are soft, about 1½-2 hours, or until peas are just cooked. Add carrots, celery, thyme, chervil and pepper to saucepan; simmer until all vegetables are tender, about 20 minutes. Puree in blender container and return to pan. Meanwhile, in small saucepan, melt margarine. Stir in flour and cook 2 minutes. Remove from heat; gradually stir in milk. Bring to the boil, stirring; cook 2 minutes. Briskly stir into blended vegetables. Add salt and heat through – about 5 minutes. Serve at once.

Makes 2 servings. *Per serving: 275 calories.*

Curried Kidney Beans
See Menu Plan for Week 13.

1 tablespoon vegetable oil

3 oz (90 g) onion, chopped

1 medium apple, cored and diced

1 clove garlic, crushed

1 tablespoon flour

2 teaspoons curry powder

8 fl oz (240 ml) chicken stock made with ½ stock cube

12 oz (360 g) canned kidney beans, drained

pinch each salt and pepper

2 tablespoons sliced spring onion

Heat oil in saucepan; add onion, apple and garlic and saute until tender. Stir in flour and curry powder and cook over low heat, stirring constantly, for 2 minutes. Stirring with a wire whisk, gradually add stock; cook, stirring constantly, until sauce thickens. Add kidney beans and cook until heated. Add salt and pepper and garnish with spring onion.

Makes 2 servings.   *Per serving: 255 calories.*

Bean and Cheese Potatoes
See Menu Plan for Week 38.

2 × 6 oz (180 g) potatoes for baking

6 oz (180 g) cooked haricot beans, drained

2 oz (60 g) Leicester cheese, grated

2½ fl oz (75 ml) low-fat natural yogurt

2 teaspoons chopped rosemary

2 teaspoons chopped parsley

1 teaspoon grated lemon rind

pinch salt and pepper

Scrub potatoes well, score with a sharp knife to prevent bursting and bake in moderate oven, 350°F, 180°C, Gas Mark 4 until cooked; approximately 1 hour. When potatoes are soft,

cut in half and scoop centres out carefully into a bowl,
reserving the skins. Mash potato in a bowl; add haricot beans,
cheese and yogurt and season with herbs, lemon rind, salt and
pepper. Pack into potato skins, mounding the filling; place on
baking tin; cover with foil and heat in oven for about 10
minutes.

Makes 2 servings.   *Per serving: 360 calories.*

Cheese and Butter Bean Peppers
See Menu Plan for Week 43.

4 × 6 oz (180 g) green peppers
4 oz (120 g) celery, diced
3 oz (90 g) onion, diced
12 oz (360 g) drained canned butter beans, mashed
8 oz (240 g) canned tomatoes, drained and chopped
1 tablespoon basil
4 oz (120 g) Cheddar cheese, grated
pinch each salt and pepper

Cut tops from peppers and remove seeds. Reserve tops. Par-
boil peppers and tops 2 minutes; drain and set aside. Combine
celery and onion in non-stick pan and cook until tender.
Transfer to a bowl; add remaining ingredients and mix
thoroughly. Spoon quarter of mixture into each pepper.
Replace tops. Place stuffed peppers in baking dish with 4
tablespoons water; cover and bake at 375°F, 190°C, Gas Mark
5 for 40–50 minutes.

Makes 4 servings.   *Per serving: 230 calories.*

Vegetables

Vegetables are about the most versatile of all of nature's gifts. There are almost as many ways to serve vegetables as there are vegetable varieties. Discover new taste treats by adding unusual vegetables to your standard repertoire. From crunchy crudites to substantial casseroles, depend on vegetable dishes for colour, texture and nutrition.

Fennel with Parmesan Cheese
See Menu Plans for Weeks 8, 27 and 50.

8 oz (240 g) fennel bulb, sliced

6 fl oz (180 ml) chicken stock made with 1 stock cube

2 teaspoons grated Parmesan cheese

1 small clove garlic, finely chopped

In saucepan combine fennel and stock; bring to the boil. Reduce heat, cover and simmer approximately 15 minutes. Drain and transfer fennel to shallow casserole. Keeping fennel slices intact if possible, sprinkle with cheese and garlic. Place under a medium grill to brown cheese and serve immediately. *Makes 2 servings.* *Per serving: 25 calories.*

Courgette Basil
See Menu Plan for Week 35.

4 teaspoons low-fat spread

2 medium courgettes, about 5 oz (150 g) each, cut into thin strips

1 tablespoon chopped fresh basil, or 1 teaspoon dried basil

pinch freshly ground pepper

Melt low-fat spread in medium pan; add courgettes and saute, tossing constantly for 5 minutes. Season with basil and pepper. *Makes 2 servings.* *Per serving: 65 calories.*

Courgettes Italian Style
See Menu Plans for Weeks 4 and 17.

2 × 5 oz (150 g) courgettes, cut into 1-inch (2.5-cm) slices
3 oz (90 g) tomato, seeded and chopped
1 clove garlic, crushed
½ teaspoon basil
½ teaspoon salt
pinch freshly ground pepper

Combine tomato, garlic and basil in small saucepan; cook gently 5 minutes. Add courgettes, salt and pepper. Cover and cook over low heat until courgettes are just tender, about 10 minutes. Serve immediately or refrigerate and serve chilled.

Makes 2 servings. *Per serving: 30 calories.*

Savoury Cabbage
See Menu Plan for Week 24.

1 lb (480 g) white cabbage, shredded
4 oz (120 g) onion, chopped
1 clove garlic, crushed
4 tablespoons chicken stock made with ½ stock cube
1 tablespoon wine vinegar
2 teaspoons lemon juice
½ teaspoon caraway seeds
1 bay leaf
salt and pepper to taste
2 tablespoons margarine, melted

Place cabbage, onion, garlic, stock, vinegar, lemon juice, caraway seeds, bay leaf and seasoning in saucepan. Bring to the boil; cover and simmer gently for about 10 minutes or until soft but still crisp. Drain. Pour margarine over cabbage and transfer to hot serving dish.

Makes 4 servings. *Per serving: 95 calories.*

Sweet and Sour Cabbage

See Menu Plan for Week 52.

2–3 tablespoons white wine vinegar

2 tablespoons brown sugar

1 teaspoon salt

pinch ground cloves

pinch each ground coriander, bay leaves and freshly ground pepper

12 oz (360 g) red cabbage, thinly sliced

4 teaspoons margarine

1 medium onion, chopped

2 medium green apples, peeled, cored and sliced

Combine first 7 ingredients; add cabbage and toss well. Set aside and allow to marinate for 1 hour. Melt margarine in medium pan. Add onion and saute until translucent. Add cabbage and marinade to pan. Cover and cook gently for about 30 minutes. Stir in apples and simmer 10 minutes longer.

Makes 4 servings.   *Per serving: 115 calories.*

Chinese Cabbage and Tomato Medley

See Menu Plans for Weeks 9, 27 and 35.

2 teaspoons olive oil

1 garlic clove, crushed

8 oz (240 g) Chinese cabbage, chopped

2 medium tomatoes, skinned, seeded and chopped

pinch each salt and pepper

Heat oil in medium saucepan; add garlic and saute, being careful not to brown. Add cabbage, tomato, salt and pepper. Cover and simmer for approximately 15 minutes or until cabbage is just tender.

Makes 2 servings.   *Per serving: 80 calories.*

Curried Vegetables
See Menu Plan for Week 24.

1½ teaspoons coriander
1 teaspoon turmeric
½ teaspoon cumin
½ teaspoon ground ginger
½ teaspoon chilli powder
8 fl oz (240 ml) boiling water
2 tablespoons onion flakes
1 lb (480 g) tomatoes, skinned and roughly chopped
1 lb (480 g) carrots, chopped
12 oz (360 g) broad beans, fresh or frozen
12 oz (360 g) potato, chopped
1 medium cauliflower, cut into florets
2 tablespoons lemon juice
salt and pepper to taste
1 tablespoon chopped parsley

Make a paste with coriander, turmeric, cumin, ginger and chilli powder and 1 tablespoon cold water. Gradually add boiling water, stirring all the time. Soak onion flakes, drain and dry-fry in non-stick pan until brown. Stir in tomatoes and curry spices; bring to the boil. Add carrots, broad beans, potatoes, cauliflower, lemon juice, salt and pepper with just enough water to cover the vegetables. Stir well and bring to the boil. Cover pan, simmer until vegetables are tender but still crisp, shaking occasionally to prevent sticking. Garnish with chopped parsley. Divide into 4 equal portions and serve as a starter or as an accompaniment to meat or poultry.

Makes 4 servings.   _Per serving: 170 calories._

Green Beans and Tomatoes Hungarian Style
See Menu Plan for Week 5.

8 oz (240 g) green beans, chopped
2 teaspoons margarine
1 small onion, chopped
8 oz (240 g) canned tomatoes, with juice, roughly chopped
¼ teaspoon paprika
pinch salt

Place green beans in saucepan with boiling, salted water to cover and blanch 5 minutes. Drain in colander and refresh under cold running water; set aside. Melt margarine in saucepan; add onion and saute until softened. Stir in tomatoes and paprika and simmer 5–8 minutes. Add beans and simmer, stirring occasionally, 5 minutes or until beans are tender-crisp; season and serve,

Makes 2 servings. _Per serving: 80 calories._

Grains, Pasta and Potatoes

It's true that 'man does not live by bread alone', but bread is still said to be the staff of life. Now you can enliven meals with some exciting new recipes featuring grains, pasta and potatoes.

Macaroni with Cheese and Peanut Sauce
See Menu Plan for Week 22.

2 oz (60 g) cooked macaroni

3 oz (90 g) cooked cauliflower florets

3 oz (90 g) cooked carrots, sliced

Sauce

3 oz (90 g) button mushrooms, sliced

2 tablespoons peanut butter

2½ oz (75 g) curd cheese

2 fl oz (60 ml) skim milk

salt and pepper to taste

sprig of parsley to garnish

Cook macaroni, cauliflower and carrots and keep warm. Poach mushrooms in 2 tablespoons water until tender. Blend peanut butter and curd cheese together then mix in milk. Stir this mixture into mushrooms. Bring to the boil, stirring; season to taste and simmer for further 2–3 minutes. Thin down if necessary with extra milk. Pour over macaroni and cauliflower; stir quickly with a fork. Garnish with parsley. Serve at once with a mixed salad.

Makes 1 serving. *Per serving: 410 calories.*

Bacon-Flavoured Potato Salad
See Menu Plan for Week 14.

6 oz (180 g) small potatoes, unpeeled

2 teaspoons vegetable oil

1 small onion, chopped

2 teaspoons imitation bacon bits

2 teaspoons red wine vinegar

pinch salt

pinch pepper

Boil potatoes in water until just tender, but not soft; about 10 minutes. Drain and allow to cool. Heat oil in small frying pan; add diced onion and saute until tender. Add bacon bits and cook 2 minutes longer. Peel potatoes and cut into cubes. Gently toss potatoes with vinegar. Add onion mixture and seasonings; toss gently to combine.

Makes 2 servings.   *Per serving: 135 calories.*

Kedgeree and Mushroom Grill
See Menu Plan for Week 22.

1 large flat mushroom

½ teaspoon vegetable oil

2 oz (60 g) cooked rice

1 oz (30 g) cooked smoked haddock, flaked

chopped chives

1 tablespoon grated cheese

Brush top sides of mushroom with vegetable oil and grill for 2–3 minutes. Meanwhile, combine rice, haddock and chives. Turn mushroom over and grill for a further 1 minute. Remove mushroom from grill, top with rice mixture, sprinkle with cheese and return to grill and cook until cheese is golden brown.

Makes 1 serving.   *Per serving: 185 calories.*

Parsley Soup
See Menu Plan for Week 31.

1 pint (600 ml) chicken stock made with 2 stock cubes

1 head lettuce, chopped

8 fl oz (240 ml) water

6 oz (180 g) potatoes, chopped

2 tablespoons chopped parsley

pinch white pepper

In saucepan combine stock, lettuce, water, potatoes and parsley. Bring to the boil; reduce heat, cover and simmer 20 minutes. Add white pepper. In several batches, puree mixture in blender container. Return soup to saucepan. Heat and serve.

Makes 4 servings.   *Per serving: 60 calories.*

Oatmeal with Spiced Fruit Ambrosia
See Menu Plans for Weeks 9, 21 and 31.

10 fl oz (300 ml) skim milk

6 fl oz (180 ml) water

1½ oz (45 g) fine oatmeal

8 oz (240 g) canned fruit cocktail

2 teaspoons sugar

pinch ground ginger and ground cinnamon

2 teaspoons desiccated coconut, toasted

Heat milk and water in heavy-based non-stick milk pan. Slowly stir in oatmeal. Bring to the boil, reduce heat and cook 10 minutes or until oatmeal is thickened, stirring occasionally. Remove from heat. Stir in sugar, ginger and cinnamon. Place half of fruit in bottom of each of 2 cereal bowls; spoon half the oatmeal over each. Sprinkle each with 1 teaspoon coconut.

Makes 2 servings.   *Per serving: 235 calories.*

Garlic Bread

See Menu Plan for Week 3.

4 teaspoons margarine
2 teaspoons chopped parsley
1 clove garlic, crushed
8 slices (½ oz/15 g each) French bread

Preheat grill. In a small bowl cream margarine with parsley and garlic. Spread each slice of French bread with an equal amount of margarine mixture. Place in grill pan; grill for 1 minute.

Makes 4 servings.   *Per serving: 105 calories.*

Salads

Fresh crisp greens, bright flavourful vegetables, aromatic herbs and spices – that's what salads are made of. Make salads a year-round part of your menu plan.

Chinese Salad
See Menu Plan for Week 47.

8 oz (240 g) skinned and boned cooked chicken meat
6 oz (180 g) Chinese leaves
3 oz (90 g) canned water chestnuts
3 oz (90 g) cucumber
3 oz (90 g) red pepper
3 oz (90 g) onion
2 tablespoons wine vinegar
2 teaspoons soy sauce
2 teaspoons olive oil
½ teaspoon ginger root, finely grated
½ garlic clove, crushed
pinch salt
pinch pepper

Slice first 6 ingredients into thin strips. Mix last 7 ingredients. Place the sliced chicken and vegetables together in a deep bowl, pour dressing over and toss well to combine.

Makes 2 servings.   *Per serving: 275 calories.*

Curried Cole Slaw

See Menu Plans for Weeks 2, 10, 15 and various other weeks.

6 oz (180 g) white cabbage, shredded

2 tablespoons green pepper, chopped

2 tablespoons carrot, grated

¼ teaspoon salt

pinch celery seed and ground pepper

4 tablespoons water

4 tablespoons cider vinegar

1 small onion, chopped

1 teaspoon lemon juice

pinch curry powder

Combine cabbage, green pepper, carrot, salt, celery seed and pepper; set aside. Combine remaining ingredients and let stand 5 minutes; add to cabbage mixture. Toss and refrigerate at least 2 hours. Toss again just before serving.

Makes 2 servings. *Per serving: 50 calories.*

Cole Slaw Vinaigrette

See Menu Plans for Weeks 4 and 37.

4 tablespoons cider vinegar

2 tablespoons plus 2 teaspoons vegetable oil

1 teaspoon celery seed

¼ teaspoon dry mustard

pinch garlic powder

9 oz (270 g) white cabbage, shredded

1½ oz (45 g) carrot, grated

2 tablespoons green pepper, chopped

Using a wire whisk, combine vinegar, oil, celery seed, mustard and garlic powder. Add remaining ingredients; toss. Chill at least 1 hour.

Makes 4 servings. *Per serving: 95 calories.*

Cucumber and Tomato Salad
See Menu Plans for Weeks 1 and 26.

1 lettuce leaf
3 oz (90 g) tomato, sliced
3 oz (90 g) cucumber, sliced
1 tablespoon wine vinegar
1½ teaspoons olive oil
1 teaspoon imitation bacon bits

Line small plate with lettuce leaf. Arrange tomato and cucumber slices on lettuce. Combine remaining ingredients. When ready to serve, pour dressing over salad.
Makes 1 serving.   *Per serving: 95 calories.*

Bean Salad
See Menu Plans for Weeks 4 and 21.

2½ teaspoons lemon juice
½ teaspoon chopped mint
2 teaspoons olive oil
½ teaspoon dill weed (optional)
10 oz (300 g) green beans, blanched and cut into 2-inch (5-cm) lengths
4 oz (120 g) celery, sliced
pinch each salt and pepper
2 teaspoons chopped parsley
3 oz (90 g) tomatoes, skinned and quartered

Combine lemon juice and mint in medium-size bowl. Set aside. In non-stick frying pan, heat oil; add dill weed if used and saute 20 seconds. Stir in beans, celery, salt, and pepper. Saute about 2 minutes. Remove from heat; add to lemon juice mixture with parsley. Toss and refrigerate. Before serving toss salad and add tomatoes.
Makes 2 servings.   *Per serving: 80 calories.*

Apple Slaw
See Menu Plans for Weeks 35 and 42.

1 lb (480 g) shredded white cabbage
2½ fl oz (75 ml) apple juice
3 oz (90 g) carrots, grated
2 tablespoons chopped green pepper
2 tablesspoon chopped celery
2 tablespoons chopped onion
4 teaspoons mayonnaise
¼ teaspoon salt
pinch white pepper
parsley sprigs to garnish

Combine cabbage and apple juice, mixing well. Put in refrigerator for ½ hour.

In another bowl combine remaining ingredients except parsley; add to cabbage mixture. Put in refrigerator for ½ hour longer. Just before serving, toss well and garnish with parsley.

Makes 4 servings.   *Per serving: 45 calories.*

Sauces, Salad Dressings and Dips

You mix and match parts of your wardrobe, adding different accessories for different occasions. You can do the same thing with the foods you eat, using sauces, dressings and dips as flavour accents.

Thousand Island Dressing
See Menu Plans for Weeks 2 and 6.

10 fl oz (300 ml) low-fat natural yogurt
2 tablespoons tomato ketchup
1 tablespoon chopped pickled cucumber
4 teaspoons mayonnaise
½ teaspoon horseradish sauce
¼ teaspoon prepared mustard
dash each salt and soy sauce

Combine all ingredients in bowl; mix well. Chill.
Makes 4 servings.   *Per serving: 50 calories.*

Mint Sauce
See Menu Plans for Weeks 24 and 34.

2 tablespoons finely chopped mint
1 tablespoon cider vinegar
1 tablespoon water
artificial sweetener to equal 4 teaspoons sugar

Combine all ingredients in small jar with lid and shake vigorously.
Makes 1–2 servings.   *Per serving: 3 calories.*

Spicy Plum Sauce
See Menu Plans for Weeks 25 and 52.

8 medium plums

pinch mixed spice

artifical sweetener to taste

2 teaspoons arrowroot or cornflour

Stone plums and cut into dice. Place in small saucepan with just enough water to cover; add spice, bring to the boil and cook until soft; add sweetener to taste. Mix arrowroot or cornflour with a little water to a thin paste; add this to plums and cook until thickened.

Makes 4 servings.   *Per serving: 35 calories.*

Creamy Yogurt Dressing
See Menu Plan for Week 52.

10 fl oz (300 ml) low-fat natural yogurt

4 teaspoons chopped fresh parsley

4 teaspoons chopped chives

4 teaspoons mayonnaise

1–2 teaspoons prepared mustard, to taste

2 teaspoons soy sauce

pinch ground ginger

Combine all ingredients; mix well. Chill.
Makes 4 servings.   *Per serving: 45 calories.*

Russian Dressing
See Menu Plans for Weeks 3, 4 and various other weeks.

2 teaspoons low-calorie mayonnaise

½ teaspoon chilli sauce

2 teaspoons relish, any type

Combine all ingredients; stir well.
Makes 1 serving.   *Per serving: 30 calories.*

Herb Dressing
See Menu Plan for Week 2.

3 tablespoons vegetable oil

2 tablespoons water

1 tablespoon wine vinegar

1 teaspoon basil

½ teaspoon chopped parsley

pinch garlic powder

pinch oregano

Combine all ingredients in jar with lid. Shake well until combined. Use immediately or store and shake before serving
Makes 6 servings.   *Per serving: 68 calories.*

Curry Dip
See Menu Plan for Week 52.

5 fl oz (150 ml) low-fat natural yogurt

¼ teaspoon curry powder

¼ teaspoon lemon juice

pinch each ground cumin, salt and white pepper

Combine all ingredients in small bowl; mix well and chill.
Makes 4 servings.   *Per serving: 20 calories.*

Vinaigrette Dressing
See Menu Plans for Weeks 1, 3, 4 and various other weeks.

4 teaspoons olive oil or vegetable oil

1 tablespoon white wine vinegar

pinch salt

¼ teaspoon prepared mustard

Combine all ingredients; mix well.
Makes 4 servings.   *Per serving: 45 calories.*

Desserts, Snacks and Drinks

Desserts and snacks should be as nourishing as everything else you eat. But that doesn't mean they have to be boring. A blend of good nutrition sense and creativity makes for a delicious selection of recipes.

Cherry Tarts
See Menu Plans for Weeks 8 and 27.

Crust

2 digestive biscuits, crushed

¼ teaspoon ground cinnamon

4 teaspoons low-fat spread, melted

Filling

8 oz (240 g) frozen dark sweet cherries; thawed and drained

4 teaspoons lemon juice

pinch ground cloves and cinnamon

2 teaspoons arrowroot, blended with 4 teaspoons water

To Prepare Crust: Combine digestive biscuit crumbs and cinnamon; add low-fat spread and mix thoroughly. Divide mixture into two 4-inch (10-cm) foil-lined Yorkshire pudding tins or aluminium foil dishes, pressing mixture firmly with back of spoon on to bottom and up sides to form crust. Chill in refrigerator.

To Prepare Filling: In a small saucepan combine cherries, lemon juice, cloves and cinnamon and cook until heated. Add blended arrowroot to saucepan, bring to the boil stirring gently so as not to crush cherries. Remove from heat, cool 10 minutes, and pour into prepared crusts. Chill.

Makes 2 servings. *Per serving: 175 calories.*

Swedish Apple Bake
See Menu Plans for Weeks 15 and 17.

1½ oz (45 g) flour
1 tablespoon sugar
¾ teaspoon baking powder
¾ teaspoon ground cinnamon
pinch each ground allspice, ground nutmeg and salt
8 oz (240 g) peeled and cored cooking apple, chopped
2 eggs, beaten with 3 tablespoons water
½ teaspoon honey
¼ teaspoon lemon juice
¼ teaspoon vanilla flavouring
ground cinnamon for topping

Combine flour, sugar, baking powder, spices and salt; sift into a medium bowl. Add apple and stir to coat with dry ingredients. Add remaining ingredients and stir to combine. Line 2-lb (960-g) loaf tin with non-stick paper. Spoon apple mixture into tin. Cover with foil and bake at 350°F, 180°C, Gas Mark 4 for 40 minutes. Let stand for 10 minutes. Sprinkle top of cake with cinnamon. Cut into slices and serve warm.

Makes 2 servings.   *Per serving: 280 calories.*

Baked Apples
See Menu Plans for Weeks 3, 4, 8 and various other weeks.

2 medium apples
artificial sweetener to equal 2 teaspoons sugar
pinch each ground cinnamon and ground nutmeg
2 fl oz (60 ml) water
1 teaspoon lemon juice

Core apples; place in ovenproof dish. Sprinkle sweetener, cinnamon and nutmeg over the apples. Add water and lemon juice and bake at 450°F, 230°C, Gas Mark 8 for 25 minutes or until tender.

Makes 2 servings.   *Per serving: 45 calories.*

Strawberry 'Cream'

See Menu Plans for Weeks 41 and 44.

2 tablespoons unflavoured gelatine
4 fl oz (120 ml) water
1¼ lb (600 g) strawberries
1 pint (600 ml) low-fat natural yogurt
artificial sweetener to equal 2 teaspoons sugar

Dissolve gelatine in water in small bowl over pan of hot water. Reserve 12 strawberries for decoration. Put rest in blender container with yogurt and sweetener and puree until smooth. Add dissolved gelatine and puree. Pour into 4 individual dishes and chill in refrigerator for 1 hour. Decorate with remaining strawberries and serve at once.

Makes 4 servings.   *Per serving: 140 calories.*

Pineapple Cheesecake

See Menu Plans for Weeks 27 and 41.

5 tablespoons plus 1 teaspoon low-fat spread
8 digestive biscuits, crumbled
6 teaspoons unflavoured gelatine
2 fl oz (60 ml) water
juice and grated rind of 1 lemon
10 oz (300 g) curd cheese
10 fl oz (300 ml) low-fat natural yogurt
8 oz (240 g) canned crushed pineapple, drained
artifical sweetener to equal 8 teaspoons sugar
2–4 drops vanilla flavouring
lemon twists to garnish

Line base of 7–8-inch (18–20.5-cm) loose-based cake tin with non-stick paper.
To Prepare Base: melt low-fat spread in basin over hot water, add crumbled biscuits and press on to base of tin. Chill.
To Prepare Filling: dissolve gelatine in water in small bowl over

pan of hot water; add lemon juice and rind. Blend cheese with yogurt, pineapple, sweetener and vanilla flavouring. Puree thoroughly in blender until all contents are smooth, add dissolved gelatine mixture and puree to mix. Pour on to biscuit base and chill until set. Carefully remove from tin. Decorate with lemon twists.

Makes 4 servings.   *Per serving: 420 calories.*

Custard
See Menu Plans for Weeks 12 and various other weeks.

10 fl oz (300 ml) skim milk
2 tablespoons custard powder
artificial sweetener to equal 1 tablespoon sugar

Heat 9 fl oz (270 ml) milk in saucepan. Mix custard powder to a cream with 1 fl oz (30 ml) skim milk. Add creamed mixture to hot milk, stirring continuously until sauce thickens. Remove from heat and add artificial sweetener.

Makes 2 servings.   *Per serving: 100 calories.*

Apple Meringue
See Menu Plan for Week 28.

4 medium cooking apples
1 teaspoon ground cinnamon
rind of ½ lemon
1 teaspoon honey
2 egg whites
1 tablespoon caster sugar

Preheat oven to 300°F, 150°C, Gas Mark 2. Peel, core and slice apples and place in a saucepan with 1 tablespoon water. Cook until tender. Stir in cinnamon, lemon rind and honey. Transfer to ovenproof dish. Whisk egg whites until stiff and then fold in caster sugar. Spoon over apple mixture. Cook in oven for about 20–30 minutes or until puffed up and pale golden.

Makes 4 servings.   *Per serving: 75 calories.*

Honey-Stewed Prunes

See Menu Plans for Weeks 2, 6, 10 and various other weeks.

8 large dried prunes
1 teaspoon honey
pinch ground cinnamon
pinch ground allspice

Place prunes in small saucepan and add water to cover. Bring to the boil; reduce heat and stir in honey, cinnamon and allspice. Cover and simmer 20–30 minutes. Serve warm.
Makes 4 servings.   *Per serving: 45 calories.*

Rich Fruit Pudding

See Menu Plans for Weeks 41 and 52.

2 slices (1 oz/30 g each) brown bread, made into crumbs
1½ oz (45 g) self-raising flour
6 tablespoons natural bran
2 oz (60 g) raisins
1 oz (30 g) currants
1 oz (30 g) sultanas
grated rind ½ lemon
grated rind ½ orange
1–2 teaspoons mixed spice
4 fl oz (120 ml) skim milk
4 teaspoons low-fat spread
1 teaspoon rum flavouring
2 oz (60 g) cooked carrots, mashed
2 tablespoons dark brown sugar

Combine first 9 ingredients in a large basin. Mix thoroughly. Put milk, 3 teaspoons low-fat spread and rum flavouring into a saucepan. Gradually heat mixture and stir until low-fat spread melts. Remove from heat, allow to cool slightly; pour into blender container, add carrots and sugar. Puree until contents are smooth. Pour this mixture on to the dry ingredients and beat thoroughly. Grease a 2-pint (1.2-litre) pudding basin, with clip-on lid, with remaining low-fat spread. Pour mixture into the greased basin, fasten lid, and then cover tightly with foil – or use greaseproof paper and then foil. Put pudding into the top of a double steamer and cook for 4½–5 hours. Allow pudding to stand for at least 5 minutes before turning out.

Makes 4 servings.   *Per serving: 275 calories.*

Fruit Sundae
See Menu Plan for Week 29.

16 oz (480 g) canned apricots

2 medium bananas, peeled and sliced

8 oz (240 g) vanilla ice cream, divided into 4

4 teaspoons chocolate sauce

Divide first three ingredients equally between four dessert dishes – top each serving with 1 teaspoon of chocolate sauce. Serve at once.

Makes 4 servings.   *Per serving: 210 calories.*

Pineapple-Orange 'Cream'
See Menu Plans for Weeks 9 and 52.

6 teaspoons unflavoured gelatine

8 fl oz (240 ml) water

8 fl oz (240 ml) orange juice

8 oz (240 g) canned crushed pineapple

articial sweetener to equal 6 teaspoons sugar

2 tablespoons lemon juice

10 fl oz (300 ml) low-fat natural yogurt

Dissolve gelatine in 4 fl oz (120 ml) water in bowl over pan of hot water. In bowl combine orange juice, pineapple and juice, remaining water, sweetener and lemon juice; stir in gelatine mixture. Chill until almost set. Whip in yogurt. Pour into dessert dishes and chill until set.

Makes 4 servings.   *Per serving: 100 calories.*

Mushroom Dip

See Menu Plan for Week 6.

4 oz (120 g) mushrooms, finely chopped

4 spring onions, finely chopped

1 teaspoon vegetable oil

5 fl oz (150 ml) natural yogurt

1 small clove garlic, crushed

pinch salt

2 sticks celery, cut into 2-inch (5-cm) lengths

2 tablespoons finely chopped fresh dill (optional)

In non-stick frying pan saute mushrooms and spring onions in oil over a moderate heat until golden brown, stirring frequently. Remove from the heat and allow to cool for 10–15 minutes. In a bowl, blend yogurt and garlic until smooth. Add the sauteed mushrooms and spring onions and sprinkle with the salt. Mix well. Cover and chill. Sprinkle with chopped dill if desired. Serve with celery sticks.

Makes 1 serving.   *Per serving: 180 calories.*

Coconut-Coffee Mounds

See Menu Plans for Weeks 2, 8 and 35.

2 oz (60 g) low-fat dry milk

artificial sweetener to equal 6 teaspoons sugar

4 teaspoons instant coffee

2 tablespoons water

½ teaspoon vanilla flavouring

2 teaspoons desiccated coconut

Combine first 3 ingredients. Sprinkle with water and vanilla. Stir until mixture forms dry paste that holds together. Wet hands and shape mixture into small balls, ½-inch (1-cm) in diameter. Roll balls in coconut to coat. Chill in freezer for at least 40 minutes. Serve or keep in refrigerator until ready to use. Makes about 16 balls.

Makes 4 servings.   *Per serving: 70 calories.*

Pear Frozen Yogurt

See Menu Plans for Weeks 3, 15, 23 and 25.

8 oz (240 g) canned pears

10 fl oz (300 ml) low-fat natural yogurt

artifical sweetener to equal 8 teaspoons sugar

2 tablespoons lemon juice

Combine all ingredients in blender container; puree until smooth. Transfer to shallow dish; place in freezer. Stir every hour to break up ice crystals until frozen, about 3 hours. Thaw for 10 minutes before serving.

Makes 2 servings.   *Per serving: 135 calories.*

Pineapple Sorbet

See Menu Plans for Weeks 10 and 35.

1 pint (600 ml) low-fat natural yogurt

1 lb (480 g) canned crushed pineapple

artificial sweetener to equal 6 teaspoons sugar

1 tablespoon lemon juice

Combine all ingredients in blender container; puree until smooth. Transfer to a shallow dish; place in freezer. Stir every hour to break up ice crystals until frozen, at least 3–4 hours. Thaw for 10 minutes before serving.

Makes 4 servings.   *Per serving: 115 calories.*

Knickerbocker Glory

See Menu Plan for Week 41.

4 digestive biscuits, crumbled

8 oz (240 g) canned peaches

10 oz (300 g) strawberries, reserve 4 for garnish

8 oz (240 g) vanilla ice cream

In 4 tall sundae glasses, layer biscuit crumbs, peaches, strawberries and ice cream. Repeat layers finishing with ice cream and decorate with reserved strawberries.

Makes 4 servings.   *Per serving: 210 calories.*

Rice Pudding

See Menu Plans for Weeks 27 and 41.

8 oz (240 g) cooked brown rice, hot

16 fl oz (480 ml) skim milk

4 eggs

4 oz (120 g) sultanas

2 tablespoons brown sugar

4–5 drops vanilla flavouring

¼ teaspoon ground cinnamon

¼ teaspoon ground nutmeg

ground cinnamon to garnish

Combine all ingredients in a mixing bowl. Pour into a baking dish, cover tightly with aluminium foil and bake at 350°F, 180°C, Gas Mark 4 for 40 minutes or until set. Sprinkle with cinnamon and serve.

Makes 4 servings.   *Per serving: 370 calories.*

Index

Weight Watchers

If you need to lose weight and want to maintain that weight loss, Weight Watchers is for you!

Weight Watchers uses the most famous and effective programme in the world, and probably has a class near you.

For information about that class, look at the Yellow Pages under 'Health Clubs'.

WEIGHT WATCHERS MAGAZINE, published bi-monthly, gives a wealth of information and tips on losing weight as well as recipes, regular features and fashion. Get your copy from your local newsagent now.

If you would like to know more about the Weight Watchers organisation, phone Windsor 56751 or write to:

Weight Watchers UK Ltd
11 Fairacres
Dedworth Road
Windsor
Berkshire
SL4 4UY

52 Collingwood
s/s.